Digital Technologies and Generational Identity

The short lifetime of digital technologies means that generational identities are difficult to establish around any particular technologies let alone around more far-reaching socio-technological 'revolutions'. Examining the consumption and use of digital technologies throughout the stages of human development, this book provides a valuable overview of ICT usage and generational differences. It focuses on the fields of home, family and consumption as key arenas where these processes are being enacted, sometimes strengthening old distinctions, sometimes creating new ones, always embodying an inherent restlessness that affects all aspects and all stages of life.

Combining a collection of international perspectives from a range of fields, including social gerontology, social policy, sociology, anthropology and gender studies, *Digital Technologies and Generational Identity* weaves empirical evidence with theoretical insights on the role of digital technologies across the life course. It takes a unique post-Mannheimian standpoint, arguing that each life stage can be defined by attitudes towards, and experiences of, digital technologies as these act as markers of generational differences and identity.

It will be of particular value to academics of social policy and sociology with interests in the life course and human development as well as those studying media and communication, youth and childhood studies, and gerontology.

Sakari Taipale works as an Academy of Finland Research Fellow at the University of Jyväskylä, Finland. He is also an Adjunct Professor at the University of Eastern Finland.

Terhi-Anna Wilska is a Professor of Sociology at the Department of Social Sciences and Philosophy, University of Jyväskylä, Finland.

Chris Gilleard is a Visiting Research Fellow at the Division of Psychiatry, University College London and a Visiting Senior Research Fellow at the Department of Social and Policy Sciences, University of Bath, UK.

Routledge Key Themes in Health and Society

www.routledge.com/Routledge-Key-Themes-in-Health-and-Society/book-series/RKTHS

Available titles include:

Empowerment
A Critique
Kenneth McLaughlin

The Story of Nursing in British Mental Hospitals
Echoes from the Corridors
Niall McCrae and Peter Nolan

Living with Mental Disorder
Insights from Qualitative Research
Jacqueline Corcoran

A New Ethic of 'Older'
Subjectivity, Surgery and Self-stylization
Bridget Garnham

Social Theory and Nursing
Edited by Martin Lipscomb

Older Citizens and End-of-Life Care
Social Work Practice Strategies for Adults in Later Life
Malcolm Payne

Digital Technologies and Generational Identity
ICT Usage Across the Life Course
Sakari Taipale, Terhi-Anna Wilksa and Chris Gilleard

Forthcoming titles include:

Identity, Ageing and Cultural Adaptation
Understanding Longevity in Crossdisciplinary Perspective
Simon Biggs

Digital Technologies and Generational Identity

ICT Usage Across the Life Course

Edited by Sakari Taipale, Terhi-Anna Wilska and Chris Gilleard

Routledge
Taylor & Francis Group

LONDON AND NEW YORK

First published 2018 by Routledge

2 Park Square, Milton Park, Abingdon, Oxfordshire OX14 4RN
52 Vanderbilt Avenue, New York, NY 10017

Routledge is an imprint of the Taylor & Francis Group, an informa business

First issued in paperback 2019

British Library Cataloguing-in-Publication Data
A catalogue record for this book is available from the British Library

Library of Congress Cataloging in Publication Data
A catalog record for this book has been requested

ISBN: 978-1-138-22597-8 (hbk)
ISBN: 978-0-367-35245-5 (pbk)

Typeset in Times New Roman
by Swales & Willis Ltd, Exeter, Devon, UK

Contents

List of figures   vii
List of tables   viii
List of editors   ix
List of contributors   x
Acknowledgements   xiv

1 **Introduction**   1
   SAKARI TAIPALE, TERHI-ANNA WILSKA AND CHRIS GILLEARD

PART I
Historical, theoretical and methodological perspectives   9

2 **The place of age in the digital revolution**   11
   CHRIS GILLEARD

3 **Generational analysis as a methodological approach to
   study mediatised social change**   23
   GÖRAN BOLIN

4 **Generational analysis of people's experience of ICTs**   37
   LESLIE HADDON

PART II
Family generations and ICT   53

5 **Mobile life of middle-aged employees: fragmented time
   and softer schedules**   55
   MIA TAMMELIN AND TIMO ANTTILA

6   Intergenerational solidarity and ICT usage: empirical insights
    from Finnish and Slovenian families   69
    SAKARI TAIPALE, ANDRAŽ PETROVČIČ AND VESNA DOLNIČAR

7   Gendering the mobile phone: a life course approach   87
    CARLA GANITO

8   How young people experience elderly people's use of
    digital technologies in everyday life   102
    LEOPOLDINA FORTUNATI

9   ICTs and client trust in the care of old people in Finland   119
    HELENA HIRVONEN

10 Mobile phone use and social generations in rural India   134
    SIRPA TENHUNEN

PART III
Consumption, lifestyles and markets   147

11 Necessities to all? The role of ICTs in the everyday life
    of the middle-aged and elderly between 1999 and 2014   149
    TERHI-ANNA WILSKA AND SANNA-MARI KUOPPAMÄKI

12 A risk to privacy or a need for security? Digital domestic
    technologies in the lives of young adults and late middle-agers   167
    SANNA-MARI KUOPPAMÄKI, OUTI UUSITALO AND TIINA KEMPPAINEN

13 Personality traits and computer use in midlife: leisure
    activities and work characteristics as mediators   183
    TIIA KEKÄLÄINEN AND KATJA KOKKO

14 Electronic emotions, age and the life course   201
    JANE VINCENT

15 Conclusions   217
    CHRIS GILLEARD, TERHI-ANNA WILSKA AND SAKARI TAIPALE

    Index   222

Figures

3.1 Three Swedish age cohorts and use of three functions of
mobile phone 2003–2013   29
10.1 Age groups according to gender in Janta   136
10.2 Illiteracy rate according to gender and caste status in Janta   139
11.1 Mean perceived necessity of PCs, cohorts aged 45 to 74,
1999–2014   156
11.2 Mean perceived necessity of home internet connection,
cohorts aged 45 to 74, 1999–2014   157
11.3 Mean perceived necessity of mobile phone, cohorts aged
45 to 74, 1999–2014   158
11.4 Mean perceived necessity of mobile internet and tablet
computers, all age cohorts in 2014   160
13.1 Hypothesised path model   188
13.2 The mediator path model between personality traits and
computer use   194

Tables

3.1	Focus group composition in Sweden and Estonia	30
5.1	Characteristics of interviewees	57
7.1	Interviewees, their age and main activity according to life stage	90
11.1	Perceived necessity of PC, the internet and mobile phone, 1999–2014, 45- to 74-year-olds	159
11.2	Perceived necessity of tablet computer and mobile internet, 2014, 45- to 74-year-olds	161
13.1	Frequencies and means with gender differences	191
13.2	Differences in personality traits between computer users and non-users	192
13.3	Correlations between personality, computer use, work characteristics, leisure activities	193
14.1	Summary of primary research sources on mobile phone and ICT users cited	203

Editors

Sakari Taipale, PhD, works as an Academy of Finland Research Fellow at the University of Jyväskylä, Finland. He is also an Adjunct Professor at the University of Eastern Finland. Presently, he is running a five-year research project on intergenerational relations in digital societies. Taipale has published on the social aspects of new media technologies and mobilities in many highly ranked academic journals, such as *British Journal of Sociology, New Media and Society, Information, Communication and Society, Social Science Research, Telecommunications Policy, European Journal of Communication*, and *Mobilities*. He is also a co-editor of *Social robots from a human perspective* (Springer, 2015).

Terhi-Anna Wilska, PhD, is a Professor of Sociology at the Department of Social Sciences and Philosophy, University of Jyväskylä, Finland. Her research interests include consumption and consumer society, lifestyles and well-being, age and generation, and the social effects of new technology. She has studied particularly the role of ICTs and online environments among young people and children. She has published in journals such as *Journal of Consumer Policy, Acta Sociologica, Childhood, YOUNG, Journal of Youth Studies*, and *Information, Communication and Society*. She is the co-editor of *The Routledge handbook on consumption*, which came out in 2017. Currently, she leads the project *DIGI50+ Mature consumers, customer experience and value creation in digital and physical environments*.

Chris Gilleard, FAcSS, PhD, is a Visiting Research Fellow at the Division of Psychiatry, University College London and a Visiting Senior Research Fellow at the Department of Social and Policy Sciences, University of Bath, UK. His principal research interests concern change and continuity in the experience and understanding of ageing and old age. He is a Fellow of the Academy of Social Sciences and author of a number of books on ageing, written with his colleague, Professor Paul Higgs, including *Cultures of ageing: self, citizen and the body* (Pearson, 2000); *Contexts of ageing: class, cohort and community* (Polity Press, 2005); *Ageing, corporeality & embodiment* (Anthem Press, 2013); and *Rethinking old age: theorising the fourth age* (Palgrave Macmillan, 2015).

Contributors

Timo Anttila, PhD, is an Academy of Finland Research Fellow at the University of Jyväskylä, Finland. His publications have focused, for example, on changing working times and time use in 24/7 societies and job quality in comparative perspective. His current projects concentrate on the changing organisation of work in Europe, time and spaces of work, and long-term consequences of social isolation.

Göran Bolin is a Professor in Media & Communication Studies at Södertörn University, Stockholm, Sweden. His research spans both media production analysis and audience studies, with a special focus on how media production and consumption are interrelated in the wake of digitisation. He is the author of *Value and the media. Production and consumption in digital markets* (Ashgate, 2011), and most recently, *Media generations: experience, identity and mediatised social change* (Routledge, 2016).

Vesna Dolničar, PhD, is an Assistant Professor at the Faculty of Social Sciences, University of Ljubljana, Slovenia. She has been involved in numerous (inter)national research projects (e.g. FP6, COST Actions, LLP, Erasmus+, Interreg, EC tenders) related to the fields of digital inequalities and ICTs for active ageing. She is a leader of the project financed by the Slovenian Research Agency and Si.mobil entitled *Digital Inclusion and Active Ageing*. She has (co)authored several scientific papers, monographs and chapters in the monographs of distinguished publishers (Wiley, Greenwood, Peter Lang, Springer).

Leopoldina Fortunati, PhD, is a Professor of Sociology of Communication and the director of the doctoral programme in Multimedia Communication and of the research laboratory NuMe at the University of Udine, Italy. She has conducted several research projects in the field of gender studies, cultural processes, and communication and information technologies. She is the author and editor of many books, associate editor of the journal *The Information Society* and serves as referee for many outstanding journals. Her research interests include the topic of generations seen through the lens of the use of technology. Her works have been published in 12 languages.

Carla Ganito, PhD, is an Assistant Professor and Coordinator of Postgraduate Studies and Advanced Training at the Faculty of Human Sciences, the Catholic University of Portugal. Her PhD in Communication Sciences tackled the gendering of the mobile phone. Her main research and teaching interests are: new media, mobile communications, gender and technology, education and technology, and digital reading. She is an MC member of the COST Action IS1404 – Evolution of reading in the age of digitisation (E-READ). Her most recent publications appear in journals such as *Feminist Media Studies* and *International Journal of Cyber Ethics in Education*.

Leslie Haddon, PhD, is a Senior Researcher and a Visiting Lecturer in the Department of Media and Communications at the London School of Economics, UK. His research over the past decades has focused on the social shaping and consumption of ICTs, especially in studies of domestication. In recent years, he was involved in the EU Kids Online and Net Children Go Mobile projects and is currently examining how very young children use smartphones and tablets. Together with Eugene Loos and Enid Mante-Meijer he edited the book *Generational use of new media* for Ashgate in 2012.

Helena Hirvonen, PhD, is a Postdoctoral Researcher and a University Lecturer of Social and Public Policy at the Department of Social Sciences, University of Eastern Finland. Her research areas include welfare state restructuring, gendered structures, and professional and organisational practices in the labour market. Besides authoring several peer-reviewed articles, she has recently co-edited the book *Interpersonal violence: differences and connections* (Routledge, 2017) and published a chapter in the book *Professionalism, managerialism and reform in higher education and the health services: the European welfare state and rise of the knowledge society* (Palgrave, 2015).

Tiia Kekäläinen is a postgraduate student in the Gerontology Research Center, Department of Health Sciences, at University of Jyväskylä, Finland. She graduated in August 2015 as a Master of Health Sciences with gerontology as a major and psychology as a minor. Her Master's thesis (2015) researched personality and muscle strength in midlife. She is currently involved in a work package related to life-span development that forms part of a multidisciplinary project called Digi50+. Her research interests include personality, leisure and well-being, especially among middle-aged and older adults.

Tiina Kemppainen is a doctoral student in Marketing at the School of Business and Economics, University of Jyväskylä, Finland. She is currently working in a Digi50+ project and writing her dissertation on customer experience in the context of different servicescapes.

Katja Kokko, PhD, is a Research Director at the Gerontology Research Center, Department of Health Sciences, University of Jyväskylä, Finland. Since 2013, she has been the principal investigator of the Jyväskylä Longitudinal Study of Personality and Social Development. Her main research areas include personality, mental well-being and working/career in a life-span perspective, adult development, and ageing. Katja Kokko has analysed these areas in collaboration with experts from various disciplines (e.g. psychology, economics, gerontology and statistics), and published around 63 international peer-reviewed articles in scientific journals, as well as book chapters, and has given dozens of presentations in international congresses.

Sanna-Mari Kuoppamäki is a doctoral student of sociology in the Department of Social Sciences and Philosophy at the University of Jyväskylä, Finland. Her research interests include consumption, life course, age and digitalising technologies. She studies values, attitudes and lifestyles of late middle-aged consumers in digitalising environments in the project Digi50+ Mature consumers, customer experience and value creation in digital and physical environments.

Andraž Petrovčič, PhD, is an Assistant Professor and a Research Fellow at the Centre for Social Informatics, the Faculty of Social Science, University of Ljubljana, Slovenia. His main research fields relate to the uses of ICTs for social support exchange and interpersonal communication, the sense of online community, and psychological empowerment in online health communities. He has published several book chapters and articles in journals such as *Quality & Quantity, European Journal of Communication, Online Information Review, Computers in Human Behaviour, The Information Society*, and *Telematics & Informatics*. He is a co-editor of *Interacting with broadband society* (Peter Lang, 2010).

Mia Tammelin, PhD, is an Adjunct Professor and an Academy of Finland Research Fellow at the University of Jyväskylä, Finland. Her publications have concentrated on work, families and time, as well as 24-hour economy and family life. Her present, five-year project 'FamilyTies', concentrates on paid work, time, family relations and ICTs.

Sirpa Tenhunen, PhD, is an anthropologist currently working as an Interim Professor and University Lecturer at the University of Jyväskylä, Finland. She has also taught anthropology at the University of Helsinki and worked as a researcher at the Academy of Finland. In addition to new media, her research interests cover gender, work and politics in India.

Outi Uusitalo, PhD, is a Professor of Marketing at the University of Jyväskylä's School of Business and Economics, Finland. Her research interests include consumer behaviour, services marketing management, customer–service firm interaction, places and spaces of consumption, and responsible consumption and marketing. She has authored research articles that have been published in journals such as *Journal of Consumer Culture, Journal of Consumer Behaviour, International Journal of Consumer Studies, European Journal of Marketing, Journal of Business and Industrial Marketing*, and *Journal of Business Ethics*.

Jane Vincent, PhD, is a Senior Researcher and holds Visiting Fellow and Guest Teacher positions at the London School of Economics and Media and Communications Department and with University of Surrey, UK's Digital World Research Centre. Prior to her academic career, she spent two decades developing and implementing mobile communications in Europe, heading up marketing and strategy teams, and negotiating 2G and 3G technologies in GSM standards and policy forums. She participates in COST Action IS1402 www.notageism.com and is an affiliate of the University of Udine, Italy's NuMe Research Group. Her publications on electronic emotions, social robots, children and mobile phones are at http://eprints.lse.ac.uk/.

Acknowledgements

Despite the numerous benefits of today's digital communication technologies, this book would not have come about without regular meetings with local co-workers, periodic face-to-face get-togethers with foreign colleagues and unexpected encounters with new people sharing the same scholarly interests. In Autumn 2015, the first two editors and a group of local colleagues realised they were running several parallel projects all dealing with the issue of digitalisation from one angle or another. Although the projects were thematically diverse, some dealing with working life and family relations, others with consumption and media usage, all shared a common interest in the adoption and use of digital technology at different phases of the life course, and especially in later life.

In November 2015, the project leaders jointly organised the *International Workshop on Generations, the Life Course and Digital Technologies* (GOLDEN) at the University of Jyväskylä, Finland. The workshop brought together a number of local and international experts, whose contributions have been incorporated in this book. After the workshop, digital technologies themselves played a major role enabling the constant exchange of messages between the editors, contributing authors, proofreader and publishers. It is fair to say that the book was born out of locally embodied connections, but was finally woven together digitally from a distance.

The editors want to express their gratitude to the University of Jyväskylä, Finland for funding the workshop, and to Ms. Armi Korhonen who assisted in many organisational matters. The sponsors of the projects that have presented some of their key findings in the book also deserve a special mention: the Academy of Finland who funded the project *Intergenerational Relations in Broadband Societies* (iGRIB), and the TEKES who funded the project *Digi50+ Mature consumers, customer experience and value creation in digital and physical environments*. In addition, we would like to especially thank all those independent reviewers for providing truly valuable and constructive feedback that helped the authors improve their contributions. Dr. Bidemi Coker's painstaking reading and language editing has made the book more coherent and polished much of its style. Last, but not least, we would like to thank Ms. Claire Jarvis, Senior Commissioning Editor of Ashgate (later part of informa group), as well Ms. Lianne Sherlock, Editor for Health and Social Care, Ms. Shannon Kneis and Ms. Georgia Priestley, both, Editorial Assistants, all from Routledge, who have gently guided us through the publishing process.

Let the life course of the book be long and eventful – as in print, so in digital.

December, 2017

The editors

1 Introduction

Sakari Taipale, Terhi-Anna Wilska and Chris Gilleard

Social generations from the life course perspective

A plunge into the literature reveals that studying digital technologies through social generations[1] is a well-established practice in social sciences and media studies. Many scholars have followed the footsteps of Karl Mannheim (1952), who proposed that age cohorts experiencing the same noteworthy historical events may develop a shared generational identity. As Mannheim considered youth as the main transformative period in fashioning such generational identities, it is no surprise that the uptake of new technologies – young people often as first-adopters – is widely considered a generational question. Several age cohorts of technology users have been named according to detected similarities among their members, such as the Net Generation (Tapscott, 1998), Digital Natives (Prensky, 2001), Nintendo or MTV generation (Guzdial and Soloway, 2002), Digital Generation (Buckingham, 2006; Taipale, 2016) or Social Media Generation (Huang, 2014). Others have considered such labels to reflect adults' stereotypes and journalists' shorthand rather than any 'revolutionary' changes in social structures (Herring, 2008).

Towards the 2010s, the simple division into technologically savvy and technologically naive generations faced increasing criticism. Such generational stereotypes stem from the idea that social generations relate to technological landscapes differently, and that technological innovations mark turning points that separate one generation from one another (Andò, 2014; Comunello *et al.*, 2016; Loos, 2012). This criticism is fuelled by the evident diversification of the media landscape, especially the rise of social media, as well as increased ICT proficiency within all age groups. Empirical research carried out in many countries has challenged the idea of a homogenous, highly skilled generation of 'technology savvy' young people, showing instead the great variation that exists in young people's skills and involvement in digital media environments (e.g. Fortunati *et al.*, 2017; Helsper and Eynon, 2010; Kennedy *et al.*, 2010; Taipale, 2016). To underline the continuity between social groups instead of clear-cut divisions, new metaphors such as digital spectrum (Lenhart and Horrigan, 2003) have been coined. White and Le Cornu (2011) speak about a continuum between Visitors, who consider digital environments as places with 'untidy gardens', and Residents, who feel at home while being online. What remain under-investigated are the more nuanced relationships between age, time period, the life course and individual life situations and their connection to social generations (Bolin, 2016).

Interestingly, Mannheim acknowledged the meaning of 'biological rhythm', including a limited life span, for the formation of social generations, but in his thinking the importance of social factors superseded biological questions related to ageing (Pilcher, 1994). He noted that generational identity is dependent on the rhythm of social change (Mannheim, 1952). All people living in the same time period do not necessarily share the same experience or understanding of historical events, leaving a distinctive generational identity underdeveloped or rendering it stratified within a generation. Considering the major socio-technological transformations that have taken place, both now and in the recent past, it appears evident why technology-based distinctions may be increasingly difficult to make between different social generations.

When older generations adopted technologies such as radio and television in the early and mid twentieth century, a large cohort of people experienced them as new technology, a fact that is easily forgotten (Berg *et al.*, 2005). It took many years before the next new mass media technologies entered the market (VCRs, CD players, etc.), and these technologies remain strong markers of shared generational experiences in various developed countries (Bolin, 2016). In contrast, the markedly shorter life span of today's new digital technologies provides a much more fragmented basis for building any generational identity. If the length of a generation is considered as a thirty-year period, at least in developed countries (Berger, 1960), each new generation experiences not just one or two epoch-making communications or media technological developments, but a multiplicity of developments across a diverse range of technologies before the next generation is born. Mobile communication serves as a great example with the rapid evolution from 1G to 4G technology within about three decades (Tondare *et al.*, 2014).

With the constant arrival of new technologies and their applications into daily life, a distinct generational consciousness may be difficult to build around any particular technologies or even a more general 'technological revolution'. Time is needed to show what kind of a basis today's extremely diverse and generative field of digital technologies can provide in the 'generationing' process. As Bolin (2016) reminds us, older generations have had more time to develop their 'we-sense', while younger generations have more time and potential to refine their self-understanding over their present and future life course.

Taking this as a point of departure, the book argues that the adoption and use of digital technologies varies across the life course in non-linear ways, influencing the sense of belonging to certain generations in a variety of ways. We take a somewhat critical stance towards the Mannheimian tradition, which considers political events as the source and youth as the phase of life that determines generation building (Corsten, 2011). Our approach to generation is more 'post-Mannheimian' since we propose that in connection to digital technologies, each stage of life can provide important building blocks in shaping generational experiences and identities. In addition to adoption and actual use, the collective attitudes of a particular age group towards and experiences of digital technologies can also serve as potential markers of generational differences, allowing the redrawing of generational lines, for example, in the latter half of life.

The shaping of generational identity in families and consumption

In addition to changes in technology and media landscapes, there are many socio-cultural processes that can shape the formation of generations and generational identities. The de-standardisation of life course, discontinuities in work and leisure, the declining role of the communities of propinquity, the growth of lifestyle politics and the blurring of cultural boundaries imply that people today no longer experience the formative influences of entry into the adult world that people did in the past. ICT contributes to this diversity of experience, by making people's lives more mobile, more individualised and more networked, and their social connections no longer organised by either time or place (Elliot and Urry, 2010; Rainie and Wellman, 2012).

This book concentrates on two domains of life where digital technologies serve as vehicles for defining generational boundaries: family and consumption. With these choices, we want to underscore the relative importance of the world of 'home and leisure' in the 'generationing' influence of these new technologies (Edmunds and Turner, 2005), compared with the greater role that was played in the past by work and labour. Ranging from electrification and cars to fixed phones, mobile communication devices and office software, 'old new technologies' were first and foremost introduced to rationalise and improve the productivity of work, hence marking the differences between generations in the labour force who either succeeded or failed in their adoption. By contrast, what is characteristic of contemporary digital technologies, both hardware and software, is that they blur the distinction between home and work. Some are targeted more towards private consumers for use in the home, by families and in people's free (non-work, non-school) time. Tablet computers, e-book readers, social networking sites, online music and movie services are just some examples of such consumer commodities. All this has been enabled on the back of the strong economic growth that took place after World War II and with it, the birth of the mass market. Over time, consumption has become an increasingly diverse arena for the reproduction of social distinction that on the one hand, strengthens generational distinctions while on the other, fosters cross-generational collaborations and shared experiences as almost everyone at almost every age, at work or at play, joins in the experience of consumerism.

Technologies in later life stages

While earlier research detected obvious generational differences in technology adoption and use (e.g. Carr *et al.*, 2012; Lunt and Livingstone, 1992), the patterns of consumption of digital technologies fluctuate over time and across the life course (e.g. Spero and Stone, 2004). Later life appears an interesting 'new' life course stage and older consumers are beginning to be targeted as potential users of new assistive technologies and applications. Older consumers are, however, not just targets of care technology, neither are they always dependent on the help of younger users (c.f. Berg *et al.*, 2005). They are also independent actors capable of using the new technologies for their own ends and to meet their own concerns, which may well be at odds with the assumptions anticipated by the developers and manufacturers of 'assistive technologies' (Neven, 2011). Many older consumers are highly networked, although often in different, non-digital ways than younger people. Family members and friends provide an important network of support that is benefitted both at home and on the market (Bakardjieva, 2005; Selwyn *et al.*, 2003).

Period effects should not be forgotten. The birth of mass markets and the individualisation that is afforded by consumption have contributed to making the experience of later life quite distinct from the old age that was institutionalised in the first half of the twentieth century (Gilleard and Higgs, 2005, p. 77). Being 'successfully aged' today means not only retaining health and independence but also having the ability and the desire to keep up with the technological developments that signify 'the new' and 'youthfulness'. Some age-related digital gaps are relatively short-lived and seem specific to certain periods of time. For example, during the first decade of the twenty-first century, age cohorts of 50 years and older caught up with younger groups year by year in terms of mobile phone use in the United Kingdom (Gilleard *et al.*, 2015). Similar trends have been found in other countries such as Finland where internet use has grown more quickly among people aged 65 or more than in any other age group (Statistics Finland, 2015). These findings suggest that generational identity, including that reflected in the integration of technology with individual lifestyles during youth, is not set in stone but keeps evolving over time and the life course.

The structure of the book

The book brings together contributions from the fields of sociology, social policy, anthropology, gender studies, communication, psychology and marketing. Although the editors made considerable efforts to streamline discipline-specific practices of doing research and reporting results, some variation in style is still detectable in the book. The chapters revolve mainly around European cultures and societies, including Finland, Estonia, Italy, Portugal, Slovenia, Sweden and the United Kingdom. We included one chapter from India, as it both highlights the limitations of generational research that is confined to the Western hemisphere and demonstrates its applicability to countries and cultures that do not provide the bulk of empirical research in this field. Clearly, there is scope for much more work from countries other than those in the West. Other characteristics of the countries represented here highlight their dissimilarities. Some of the countries have the most rapidly ageing population in the world, such as Italy, Finland and Portugal (UN, 2015). Sweden, Finland, the UK and Estonia are ranked among the top seven EU countries on *The Digital Economy & Society Index* for 2016, while Portugal is close to the EU28 average, Slovenia slightly below, and Italy placed only 25th. Institutional arrangements to adjust to the changes of ageing societies are profoundly different in the studied countries, ranging from (still) largely publicly provided welfare services in Finland and Sweden to the mixed public-private model of the UK to the family-oriented Mediterranean welfare models of Italy and Portugal and post-socialist Estonia and Slovenia (e.g. Ferrera and Hemerijck, 2003; Rechel *et al.*, 2013). Hence even within the narrow geographical boundaries of Europe, considerable diversity exists.

The book is organised into three parts. The first, *Historical, theoretical and methodological perspectives*, situates the book in the wide field of generation and life course studies. *Chris Gilleard*'s chapter considers the confluence between the emergence of the new ICT and changes taking place in the nature of later life. It considers changes in later life itself, the penetration of technology into the worlds of home and work as part of modernity, and the emergence of new social divisions within later life that seem to be replacing those between working life and later life. *Göran Bolin* elaborates on the question of mediatisation from historical and methodological perspectives. He presents generational theory combined with interviews and focus groups as a methodological solution to clarify the role of the media over the entire life course, especially after the alleged formative period of youth. *Leslie Haddon* discusses the relevance of earlier life and ICT experiences for understanding current generational differences in the adoption and use of ICTs. Moreover, his study sheds light on the applicability of cohort analysis in the future.

The second part, *Family generations and ICT,* deals with practices that either reinforce or bridge generational gaps inside the family. The focus is especially on the life stages after youth and the intergenerational relations within families. *Mia Tammelin* and *Timo Anttila*'s chapter analyses ICT use by late middle-aged employees in Finland, the group of people who do not easily fall into any well-defined social generation. Their ICT use is very varied and strongly determined by their life situation, especially as regards children and the nature of their work. *Sakari Taipale, Andraž Petrovčič* and *Vesna Dolničar*'s chapter makes comparisons between Finnish and Slovenian families with regard to the use of ICTs in extended families. They argue that normative expectations concerning ICT use are higher and intergenerational assistance in ICT use stronger in Slovenia when compared with Finland. The latter country seems to blur generational boundaries more, intensifying cross-generational interaction within families. *Carla Ganito*'s chapter provides a detailed description of the reasons and ways in which women's mobile phone use varies across the life stages in Portugal. The intensity of and reasons for mobile phone usage alter considerably over the life course, primarily due to work and family situations. As in Tammelin and Anttila's chapter, belonging to a certain societal generation or age cohort appears a less decisive factor than people's stage in the life course. *Leopoldina Fortunati* argues that a new form of domestic labour referred to as 'digital housekeeping' has been assigned for youth, changing the division of immaterial labour in families. She advocates the idea of digital housekeeping as an intergenerational practice, bringing the generations closer together rather than tearing them apart. Following Fortunati's chapter, *Helena Hirvonen* presents an important theoretical window to the study of social relations and ICT from the concept of trust. Using ICTs in elderly care provision as an example, she shows how they can work as a nexus between older people, their family members and care providers. ICTs can reinforce interaction and hence trust between people involved, but this is the case only if ICTs are not harnessed simply to serve the needs for efficiency of work and accountability. This part ends with *Sirpa Tenhunen*'s study on mobile phone use in rural India. Based on her long-term fieldwork, she describes the limits and the possibilities of a classical generational approach in the Indian context, where the caste system typically overrides most other mechanisms for social distinction.

The third part, *Consumption, lifestyles and markets*, investigates the role of the market as a source of generation formation. *Terhi-Anna Wilska* and *Sanna-Mari Kuoppamäki*'s chapter opens this part by studying whether ICTs are regarded as necessities by all age cohorts. Based on nationally representative repeated cross-sectional survey data, they show how differences between age cohorts have largely evened out, while the impact of life course stage and everyday practices remain rather pronounced. *Sanna-Mari Kuoppamäki, Outi Uusitalo* and *Tiina Kemppainen* add to this theme by analysing generational differences in housing preferences focusing particularly on domestic technologies and the attitudes and experiences of two age groups: young adults and people in late middle-age. *Tiia Kekäläinen* and *Katja Kokko* raise the question of individual differences in ICT use and adoption, bringing to bear the perspective of personality psychology. Employing a longitudinal study design, they explicate how different personality traits predict the use of computers in midlife as part of leisure time use and leisure activities. The third part ends with a chapter by *Jane Vincent*, who, motivated by her remarks on mobile phone marketing activities, examines the nature of 'electronic emotions' in connection to life stages and transition periods. She asks whether the electronic emotions experienced by respondents from different generations of ICT users are similar. Her conclusions are qualified, reflecting the contingencies that permeate this field of research. Lastly, the editors, *Chris Gilleard, Terhi-Anna Wilska* and *Sakari Taipale* outline implications for further research drawing upon the themes of home, family and the omnivorous market.

Note

1 We are following here Pilcher's (1994) distinction between 'generation' and 'social generation' where generation refers to kinship-based relationships, and social generation is used when referring to the collective experiences of particular birth cohorts.

References

Andò, R., 2014. What does TV actually mean? New consumer experience and generations. *Participations*, 11(2), pp. 156–181.
Bakardjieva, M., 2005. *Internet society: the internet in everyday life*. London: SAGE.
Berg, E., Mörtberg, C. and Jansson, M., 2005. Emphasizing technology: socio-technical implications. *Information Technology & People*, 18(4), pp. 343–358.

Berger, B. M., 1960. How long is a generation? *The British Journal of Sociology*, 11(1), pp. 10–23.

Bolin, G., 2016. *Media generations: experience, identity and mediatised social change*. London: Routledge.

Buckingham, D., 2006. Is there a digital generation? In: D. Buckingham and R. Willett, eds. *Digital generations: children, young people, and new media*. London: Routledge, pp. 1–17.

Carr, D. J., Gotlieb, M. R., Lee, N. J. and Shah, D. V., 2012. Examining overconsumption, competitive consumption and conscious consumption from 1994 to 2004: disentangling cohort and period effects. *The Annals of the American Academy of Political and Social Science*, 664(1), pp. 220–233.

Comunello, F., Ardèvol, M. F., Mulargia, S. and Belotti, F., 2016. Women, youth and everything else: age-based and gendered stereotypes in relation to digital technology among elderly Italian mobile phone users. *Media, Culture & Society*. http://dx.doi.org/10.1177/0163443716674363.

Corsten, M., 2011. Media as the historical new for young generations. In: F. Colombo and L. Fortunati, eds. *Broadband society and generational changes*. Frankfurt am Main, Germany: Peter Lang, pp. 37–49.

Edmunds, J. and Turner, B., 2005. Global generations: social change in the twentieth century. *The British Journal of Sociology*, 56(4), pp. 559–577.

Elliot, A. and Urry, J., 2010. *Mobile lives*. London: Routledge.

Ferrera, M. and Hemerijck, A., 2003. Recalibrating Europe's welfare regimes. In: J. Zeitlin and D. M. Trubek, eds. *Governing work and welfare in a new economy*. Oxford, UK: Oxford University Press, pp. 88–128.

Fortunati, L., Taipale, S. and De Luca, F., 2017. Digital generations, but not as we know them. *Convergence*. https://doi.org/10.1177/1354856517692309

Gilleard, C. and Higgs, P., 2005. *Contexts of ageing: class, cohort and community*. Cambridge, UK: Polity.

Gilleard, C., Jones, I. and Higgs, P., 2015. Connectivity in later life: the declining age divide in mobile cell phone ownership. *Sociological Research Online*, 20(2). http://www.socresonline.org.uk/20/2/3.html.

Guzdial, M. and Soloway, E., 2002. Teaching the Nintendo generation to program. *Communications of the ACM*, 45(4), pp. 17–21.

Helsper, E. J. and Eynon, R., 2010. Digital natives: where is the evidence? *British Educational Research Journal*, 36(3), 503–520.

Herring, S., 2008. Questioning the generational divide: technological exoticism and adult constructions of online youth identity. In: D. Buckingham, ed. *Youth, identity, and digital media*. Cambridge, MA: MIT Press, pp. 71–92.

Huang, H., 2014. *Social media generation in urban China. A study of social media use and addiction among adolescents*. Berlin: Springer.

Kennedy, G., Judd, T. and Dalgarno, B., 2010. Beyond natives and immigrants: exploring types of Net Generation students. *Journal of Computer Assisted Learning*, 26(5), pp. 332–343.

Lenhart, A. and Horrigan, J. B., 2003. Re-visualising the digital divide as a digital spectrum. *IT & Society*, 5, pp. 23–39.

Loos, E., 2012. Senior citizens: digital immigrants in their own country? *Observatorio (OBS*)*, 6(1), pp. 1–23.

Lunt, P. and Livingstone, S., 1992. *Mass consumption and personal identity*. Milton Keynes, UK: Open University Press.

Mannheim, K., 1952. The problem of generations. In: K. Mannheim, ed. *Essays of the sociology of knowledge*. Oxford, UK: Oxford University Press, pp. 276–322

Neven, L., 2011. *Representations of the old and ageing in the design of the new and emerging*. Published thesis. Twente, The Netherlands: University of Twente. https://doi.org/10.3990/1.9789036532242.

Pilcher, J., 1994. Mannheim's sociology of generations: an undervalued legacy. *British Journal of Sociology*, 45(3), pp. 481–495.

Prensky, M., 2001. Digital natives, digital immigrants. *On the Horizon*, 9(5), pp. 1–6.

Rainie, L. and Wellman, B., 2012. *Networked: the new social operating system*. Cambridge, MA: MIT Press.

Rechel, B., Grundy, E., Robine, J. M., Cylus, J., Mackenbach, J. P., Knai, C. and McKee, M., 2013. Ageing in the European Union. *The Lancet*, 381(9874), pp. 1312–1322.

Selwyn, N., Gorard, S., Furlong, J. and Madden, L., 2003. Older adults' use of information and communications technology in everyday life. *Ageing and Society*, 23(5), pp. 561–582.

Spero, I. and Stone, M., 2004. Agents of change: how young consumers are changing the world of marketing. *Qualitative Market Research: An International Journal*, 7(2), pp. 153–159.

Statistics Finland, 2015. *More mobile internet use, more personal devices*. http://tilastokeskus.fi/til/sutivi/2015/sutivi_2015_2015-11-26_tie_001_en.html.

Taipale, S., 2016. Synchronicity matters: defining the characteristics of digital generations. *Information, Communication & Society*, 19(1), pp. 80–89.

Tapscott, D., 1998. *Growing up digital: the rise of the Net Generation*. New York: McGraw Hill.

Tondare, S., Panchal, S. and Kushnure, D., 2014. Evolutionary steps from 1G to 4.5G. *International Journal of Advanced Research in Computer and Communication Engineering*, 3(4), pp. 6163–6166.

UN, 2015. *World population ageing*. New York, NY: United Nations.

White, D. S. and Le Cornu, A., 2011. Visitors and residents: a new typology for online engagement. *First Monday*, 16(9). http://firstmonday.org/ojs/index.php/fm/article/view/3171/3049.

Part I

Historical, theoretical and methodological perspectives

2 The place of age in the digital revolution

Chris Gilleard

Introduction

This chapter addresses the confluence between developments in the information and communication technologies (ICTs) of the late twentieth century and contemporary changes in the social nature of later life. Beginning in the 1980s, an expanding array of digital technologies moved the world toward an increasingly 'networked' society (Castells, 1996; Rainie and Wellman, 2012). Communities presaged upon regular, face to face encounters – what Calhoun called the old 'communities of propinquity' (Calhoun, 1998) – became less influential as new possibilities emerged for families, friends, civic and state actors to maintain contact with each other with little consideration of distance. While traditionally it had been assumed that modern technologies were first adopted by and impacted upon those with the time and the money to spend on them, changes in technology and society in the late twentieth century reduced the influence of particular groups or classes in generating distinct lifestyles. Society became progressively individualised as everyone 'connected' to their own, self-selected community (Beck and Beck-Gernsheim, 2001; Rainie and Wellman, 2012). The time when modernity created distinct 'generational' divides seems to be passing. Now, when such divides emerge, almost before they can be crystallised into a distinct generational field, their boundaries, whether of age, class or life stage, start to dissolve. These new transformative powers form the main concern of this chapter. Its aim is to examine how, in the context of a different modernity, forms of communication associated with 'network society' affect and impact people at all stages of life; how this relates to the 'destandardisation' of the life course (Kohli and Rein, 1991); and how, in particular, this contributes to the refashioning of later life (Gergen and Gergen, 2000).

Whether framed as a new, liquid or reflexive modernity, the idea that there has been a distinct, 'post-modern' change in society has been developed by a number of writers (Bauman, 2000; Beck *et al.*, 2003; Giddens, 1991). While recognising that these views do not command full acceptance (Atkinson, 2007; Outhwaite, 2009) I will draw upon the work of the late Ulrich Beck, particularly in his analysis of the 'post-modernisation' of society, for the background context in understanding this 'new' form of modernity (Beck *et al.*, 2003). In a series of papers, Beck and his colleagues have set out a research programme to distinguish those features of what he termed 'second' modernity that set it apart from the earlier 'first' modernity whose contours were explored by sociology's 'founding fathers' (Durkheim, 1984; Mannheim, 1997; Tönnies 1958; Weber, 1978).

For Beck, three features exemplify the role of 'second' modernity in de-standardising the life course. In the first place, the processes of individualisation have hollowed out many of the institutions and structures that once defined what it was for a society to be modern – particularly the role once played by the systems of production in organising social relations. In the second place have come changes in gendered relations and the undermining of the previous distinction between productive and reproductive labour that was such a dominant feature of industrialisation. Third, has been the expansion of markets into ever wider areas of personal life, as consumption has become the major arena where identities and lifestyles are realised (Beck and Beck-Gernsheim, 2001; Beck and Grande, 2010; Beck and Lau, 2005; Beck *et al.*, 2003).

In earlier analyses of industrial society, concepts such as class, community and cohort (generation) were widely deployed as terms or tools for defining and understanding modernity (Durkheim, 1984; Mannheim, 1997; Tönnies, 1958; Weber, 1978). These analyses underplayed the role of technology, and emphasis was placed on work, labour and economic relations. Mass production, class consciousness and the transformation of traditional (folk) into popular (mass) culture were, to the founding fathers, key in what constituted 'modern' life. Trains, cars and aeroplanes, radios, telephones and the cinema were recognised as symbols of modern life, but they were still largely viewed as the superstructure, not the determinants of culture and society.[1] The divisions of gender and the organisation of the life course were regulated by the needs of capital for labour. Technology served this cause, enabling people to get to work on time, to have their work organised on time and their productivity enhanced over time, through electrification, mechanisation and regulation. Technology symbolised but remained subservient to the modernity of mass production.

In second modernity, this pattern began to unravel. Technology expanded the number and range of goods and services available outside the work place as much as it transformed the workplace (Lunt and Livingstone, 1992; Miles, 1998). The media became increasingly important in shaping the identities and lifestyles of workers and their families. Mass consumption first matched then exceeded mass production; mass consumption became mass consumerism. This affected life inside and outside of work. The home became as much a site of modernity as the workplace. The marketing and sales of white goods such as fridge freezers, tumble dryers, vacuum cleaners and washing machines blurred the distinctions of class while changing the nature and form of reproductive labour. (Benson, 1994; Bowden and Offer, 1994; Lunt and Livingstone, 1992; Miles, 1998). The expanding leisure and entertainment industries progressively individualised lifestyles, from the communal radio and the gramophone to portable record players, cassette and CD players, to digital downloads, from limited channel terrestrial TVs to VCRs then DVDs, and from cable TV to online entertainment systems. While many of these developments have created new industries and expanded new systems of production, their greatest impact has been on expanding the possibilities of a more individualised consumer life style inside and outside the home (Beck and Beck-Gernsheim, 2001).

As the dynamic shifted from a first to a second modernity, so have the organising principles of work (Beck and Beck-Gernsheim, 2001). The job a man does no longer determines his place in the world or that of his family. Men and women are equally likely to provide the source of income for the home; the fixed communities that were associated with factory work or primary industries like farming, fishing or mining have become less dominant and the spatial connection between home and work attenuated. Working parents' children are exposed to a diversity of influences and role models that exceed by far those once provided by their parents and the local school, while household structures are no longer held together in the ways they once were by the farm or the factory, the mine or the mill. A plethora of influences impinge upon people at all stages of their life, before, during and after working life. Consumerism shapes the lives of primary school children and pensioners as much as it does those of 'working age' (Jones *et al.*, 2008; Kline, 1994).

Framing this transition as one from first to second modernity provides the general context for this chapter. Its particular focus is upon how the changing nature of later life is realised by and within the new 'domestic' technologies that are an increasingly important part of second modernity, and that help realise it as both a 'networked' society and a society of 'networked individualism' (Rainie and Wellman, 2012). The aim is to periodise some of the key changes in this process, to outline the relevance of these new technologies in these changes and to identify their role in contributing to – or in constraining – the 'post-modernisation' of later life.

The new ageing: a conceptual framework

The conditions establishing the new ageing can be traced to 'the long sixties' and its associated consumer revolution (Marwick, 1998). Those born in and just after the Second World War are perhaps its vanguard birth cohort, emerging as the offspring of a cultural revolution that offered access to new media, new forms of popular entertainment and the novelty of having, as teenagers, discretionary spending power. The post-war economies were expanding and new opportunities arose for young people to express their distinctiveness as a generation – through music, fashion, hairstyles, clubs and coffee bars. Linked to, though distinguishable from this cultural 'turn' were changes in lifestyle, the celebration of difference, and the embodied identities and practices of ethnicity, gender and sexuality (Gilleard and Higgs, 2013).

If the sixties and seventies laid the foundation for such changes, the eighties saw them embedded across the life course. Just as the bands of the sixties kept on rocking into mid-life, so too did their fans. The marketing of 'youth' extended beyond the expenditure of young people as issues of consumerist distinction moved downwards into childhood and upwards into and beyond middle age. No longer youth but youthfulness was bought and sold through an ever-increasing range of goods and services, part of a 'rebel sell' that was beginning to incorporate not just resistance to the old but liberation from agedness itself (Gilleard and Higgs, 2013, p. 31).

As part of this cultural turn, the body became subject to an ever-widening range of 'somatic technologies' or, in Foucault's terms, technologies of the self (Foucault, 1988). Their points of reference soon outgrew their narrow 'commoditisation' within the 1960s counter-cultures and sub-cultures. No longer so carefully policed and bound, as they first were by age and generation, these variously expressed forms of 'appearance management' (Cahill, 1989), 'body maintenance' (Featherstone, 1982), or 'body work' (Gimlin, 2007) made fashioning and refashioning the body a lifelong enterprise; and, for some, a lifelong chore. The greater their penetration into everyday life, the more they undermined the stability previously attached to identities that were once embodied as 'foundationalist' social forms. The result was a greater individualisation of the body, rendering it subject to the processes of 'lifestyle' rather than 'life stage' fashioning (Lipovetsky, 2002, p. 5), that was without any obvious ending.

Nowhere was this turn from the distinctions of youth to the demonstration of youthfulness better marked than by the Jane Fonda body work-out video tapes first marketed in the 1980s (Dinnerstein and Weitz, 1994). Here in condensed form were the corporate technologies of self, marketed to the baby boomers, in celebration of the values of choice, autonomy, self-expression and pleasure (Fonda, 2011, p. 88). Here was the generational divide that had first emerged in 1960s youth working its way across the life course. In the process, those approaching later life were gradually fashioning (and being fashioned into) a new generational field, that of the third age, enacted in front of their TV screens.

The idea of the third age was introduced into the field of ageing studies during the late 1980s in Peter Laslett's book *A fresh map of life* (Laslett, 1989). Representing the third age as a generational field rather than, as Laslett had proposed, a stage of life, was proposed a decade later by Gilleard and Higgs (2002). Drawing on the work of Karl Mannheim and Pierre Bourdieu, Gilleard and Higgs integrated Bourdieu's concepts of fields and habitus with Mannheim's concept of a generational unit and generational 'entelechy' to construct the idea of the third age as a 'generational field'. United by the logic of mass consumerism and the valorisation of choice, autonomy, self-expression and pleasure, they argued that the third age emerged as a specific generational field where *distinction, identity* and *lifestyle* were realised through a combination of rising living standards, progressive exposure to consumption, the continuing penetration of the system world into the life world and the historical legacy of the 'long sixties' and its ideology of personal and political liberation (Gilleard and Higgs, 2011).

Technological generations, new eras and second modernity

Just as it is possible to chart the emergence of the third age as a generational field reflecting the dissolution or destandardisation of the 'traditional' institutional structures of industrial society, so it is possible to consider the emergence of a distinct technological habitus associated with the new ICTs as constituting another feature of this emergent cultural field. Over time, each modifies the other as technology and lifestyle are slowly fashioned by and adapt to each other at different points and in different ways across the life course. Within the changing fields of technology and the life course, it is possible to discern a common modernising process at work, one that first set up and then dissolved the organising principles of lives and institutions of first modernity, laying the foundations for its emergence in a second, more liquid form (Bauman, 2000, 2005).

Beyond such generalities, it is possible to explore a slightly different periodisation, contrasting the technological changes that accompanied first modernity, with those that democratised and then dissolved it. In keeping with Beck's dichotomy between a 'first' and a 'second' modernity, the first two periods to be discussed may be thought of as corresponding with 'first' modernity; the third with 'second' modernity. But before joining together these periods of social and technological change, let us consider the idea that there may be distinct 'technological' generations, not just distinct eras. According to Sackmann and Winkler, 'the concept of technology generations was developed by German sociologists in the early 1990s' (Sackmann and Winkler, 2013, p. 493). The term refers not to the technology itself but to the birth cohorts that adopt it. Its boundaries are determined, according to these authors, 'when a technology reaches a 20 per cent threshold in households in the relevant formative years (*c.* 15–25 years)' (Sackmann and Winkler, 2013, p. 494). In fact, however, much of these authors' work has concentrated on a distinction between the technological habitus of older people born before the 1960s, with that of 'a computer generation' born in the 1960s/1970s, a division that inevitably risks confounding simple age effects with 'cohort' or 'generational' effects.

Rather than getting lost in this kind of 'is it age or is it cohort' dilemma, it may be preferable to focus upon technological change as indicative of general period or era effects – that is to acknowledge that distinct technological formats or features arise within particular time periods, as a function of both what has gone before and what is new – than to define a generation by the technologies of its time. The extent to which such changes affect or are adopted by particular groups, including particular age groups, is contingent, not subject, to universal rules. Only the temporality of change is constant. Particular technological systems necessarily persist until they are replaced or overtaken by newer ones. These changes may affect different age groups, but do so not as a consequence of generational cohorts, but because when earlier technologies are superseded by later technologies, they not only change the form but expand the range of functions that are rendered possible by the newer technologies. This alters access and usability, creating new or different groups of potential users, while growing familiarity, reduced costs and further adaptations expand the user base. In short, technological change may be better viewed as periodised by time, form and function rather than being associated with a particular cohort class or community.

As far as forms of communication have been enhanced and expanded, and notions of community changed by technology, it is possible to discern three distinct periods that mark the transition from first to second modernity. The emergence of modern communication technology, exemplified by the telephone and telegraph, appeared during the late nineteenth century and arguably continued up to the 1930s, located very much in the time frame of first modernity. Future developments beginning just before but extending particularly after the Second World War saw the democratisation of this electrical technology, when between 1930 and 1975 more homes were connected and telephones and radios became part of the household furniture for the majority of the population. The third era is exemplified by the transition from electrical to electronic technologies. This period, from the late 1960s/early 1970s onward, witnessed the arrival of the transistor and the semi-conductor, the integrated circuit, the microprocessor and the rapid evolution of electronic machine language. This new technological era was built upon the already democratised systems of first modernity that had ensured electrical power supplies in most homes and widespread access to radios, televisions and telephones. Developments in electronics witnessed a range of new portable, personalised devices such as the cell phone, the microcomputer and the internet. This development helped define the transition into a second modernity, permitting further individualisation, rendering communities more liquid and more mobile, and pervasively 'in touch' (Chen, 2012).

Technological eras, generational divisions and age divides

This no doubt over-simplified picture of technological change can be summarised by stating that the rise of mass society – with its democratisation of consumer culture, politics of liberation and securitisation of a degree at least of disposable income for all – created the conditions for its unravelling. The process of securitisation and the accompanying standardisation of the life course into youth, working life and retirement, like much else in modernity, was achieved by and largely for the interests of white, heterosexual males, via the male breadwinner model of the modern economy. This achievement enabled a second, less solid type of modernity to emerge which has replaced the structures of first modernity. The old solidarities have dissolved as neglected minorities have acquired the beginnings, at least, of a voice that challenges the 'old' certainties established by first modernity (Bauman, 2000, 2005). From a widening range of sources, and spurred on by the expansion of the market into ever more aspects of the life world, more diverse, multi-directional modernities have been fashioned. Whereas once, the dynamic driving these new social movements was articulated primarily by the young and the old were left behind, later life has acquired, in modernity two, a new place for itself; not in the old shape of pensioners quietly secure in their relative poverty, but within the diverse communities and later lifestyles that constitute the cultures of a third age.

As the retired population continues to grow in size and in cultural and social salience, the diversity as well as the divisions within this community are becoming more apparent. The old divisions of modernity that were associated with occupational class and place are increasingly challenged by the new more unstable divisions of identity and lifestyle that ebb and flow past those old divisions. The distinctions and divisions of the third age are captured by the market rather than secured by the state. Catch up has seen a new rhetoric of active, healthy, productive, 'successful' ageing that is now framed not just as a market segment but as a target for the new governmentality of later life that jostles with the earlier rhetoric of care, dependency and need. Not that the former political discourse has replaced the latter; but within the revived neo-liberal state, it is fast overtaking it (Macnicol, 2015).

But though the distinctions of the old life course have become less salient and less solid, new divides seem to be emerging that are of particular relevance to the digital era: that between a third and a fourth age. The old life stages divide between 'student', 'worker' and 'pensioner' has lessened much like that between 'working' and 'middle' class. In their place is a new divide that separates an age denying, age defying cohort and community who shop, chat and travel relatively freely and at relative ease with the new technosphere, from another, inescapably aged population. The latter have, in many ways, become more isolated and more excluded from contemporary culture than the pensioners of the past, trapped within what has been termed the social imaginary of the fourth age (Gilleard and Higgs, 2010).

The social imaginary of the fourth age can be seen as one of the unintended consequences of the emergence of the third age. Rejecting 'old' and 'agedness', the cultures of the third age have inadvertently rendered old age darker and more undesirable; as an 'imaginary' of a real old age the fear of a fourth age acts as a spur toward new desires, new opportunities and new imperatives to stay young, keep fit and be forever functional (Marshall and Katz, 2002). Unlike the realisation of the various cultures and lifestyles that mark out the cultural field of the third age, including those determined by the new ICT, the fourth age functions less as a social space or 'actor network', but operates, in Castoriadis' terms,[2] as an imaginary whose malignant significations exceed the confines of any old age associated practice or institution (Gilleard and Higgs, 2013; Higgs and Gilleard, 2015).

This divide is recreated within the cultural and social relations marked by contemporary ICT. The third age Skypes, joins online communities, shops and networks online and travels into the unknown with a smart phone in hand, active and evolving participants in the cultures of the third age. The fourth age does none of these. Instead, they are regarded primarily as potential candidates for various so-called adaptive digital technologies – technologies that are more clever and more capable than they. This division is not just a digital divide – though it can be seen to map onto such models – neither is it reducible to the difference between two cohorts sharing different habitus or products of different 'generational technologies'. In second modernity, such divides soon lessen (Gilleard *et al.*, 2015). More than anything else, it is a division between those who can and those who cannot participate, share and help realise an identity and a lifestyle within and by means of the material resources and cultural capital that have been generated by second modernity.

Technological frames for the third age and the fourth age

This leads me to consider, in this final section of the chapter, some of the direct consequences that link this critical distinction between third age cultures and a fourth age imaginary, and the use and application of the new ICT. How do the new divides of modernity two influence later life and the place of the new technologies in contributing to – or constraining – this fracturing of old age? One set of studies that might be considered a research programme for technology and third age studies might seek to discover what consumerist habitus distinguishes adopters and non-adopters of new technologies within or between age cohorts or groups of retired people varying in their style and extent of consumerism. Such research might seek to explore, for example, what distinguishes later life 'players' and later life 'communicators' from those who remain mostly 'watchers' or 'listeners' (e.g. those using old style mobile phones to keep in touch or for 'emergencies' vs. those using smart phones to play, shop or travel). Similarly, useful research may explore how many grandparents are bought digital technology by their grandchildren and how these particular grandparents differ from those who buy new digital technology for themselves and their grandchildren.

Likewise, within the same 'third age' framework, one might want to inquire into patterns of recycling and upgrading. Who and how many make the upgrade from mobile to smart phone; from using mobile phones for communication only to using them to conduct online banking, play games or go surfing the supermarket online? Who learns how to Skype, how do they learn and why? Who acquires technological expertise from their peers, from friends, partners and colleagues, and who does so via the vertical relationships of kith and kin? Likewise, for social media, who learns to book Facetime and how do they learn? These examples can be multiplied over and over, but the point remains the same – the need to promote research presaged upon the role of the new technology in extending, expanding and shaping the cultures of the third age, including expanding the ways of having fun online (e.g. Marston and Graner Ray, 2016; Rogers *et al.*, 2014).

Such research seems much rarer than that conducted to assist or help older people use ICT (Arthanata *et al.*, 2016), 'adapt' the technology for 'older people' (Díaz-Bossini and Moreno, 2014) or discover whether using the new technology is 'good for them' (Bobillier Chaumon *et al.*, 2014); for example, if it 'prevents dementia' (Kenigsberg *et al.*, 2016) or if it reduces depression (Elliot *et al.*, 2014). This way lies the social imaginary of old age. The fourth age and fourth age studies in digital technology have a very different agenda to the sort of questions posed earlier. A kind of shift can be observed from what appear to be 'third' age concerns based on 'enablement' but presaged upon disablement (preventing dementia with memory games; mind fitness training, etc.) to frankly fourth age pre-occupations, such as the use of mobile and smart phones as alarm bracelets, or memory and orientation aides, or the development of information systems to monitor the older person at risk, or to support and enhance the work of human 'care' providers through 'robotic' aides (Angelini *et al.*, 2013; De San Miguel and Lewin, 2008; Granat *et al.*, 2013; Gschwind *et al.*, 2015; Schneider and Henneberger, 2014).

By examining the development of different 'gerontechnologies' it is possible to discern how far digital technology researchers – as well as the technologies themselves – prevent, and how far they bring about, the 'frailing' of old age. Just as the visibly prominent hearing aid marks out the wearer as 'deaf', or the push-chair style wheelchair marks its passenger as 'immobile', so the necklace with the alarm or the electronic care plan in the kitchen mark out the householder or resident as impaired; as having something 'wrong' with them. The challenge is one that researchers in disability studies have been engaged with for some time, namely how and in what ways it is possible to design technologies that mark the person or user as 'enhanced' or 'augmented' rather than made less or belittled by their use. Reflexively viewing the changing concepts of modernity and the changes that have taken place in the organisation and experience of later life from 'first' to 'second' modernity, it is possible to develop a more critical analysis of the role of ICTs in fashioning the kind of later life that our present and future age-ing societies are on the point of realising. Recognising that these processes not only create new potentials but also present new pitfalls, it is important to retain that mix of optimism of the will and pessimism of the intellect when judging the future of ageing and technology and their complex, evolving relationship.

Notes

1 An exception could be made for the writing of Georg Simmel whose fascination for the cultural aspects of modernity set him apart from "the sociology taking shape in the late nineteenth and early twentieth century" (Connor, 1996, p. 341).
2 Castoriadis' use of the term 'imaginary' and 'social imaginary significations' are out-lined in detail in his book, *The Imaginary Institution of Society* (Castoriadis, 1987).

References

Angelini, L., Caon, M., Carrino, S., Bergeron, L., Nyffeler, N., Jean-Mairet, M. and Mugellini, E., 2013, September. Designing a desirable smart bracelet for older adults. In: *Proceedings of The 2013 ACM Conference on Pervasive and Ubiquitous Computing*. Adjunct publication. New York: Association for Computing Machinery, pp. 425–434.

Arthanata, S., Vromana, K. G. and Lysackb, C., 2016. A home-based individualized infor-mation communication technology training program for older adults: a demonstration of effectiveness and value. *Disability and Rehabilitation: Assistive Technology*, 11(4), 316–324.

Atkinson, W., 2007. Beck, individualization and the death of class: a critique. *The British Journal of Sociology*, 58(3), pp. 349–366.

Bauman, Z., 2000. *Liquid modernity*. Cambridge, UK: Polity.

Bauman, Z., 2005. *Liquid life*. Cambridge, UK: Polity.

Beck, U. and Beck-Gernsheim, E., 2001. *Individualisation: institutionalised individualism and its social and political consequences*. Cambridge, UK: Polity.

Beck, U. and Grande, E., 2010. Varieties of second modernity: the cosmopolitan turn in social and political theory and research. *British Journal of Sociology*, 61(3), pp. 409–443.

Beck, U. and Lau, C., 2005. Second modernity as a research agenda: theoretical and empirical explorations in the 'meta-change' of modern society. *The British Journal of Sociology*, 56(4), pp. 525–557.

Beck, U., Bonss, W. and Lau, C., 2003. The theory of reflexive modernization problematic, hypotheses and research programme. *Theory, Culture & Society*, 20(2), pp. 1–33.

Benson, J., 1994. *The rise of consumer society in Britain, 1880–1980*. London: Longman.

Bobillier Chaumon, M. E., Michel, C., Tarpin Bernard, F. and Croisile, B., 2014. Can ICT improve the quality of life of elderly adults living in residential home care units? From actual impacts to hidden artefacts. *Behaviour & Information Technology*, 33(6), pp. 574–590.

Bowden, S. and Offer, A., 1994. Household appliances and the use of time: The United States and Britain since the 1920s. *Economic History Review*, 47(4), p. 725–748.

Cahill, S. E., 1989. Fashioning males and females: appearance management and the social reproduction of gender. *Symbolic Interaction*, 12(2), pp. 281–298.

Calhoun, C., 1998. Community without propinquity revisited: communications technology and the transformation of the urban public sphere. *Sociological Inquiry*, 68(3), pp. 373–397.

Castells, M., 1996. *The rise of the network society: Vol. I. The information age: economy, society and culture*. Oxford, UK: Blackwell.

Castoriadis, C., 1987. *The imaginary institution of society*. Cambridge, UK: Polity Press.

Chen, B. 2012. *Always on: how the i-phone unlocked the anything-anytime-anywhere future*. Boston, MA: Da Capo Press.

Connor, S., 1996. Cultural sociology and cultural sciences. In: B. S. Turner, ed. *The Blackwell companion to social theory*. Oxford, UK: Blackwell, pp. 340–368.

De San Miguel, K. and Lewin, G., 2008. Personal emergency alarms: what impact do they have on older people's lives? *Australasian Journal on Ageing*, 27(2), pp. 103–105.

Díaz-Bossini, J. M. and Moreno, L., 2014. Accessibility to mobile interfaces for older people. *Procedia Computer Science*, 27, pp. 57–66.

Dinnerstein, M. and Weitz, R., 1994. Jane Fonda, Barbara Bush and other aging bodies: femininity and the limits of resistance. *Feminist Issues*, 14(2), pp. 3–24.

Durkheim, E., [1893] 1984. *The division of labour in society*. Basingstoke, UK: Macmillan.

Elliot, A. J., Mooney, C. J., Douthit, K. Z. and Lynch, M. F., 2014. Predictors of older adults' technology use and its relationship to depressive symptoms and well-being. *The Journals of Gerontology Series B: Psychological Sciences and Social Sciences*, 69(5), pp. 667–677.

Featherstone, M., 1982. The body in consumer culture. *Theory, Culture & Society*, 1(2), pp. 18–33.

Fonda, J., 2011. *Prime time: making the most of all of your life*. London: Vermillion,

Foucault, M., 1988. Technologies of the self. In L. H. Martin, H. Gutman and P. H. Hutton, eds. *Technologies of the self: a seminar with Michel Foucault*. Amherst, MA: University of Massachusetts Press, pp. 16–49.

Gergen, K. J. and Gergen, M. M., 2000. The new aging: self construction and social values. In: R. W. Schaie and J. Hendricks, eds. *The evolution of the aging self: the societal impact on the aging process*. New York, Springer, pp. 281–306.

Giddens, A., 1991. *Modernity and self-identity: self and society in the late modern age*. Stanford, CA: Stanford University Press.

Gilleard, C. and Higgs, P., 2002. The third age: class, cohort or generation. *Ageing & Society*, 22(3), 369–382.

Gilleard, C. and Higgs, P., 2010. Ageing without agency: theorising the fourth age. *Aging & Mental Health*, 14(2), pp. 121–128.

Gilleard, C. and Higgs, P., 2011. The third age as a cultural field: In: D. Carr and K. Komp, eds. *Gerontology in the era of the third age*. New York: Springer, pp. 33–50.

Gilleard, C. and Higgs, P., 2013. *Ageing, corporeality and embodiment*. London: Anthem Press.

Gilleard, C., Jones, I. and Higgs, P., 2015. Connectivity in later life: the declining age divide in mobile cell phone ownership. *Sociological Research Online*, 20(2). http://www.socresonline.org.uk/20/2/3.html.

Gimlin, D., 2007. What is 'body work'? A review of the literature. *Sociology Compass*, 1(1), pp. 353–70.

Granat, C., Pino, M., Legouverneur, G., Vidal, J. S., Bidaud, P. and Rigaud, A. S., 2013. Robot services for elderly with cognitive impairment: testing usability of graphical user interfaces. *Technological Health Care*, 21(3), pp. 217–231.

Gschwind, Y. J., Schoene, D., Lord, S. R., Ejupi, A., Valenzuela, T., Aal, K., Woodbury, A. and Delbaere, K., 2015. The effect of sensor-based exercise at home on functional performance associated with fall risk in older people: a comparison of two exergame interventions. *European Review of Aging and Physical Activity*, 12(11). https://doi.org/10.5817/CP2012-2-3.

Higgs, P. and Gilleard, C., 2015. Fitness and consumerism in later life. In: E. Tulle and C. Phoenix, eds. *Physical activity and sport in later life: critical perspectives*. London: Palgrave Macmillan, pp. 32–42.

Jones, I. R., Hyde, M., Victor, C., Wiggins, R. D., Gilleard, C. and Higgs, P., 2008. *Ageing in a consumer society: from passive to active consumption in Britain*. Bristol, UK: Policy Press.

Kenigsberg, P. A., Aquino, J. P., Berard, A., Gzil, F., Andrieu, S., Banerjee, S., Brémond, F., Buee, L., Cohen-Mansfield, J., Mangialasche, F. and Platel, H., 2016. Dementia beyond 2025: knowledge and uncertainties. *Dementia*, 15(1), 6–21.

Kline, S., 1994 Toys, socialization and the commodification of play. In: S. Strasser, C. McGovern and M. Judt, eds. *Getting and spending: European and American consumer societies in the twentieth century*. Cambridge, UK: Cambridge University Press, pp. 339–358.

Kohli, M. and Rein, M., 1991. The changing balance of work and retirement. In: M. Kohli, M. Rein, A-M. Guillemard and H. M. Gunsteren, eds. *Time for retirement: comparative studies of early exit from the labor force*. Cambridge, UK: Cambridge University Press, pp. 1–35.

Laslett, P., 1989. *A fresh map of life: the emergence of the third age*. London: Weidenfeld and Nicholson.

Lipovetsky, G., 2002. *The empire of fashion: dressing modern democracy*. Princeton, NJ: Princeton University Press.

Lunt, P. K. and Livingstone, S., 1992. *Mass consumption and personal identity: everyday economic experience*. Buckingham, UK: Open University Press.

Macnicol, J., 2015. *Neoliberalising old age*. Cambridge, UK: Cambridge University Press.

Mannheim, K., [1952] 1997. On the problem of generation: In M. A. Hardy, ed. *Studying aging and social change: conceptual and methodological issues*. London: SAGE, pp. 22–65.

Marshall, B. and Katz, S., 2002. Forever functional: sexual fitness and the aging male body. *Body & Society*, 8(4), pp. 43–70.

Marston, H. R. and Graner Ray, S., 2016. Older women on the game: understanding digital game perspectives from an ageing cohort. In: E. Domínguez-Rué and L. Nierling, eds. *Ageing and technology: perspectives from the social sciences*. Bielefeld, Germany: Transcript-Verlag, pp. 67–91.

Marwick, A., 1998. *The sixties: cultural revolution in Britain, France, Italy, and the United States, c. 1958–c. 1974*. Oxford, UK: Oxford University Press.

Miles, S., 1998. *Consumerism as a way of life*. London: SAGE.

Outhwaite, W., 2009. Canon formation in late 20th-century British sociology. *Sociology*, 43(6), pp. 1029–1045.

Rainie, L. and Wellman, B., 2012. *Networked: the new social operating system*. Cambridge, MA: MIT Press.

Rogers, Y., Paay, J., Brereton, M., Vaisutis, K. L., Marsden, G. and Vetere, F., 2014. Never too old: engaging retired people inventing the future with MaKey MaKey. In: *Proceedings of the SIGCHI Conference on Human Factors in Computing Systems*. ACM, pp. 3913–3922.

Sackmann, R. and Winkler, O., 2013. Technology generations revisited: the internet generation. *Gerontechnology*, 11(4), 493–503.

Schneider, C. and Henneberger, S., 2014. Electronic spatial assistance for people with dementia: choosing the right device. *Technologies*, 2(2), 96–114.

Tönnies, F., [1886] 1958. *Community and association*. London: C. P. Loomis, Routledge and Kegan Paul.

Weber, M., [1922] 1978. *Economy and society*. Berkeley, CA: University of California Press.

3 Generational analysis as a methodological approach to study mediatised social change

Göran Bolin

Introduction

Time and again, it is said that we are living in an era of rapid technological change, or even one of increased acceleration (Rosa, 2013 [2005]). This idea of accelerating technological change, especially that involving media technologies, also serves as a basis for contemporary theories of 'media generations'. These theories argue that in contrast to previous generations who were socialised into print media culture, those born over the past 50–60 years have seen a much more rapid transformation of technologies, impacting more strongly on the formation of generational identity. According to Gary Gumpert and Robert Cathcart, the faster pace of technological change leads to the formation of distinct media generations.

> Prior to the late nineteenth century media explosion, generations came and went, all exposed to and acquiring the same print grammar. Thus media seemed to have little bearing on human time relationships. Though we still think of people as related, or separated in chronological generation time, the rapid advent of new media and the acquisition of new media grammars implies new alignments, shorter and more diverse than those based on generations.
>
> (Gumpert and Cathcart, 1985, p. 31)

Theories of generation were formulated first in the early 1900s by theorists such as Spanish philosopher José Ortega y Gasset (1931 [1923]) and German sociologist Karl Mannheim (1952 [1928]) in order to understand why and how societies change. In a more general sense, it could be argued that the theory of generations is a theory of time; trying to come to grips with 'the rhythm of ages' (Ortega y Gasset, 1931 [1923], p. 18; cf. Ricoeur, 1990 [1985]; Bolin, 2016b). Although generational theory has been refined and developed in the wake of Mannheim, Ortega y Gassett and others within sociology (e.g. Kertzer, 1983; Pilcher, 1998; Corsten, 1999), and also in media studies (Gumpert and Cathcart, 1985; Colombo and Fortunati, 2011), general methodological principles for how to analyse generations, and thus media-related social change, have been less discussed.

Media-related social change is at the heart of theories on mediatisation. The concept of mediatisation has been developed to address these changes and understand how media technologies have come to play an increasingly important role in everyday life (e.g. Lundby, 2009; Hjarvard, 2013). In its institutional conceptualisation, it has been argued that the media impact on other societal institutions (Hjarvard, 2013), making them adjust to the logics of the media (Altheide and Snow, 1979). In a social-constructionist version of this theory, the media is presented as a more general 'moulding force' (Hepp, 2013), while in semiotic or structuralist accounts the media are seen as becoming increasingly influential for the signifying systems by which human communication occurs (Bolin, 2014a).

While the concept of mediatisation has been met with enthusiasm, it also has its critics. One criticism concerns the relative lack of temporal perspectives. The concept of mediatisation like other '-isation' concepts, such as globalisation, individualisation and commercialisation, suggests historical change, but as Deacon and Stanyer (2014) have pointed out 'much mediatization research depends on a presumption rather than the demonstration of historical change, projecting backwards from contemporary case studies rather than carefully designed temporal comparisons' (Deacon and Stanyer, 2014, p. 1037).

In this chapter I suggest that an analytical perspective that focuses upon generations can work as an aid in studying historical change, and that it can help provide empirical substance to mediatisation theory. The chapter draws on empirical material from a project on generations, media and historical change that was carried out in Sweden and Estonia between 2002 and 2012. Data collected using quantitative survey methodology have been combined with qualitative focus group interviews to address various opportunities and obstacles that a such multi-method approach entails for the analysis of generations.[1]

By coupling this methodological approach with a comparative intergenerational analysis, the chapter shows how media memories from childhood and from the formative years of youth reveal specific traits in the historical process, and on how the role of the media has changed over time in the minds of different generations. The chapter explains how the passage of calendar time gradually forms generations in what may be termed a 'generationing' process (Siibak and Vittadini, 2012). Analysing this process, it is argued here, is also to analyse social change, including its media-related dimensions. Elsewhere, I have discussed this in terms of a specific generational 'rhythm of ages', where the theoretical underpinnings of my argument are developed (Bolin, 2016a). Here, I have focused upon a more elaborate discussion of analytical approaches and empirical implications. I have also played down the cross-cultural comparisons that were made in the larger project in order to focus more specifically on the issue of social change. The cross-cultural dimension is more elaborated in Bolin (2016b).

The chapter is organised in four sections. First, the theory of generations is elaborated on to establish a general framework for the study. Second, a specific analytical approach is presented. Third, the benefits and drawbacks of these methodological choices are discussed, and the method is critically evaluated, and in the final section the methodological opportunities and challenges that a generational perspective allows for in the study of mediatised social change are then summarised.

Generation theory and time

Following Karl Mannheim's seminal paper (Mannheim, 1952) a founding idea in generational theory is that generations are formed through the common experiences of coevals, located in the same place in the historical process. The relation to the historical context is important, and Mannheim made a major distinction between generation as 'location' and as 'actuality'. In an analogy with Marx's theory of class, Mannheim defined generation as "the certain 'location' (*Lagerung*) certain individuals hold in the economic and power structure of a given society" (Mannheim, 1952, p. 289). The basis for this generational location is year of birth, where all people born in the same year have a "common location in the historical dimension of the social process" (Mannheim, 1952, p. 290). However, location in time is not enough since it would reduce a generation to being nothing more than an age cohort. To explain the basis of generations in common experience, Mannheim introduced the concept of generation as *actuality*, that is, when people born around the same time have similar experiences and also perceive themselves as thereby constituting a generation. The process of acquiring such a 'generational consciousness' is termed 'generationing' (Siibak and Vittadini, 2012). This alludes to "the result of the interaction between contextual and fixed traits (such as historical, cultural and social events and experiences) and a cultural process of identity formation developed over time (including narratives, performances and rituals)" (Siibak and Vittadini, 2012, p. 3; Siibak *et al.*, 2014). According to this perspective, people are not born into a generation, but form their generational identity over time. Hence it is easier to detect clear-cut generational formations among older generations who have lived longer than those whose identity is only emerging (Bolin, 2016a, pp. 124ff).

Mannheim argued that the most important experiences that bring a generational formation together are those that are acquired during the formative years of youth. Making 'fresh contact' with specific phenomena binds people together in their common experiences and makes them act in relation to these things or phenomena in similar ways. Their responses to societal events need not be the same and may produce different generational units (for example, men and women might react differently), but they are all triggered by major societal events. Mannheim thought of such events as wars, famine, uprisings and major catastrophes, but later research has proposed that the media can also be an important source in the development of generational consciousness (see the earlier quote from Gumpert and Cathcart, 1985).

Whether change occurs, and if so at what speed and with what consequences, can of course be debated. Furthermore, as Marshall Berman (1988 [1982]) points out, change is itself the dominant mode of experience in modernity. Although most people perceive their specific era as the most revolutionary in human history when it comes to change, there are qualitative differences related to different (media) technologies, depending on the level that one enters into the analysis. If we agree with Marshall McLuhan (1964) that "the medium is the message", it will indeed matter to this message *which* specific medium provokes the change.

Generations are thus formed in relation to the experience of various phenomena in society. Among these is the range of media technologies, media contents and the media's capacity to provide people with the means to communicate with one another. Individual subjects react to and act against these structures, much depending on how the subjects perceive them. This produces the subjective apprehension of the 'objective' structure. It is a commonly shared subjective apprehension that lies at the bottom of the generational experience, and which can result in the actualisation of a generational consciousness.

The generational theory of Mannheim and others focuses on coevals, people born around the same time. As a result of having similar experiences, a specific generational consciousness is formed that renders such a generation as a social formation. However, people do not confront media technologies, content or services in the same way. Individuals make fresh contact with the media landscape at different ages and from the vantage point of different life-phases and situations. Being confronted with the Beatles at the age of 16 in the midst of the teenage years means something entirely different from having been introduced to them as a 45-year-old parent (cf. Corsten, 1999). There is thus a need for coupling the synchronic approach of Mannheim and his followers, with the diachronic approach of, for example, Margaret Mead (1970), who emphasised intergenerational relations, that is, how younger and older generations relate to one another, with the potential of such relations producing a 'generation gap'. Such gaps can stem from such differences in life situation and age, which may inform the ways in which one appreciates the media, and which may influence the type of impact this meeting may have on one's generational self-perception. Life phase, life situation and age thus need to be related to the generationing process. In order to capture this process, a particular methodological approach was developed.

Analytical approach

One way of analysing generationing as a temporal process, as the meeting between a social collective and a techno-cultural structure, is to adopt a cross-generational comparative approach, whereby different generational formations can stand out against each other. In this case, the background to such a comparative analysis came from a larger project, initiated with colleagues at Södertörn University, Sweden, and Tartu University, Estonia, in 2001. Its aim was to study the processes of mediatised change, for which the comparison between Sweden and Estonia was considered fitting. The point of departure, described in more detail in Bolin (2003, 2005), was that while the developments in media technologies were similar in both cultural contexts (i.e. media technologies arrived and were established at approximately the same time), the historical and geopolitical context for that encounter was dramatically different in the two media landscapes. There were also varieties in contents between the two cultural contexts. The basic hypothesis was that these differences should have made an impact on the ways in which media were adopted and used in each of these national settings. However, the aim was not to establish if this was the case or not, but rather to specify variations in the ways in which the media were 'domesticated' in each country and what relations citizens in both countries had with the media. Our conception of 'the media' was broad, and included all kinds of communication technologies from books, records, the traditional mass media and the digital media of the present.

As James Beniger (1992) pointed out, all research in the social sciences is comparative, and thus the comparative dimension of research is more a matter of specifying exactly how such comparisons are made. I have discussed the benefits of adopting a comparative perspective at length in Bolin (2016a, pp. 15ff), so for this context I will simply point out that in this specific case, the comparative approach aimed to identify on which occasions we could recognise the impact of different cultural-historic circumstances.

The concept of *media landscape* was chosen for the 'objective' structure of technologies, contents and communication opportunities, over similar competing concepts such as 'media ecology', or 'media environment', which, although having their specific merits, through their biological connotations point to developments of an organic nature. The concept of landscape, on the contrary, points to the constructedness of the media as a specific combination of technologies and contents, formed socially and used and appropriated socially (Bolin, 2003, 2006). It points to the ensemble of media that is present at any one point in time in a society. It is the technological and symbolic media structure, the amount of technologies and contents (signs, messages) that an individual can react to, act against, or ignore. Some of these technologies and semiotic structures are more accessible than others, and, depending on the individual trajectory that people have through these landscapes and the experiences they have acquired, the landscape will privilege certain types of approaches over others.

The metaphor of media landscape thus refers to the mediatised space in which people live and act. It is a spatial metaphor that indicates a phenomenological 'world' perspective. It first appeared as a technical term for painters and was thus connected to representational practices (Adams, 1994). But so too are geographical landscapes – these are also formed by individual or collective subjects, acting on the surrounding physical environment. Thus, both the symbolic and the physical landscape are (re)presented for us (Casey, 2004), are shaped by someone, for some purpose, and are *cultivated* into different shapes and forms. It is thus both something constructed for us by, for example, a landscape artist, representing the world for us in painted form, but also it is a space shaped by the hands of a landscape gardener, where we can act individually as well as socially. Our actions in a landscape also impact on it. People may not always follow the paths through a garden, for example, but make short-cuts over the lawn, producing a path that was not foreseen or intended by the landscape gardener. Eventually, such actions impact on the landscape itself. This metaphor of landscape, in short, allows for thinking about the media in ways that transgress the structure-agency dichotomy and make it possible to see actions structured by frameworks that were produced by previous social actions, by preceding others. Those structures, however, never determine the scope of individual action.

Empirical approach

In line with Henri Lefebvre (1991), we can think of time as movement in space. The trajectory of a social formation through the spatial unit that is the media landscape thus produces time, both in its linear conception as calendar time and also in its sense of punctual time, that is, time that is defined by its specific quality. While individuals move about in the technological and symbolic landscape of the media, their movements give both this space and this time a unique quality that would not have been there had it not been for the social actions of these individuals. But time is not produced solely through movement in space; it is also formed in our discursive constructions of the past, in relation to the present. This apprehension of time is relatively freed from the cosmic time of the calendar, since it can produce prosthetic memories (Landsberg, 1995), things that have not actually happened, or that have happened in another way than that in which it is remembered.

The empirical material of this study consists of both quantitative and qualitative data. For the quantitative part, biennial surveys were made from 2002 to 2012, initially together with researchers at the Department of Journalism and Communication at Tartu University. Questions focused on access and use of media, as well as attitudes to media use. The survey included themes concerning both traditional mass media but had a slight bias towards digital media. The sample was national in Estonia, and regional in Sweden, restricted to the South Stockholm region of Södertörn.[2] The aim was not to compare countries, but to analyse processes of change, framed by historical circumstance and occurring in a specific cultural context. This context includes differences in political and cultural autonomy, where change in Estonia was framed by its short history of national sovereignty, having been under Soviet rule since World War II. However, the context also includes differences in living standards, especially historically, for the older age groups. Although this is clearly insufficient for laying bare long-term, generationally formed patterns of media usage (and general social behaviour), it can reveal if there are consistencies among cohorts over the period of one decade. It can also be used to identify 'break points' between age cohorts. Regarding the first point, the research material allows for following specific age cohorts over a ten-year period, trying to look for consistency in these cohorts' media behaviour. In terms of the cross-cultural inquiry, such national consistencies can also be explored, but these have not been emphasised so much here (see more, Bolin, 2016a, 2016b).

Most cross-generational analysis that uses statistical methods divides generational cohorts along a continuum, where each cohort starts the year after the older one ends. A common such generational typology is built on Zukin *et al.*'s (2006) division of US political generations into people born pre-1945 ('the dutifuls'), those born after World War II, 1946–64 ('the baby-boomers'), those born between 1965–76 ('generation X') and those born in 1977 and after ('the dotnets'). Such a conceptualisation of generations warrants an elaborate discussion about why someone born in December 1945 would have a dramatically different experience of societal events compared with someone born in January 1946, or, for that matter, why someone born in 1946 would share the

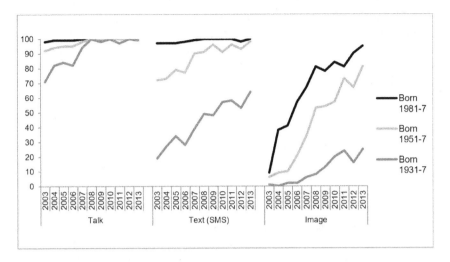

Figure 3.1 Generation as location: three Swedish age cohorts and their use of three functions of the mobile phone 2003–2013 (%). Adapted from the national SOM Institute.

Note: Statistics from the national SOM Institute surveys 2003–2013. Use defined as several times per month or more often.

same experiences of societal and cultural events with someone born almost two decades later, in 1964. If for no other reason than for analytical clarity, it might be better to work with people born within a more delimited period and also to separate generational cohorts statistically. One such attempt at the construction of discrete generational cohorts is shown in Figure 3.1, represented by people born in 1931–1937, 1951–1957 and 1981–1987.

As can be seen from Figure 3.1, older generation cohorts use each of the functions on the mobile phone less than the younger ones, and even if all cohorts increase their use over the years, the increase is similar in relation to the other two cohorts. One can therefore conclude there are clear generational patterns of use. If we reflect further on the age group distinction made in Figure 3.1, we can of course claim that this construction of cohorts is also arbitrary. Although the goal of analytical clarity might be achieved with this separation of cohorts, the differences in user patterns are not really indicative of any differences in generational experience, but just present generations as a location, situated in a similar position in the historical process. This locatedness does, admittedly, result in different responses to the introduction and establishment of the mobile phone (or whatever medium or phenomenon one measures in relation to the cohorts), but this is hardly evidence of the existence of a self-perceived social formation that considers itself as a generation – that is, of a generation as actuality. So, in order to grasp this experiential dimension, a series of focus group interviews in each country was organised.

From the statistical material, in conjunction with an historical analysis that aimed to identify major societal events including media events (Dayan and Katz, 1992), four age groups were outlined, where one could identify changes, albeit modest, in media behaviour. Media behaviour focused specifically on differences in the reading of news in print and in online forms. This was coupled with an analysis of the different historical circumstances, especially as related to media, in the two countries. Based on this analysis, it was decided to construct focus groups of people born in the early 1940s, early 1960s, late 1970s and early 1990s. Some of these age groups were wider age-wise than others (see Table 3.1).

The basic idea for forming these focus groups was to see if participants had common shared experiences and, if so, how this would be articulated in the interviews. The focus group discussions were structured around thematic areas such as early media memories, contemporary media use, mobile media use, news consumption, print vs. online media, and specific media events around the time of the interview.[3] In order to capture these potentially shared experiences that would bind people together in a generation as actuality, each focus group discussion was introduced through such prompting questions as "Which media did you have in your home as a child? Can you tell us about your earliest media memories?" This proved an effective start to the conversation, and in most groups resulted in someone mentioning certain media content from their early years.

> *Michael:*   Well, if we jump very far back . . . what I remember actually, and if we are talking media, then it's the moon landing. This is perhaps the first when it comes to media, the memories that remain. That it was so special, that thing.
>
> *John:*   Sixtynine.
>
> *Michael:*   Yes, sixtynine, yes.
>
> *Anne:*   That it was live transmission?
>
> *Michael:*   Live transmission, exactly.
>
> (Focus group born 1962–1964, Sweden)

From the turn-taking in the quote (anonymised and slightly edited for readability here, as they spoke over each other) we can see that there is a shared experience of this media event. Interestingly enough, a few moments later, in the

Table 3.1 Focus group composition in Sweden and Estonia.

	Sweden	Estonia
Early 1940s	1940–1945 (N=4)	1939–1946 (N=5)
Early 1960s	1962–1964 (N=4)	1959–1966 (N=8)
Late 1970s	1977–1981 (N=4)	1976–1980 (N=5)
Early 1990s	1991–1995 (N=5)	1990–1995 (N=5)

Notes

a   Interviews made in late 2011 (Estonia) and early 2012 (Sweden).

b   N in parenthesis indicates the number of participants in each focus group. All groups were balanced when it comes to the gender mix, except the Estonian early 1960s group, which consisted of seven females and only one male.

same interview, it was revealed that Anne had grown up without a television set, as her parents were stationed in an African country during her earliest years. Nonetheless, the moon landing as a media event was also a reference point for her, although she had no first-hand experience of it. Note, for example, that she emphasises the liveness quality of the situation, although she explicitly stated later that she had not seen it. The moon landing was a media event (Dayan and Katz, 1992) in the capacity of not only cutting across all mass media (radio, television, press), but also appearing as a theme in the general popular culture.

> *Michael:* Well, it was all the things around . . . in magazines, I remember there were these plastic stickers you could rub onto things, to build a scenario for a moon landing yourself, and a lot of such stuff around the whole thing.
>
> (Focus group born 1962–1964, Sweden)

Such media events impact on those who did not explicitly watch the live broadcast. Media events of this magnitude seem to set their mark on all individuals within a certain society. For example, the interviewees who lived in remote areas where television arrived several years later compared their experiences with those who lived in the cities. Of course, interviewees who lived in the geographical periphery knew about the medium, and thus it also affected them. This resonates perfectly with McLuhan's (1964) famous dictum that "the medium is the message".

The focus group quoted above consisted of four people, three of whom were born in 1962 and one in 1964. Karin, who was the youngest, was very silent during the discussion of the moonlanding, and in fact admitted that she remembered nothing of it. She was two years younger than the other three in the group, who all vividly remembered and discussed it. The interesting issue here is the ways in which media events stretch out, transcending any single medium to define experience in a broader way. The combination of the actual live transmission, and its reporting in the press and radio, combined with its reference points in popular culture (the stickers) produced a context in which people of approximately the same age are included in a common experience. But as the discussion in the focus group also reveals, it does not reach everybody. Karin actually showed signs of being embarrassed for not being able to be included in the common experience, and even excused herself for having such a low interest in the media.

The commonality described above is produced through what I have called *indirect generational relations*, as there are no specific or direct distinctions towards, or reference to, other generations. The commonality consists of the confirmations of the experience of other individuals, present in the situation at hand. In fact, we could argue that this is one of many moments in which a generation becomes realised or actualised, in common understanding and the acknowledgement of shared experience. The situation here was a focus group interview, but it could just as well have been a family or school-class reunion, meeting a friend one hasn't met for a long time, looking through a family photo album, etc. For each and every one of these occasions, the generationing process deepens, and a generational identity accumulates.

This may be why research seems to find it easier to track generational identities among baby-boomers than among people of younger groups. The baby-boomers have rehearsed their identity over the years, and have seen it represented in newspaper features, in academic analyses, etc. (e.g. Jamison and Eyerman, 1994; Bristow, 2015). They are constantly reminded of their position in the historical process and have gradually internalised this knowledge into their generational consciousness.

Besides such indirect generational references, there are, quite naturally, also *direct generational distinctions* made between other generations in the interviews. When interviewees referred to older or younger generations by comparison, they would single out traits among these other generations that differ from their own generation. Thus, one could talk about the lack of digital competences among the older generations, but also point to how superficial younger generations are in their digital habits. The two quotes below illustrate these two positions.

> Our generation seems to have quite a lot of similarities in their media use. When you look at people who are 10–15 years younger, they are many times more superficial. It's another world actually.
>
> (Focus group, Estonia, born 1976–1980)

> *Kajsa:* What I remember is when my sister and I went up north to see my mother, when she had ... my sister had gotten herself a mobile phone. And mum, she just couldn't understand how she could ... We were in a grocery store and then my sister called her husband to ask if there was anything specific she should buy, and she said: "But can she really talk with Kjell here in the store? Don't we have to get back home first?" It was really difficult for her to grasp that this telephone could connect from wherever you were.
>
> *Leif:* It was the same with the television. Many believed that the TV signal came through the electric wall socket.
>
> (Focus group, Sweden, born 1940–1945)

Where the first excerpt illustrates the relation to younger generations, the second quote captures the way in which many relate to the older parent generation. Both quotes are examples of constructing one's own generational belonging in relation to competences that are considered lacking among other generations, that is a kind of generational consciousness forming by way of negation.

> *Anne:* Today they just sit online, and on Spotify, and I get totally confused, because I'm there myself, and I think ... God, I can download anything and listen to it. And that stresses me out, because you somehow lose your grip on ... And there they are online all the time, and all of this with three hundred friends on Facebook, or you have a whole world on your computer, and what not.
>
> (Focus group, Sweden, born 1962–1964)

The interesting thing with this quote is the way in which the interviewee Anne related her own use of Spotify to that of younger generations, here partly represented by her two sons who were in their early twenties at the time of the interview, and acknowledged the difference in approach between her and younger generations. She admittedly uses both streaming services like Spotify and social networking sites such as Facebook, but she realised that her use differed from that of younger users, in both quantitative and qualitative terms. Her use was more instrumental, and since she grew up in a foreign country and her childhood and teenage friends are scattered all over the world, so Facebook provides her with a tool for keeping in contact with them.

> *Anne:* Yes, I'm on Facebook and LinkedIn and I am very provoked by the fact that Facebook somehow uses your profile for sending ads to you, adjusted to your interests . . . that suddenly pop up, and then you feel . . . Well, I don't really like that. But to me it is a very important channel, because I have recreated contacts with my childhood friends, so to me it is very nice to be able to chat with people in England and the USA . . . well in other countries, that I haven't . . . that type of contact was not possible before. So, I found a lot of childhood friends thanks to Facebook, so to me it's . . . really important. For the rest part . . . I hide certain friends because I do not want to see these meaningless posts.
>
> (Focus group, Sweden, born 1962–1964)

By meaningless posts, Anne meant posts of what people had for breakfast or lunch and other, more 'phatic' functions of social networking media. This indicates her more instrumental approach to the medium. Of course, this was partly triggered by the interview situation where you do not readily admit to engaging in meaningless activities, but construct each action as meaningful and therefore justifiable. Nonetheless, even if in the interview situation she emphasised her rational behaviour, there is nothing indicating that she does not have that side to her usage. The direct intergenerational references also reveal what could be called a pre-figurative cultural form of learning, where "young people everywhere share a kind of experience that none of the elders ever have had or will have" (Mead, 1970, p. 64):

> *Interviewer:* Do you sometimes watch together with siblings or parents?
> *Eva:* Yes, I do. I mostly watch with my sister. But also with daddy. I have taught him how to connect the laptop to the TV so we can watch SVT Play on the TV.
> *Interviewer:* OK, so you watch on a larger screen?
> *Eva:* Yes, and then it is like watching in the ordinary way. Then I watch with him.
>
> (Focus group, Sweden, born 1991–1995)

The 'generation gap', as theorised by Margaret Mead (1970), is produced by the fact that from around World War II, generational change has been more dramatic due to the depth and pace of the changes in society. Although one could argue that her analysis was exaggerated in that she saw an abrupt change in the direction of learning, it is nonetheless illustrative of the smaller reversals of learning related to new media technologies that we can see from the earlier quote. Such changes, quite naturally, sensitise those involved to the passing of time, and reveal how past habits have become outdated in orienting people towards the new media landscape. The combination of the synchronic generation as social formation in the Mannheimian sense, with generation as succession in Mead's analysis where it is the intergenerational relations that are the focus, are instructive for this analysis.

Conclusions: generation theory and social change

Above I have described a model for studying generational relations and by doing so have tried to say something about the nature of time and social change. In these last paragraphs, I will summarise my main arguments.

First, I have illustrated the value, indeed the necessity, of analysing generation both in its synchronic and its diachronic senses, as the combination of a social formation moving with time, and the meeting between different generations in the succession order. The argument of this chapter is that generational theory, combined with historically oriented focus group interviews and longitudinal, quantitative data, provides one suggested methodological solution to the problem of studying long-term social and cultural change, and the process of mediatisation. Where quantitative data can say something about the ways in which age groups, or cohorts, respond to changes (or stability) in the media landscapes, the qualitative material can say something about how this landscape is perceived, and reveal responses based on the actual experience of these landscapes.

Second, I have provided some methodological examples of how empirically to approach generations through the use of focus group interviews, with a specific focus on media use over the life course. The prompting question used to open the focus group interviews proved to be valuable for how the interviews then unfolded. In most interviews the discussion took off in a lively manner, and early memories provoked discussions where the interviewees confirmed their shared memories. Quite naturally, the distinctions between the generations – both younger and older – were an effect of the focus group setting, and one could hypothesise that a mixed age composition in the focus groups might not have warranted what I called the making of direct generational distinctions. Thus, the methodology privileged the respective focus groups to look for similarities inwards, among themselves, and distinctions outwards with other age groups. This is, however, not an indication that the generation identities revealed were merely a fabrication of the focus group setting, but that the focus group context served more as a trigger of the hibernating generational identity.

Third, and relatedly, the generationing process makes older generations stand out more clearly in the qualitative material, since this group of interviewees has had more occasions to rehearse its generational identity, having been faced over the years with descriptions of themselves as baby-boomers, distinct from other (earlier) generations, not least in the media (films, features in the press and academic writing), but also through various social occasions such as class reunions, or in reconnecting with older friends on social networking media, or being confronted with other generations' media use. This confrontation produces the self-awareness that is needed for a generation as location to become a generation as actuality, that is, for the self-understanding of oneself as belonging to a generation with a common understanding of the media landscape. On all these occasions a generational identity is activated, and where present is further strengthened and brought to the surface in the analysis of social change.

Notes

1 The project was funded by The Baltic Sea Foundation, and carried out together with Signe Opermann, who wrote her PhD thesis within the project (Opermann, 2014).
2 The Södertörn region includes 9 municipalities, including Stockholm. For more detailed information on sampling procedures in both countries, see Bolin (2005). On the general, response rates were satisfactory, and similar to larger surveys (e.g. the national surveys by the SOM Institute in Sweden).
3 Interviews were made by Bolin in Sweden, and Signe Opermann in Estonia, recorded and transcribed and in the case of the Estonian interviews translated to English.

References

Adams, A. J., 1994. Seventeenth-century Dutch landscape painting. In: W. J. Thomas Mitchell, ed. *Landscape and power*. Chicago, IL: Chicago University Press, pp. 35–76.

Altheide, D. L. and Snow R. P., 1979. *Media logic*. Beverly Hills, CA: SAGE.

Beniger, J. R., 1992. Comparison, yes, but – the case of technological and cultural change. In: J. Blumler, J. M. McLeod and K. E. Rosengren, eds. *Comparatively speaking: communication and culture across space and time*. London: SAGE, pp. 35–50.

Berman, M., 1988 [1982]. *All that is solid melts into air: the experience of modernity*. New York: Penguin.

Bolin, G., 2003. *Variations, media landscapes, history. Frameworks for an analysis of contemporary media landscapes*. Huddinge, Sweden: MKV.

Bolin, G., ed., 2005. *The media landscape of Södertörn 2002: media use, values and everyday life in southern Stockholm*. Huddinge, Sweden: MKV.

Bolin, G., 2006. Electronic geographies: media landscapes as technological and symbolic environments. In: J. Falkheimer and A. Jansson, eds. *Geographies of communication: the spatial turn in media studies*. Gothenburg, Sweden: Nordicom, pp. 67–86.

Bolin, G., 2014a. Institution, technology, world: relationships between the media, culture and society. In: K. Lundby, ed. *Mediatization of communication*. Berlin and Boston, MA: De Gruyter Mouton, pp. 175–197.

Bolin, G., 2014b. Generationsskiftningar i mobillandskapet. In: A. Bergström and H. Oscarsson, eds. *Mittfåra & marginal*. Gothenburg, Sweden: SOM-Institutet, pp. 229–237.

Bolin, G., 2016a. *Media generations: experience, identity and mediatised social change*. London and New York: Routledge.

Bolin, G., 2016b. The rhythm of ages: analyzing mediatization through the lens of generations across nations. *International Journal of Communication*, 10, pp. 5252–5269.

Bristow, J., 2015. *Baby boomers and generational conflict*. Basingstoke, UK: Palgrave Macmillan.

Casey, E. S., 2004. Mapping the world in works of art. In: B. V. Folz and R. Frodeman, eds. *Rethinking nature: essays in environmental philosophy*. Bloomington, IN: Indiana University Press, pp. 260–269.

Colombo, F. and Fortunati, L., eds., 2011. *Broadband society and generational changes*. Frankfurt am Main, Germany: Peter Lang.

Corsten, M., 1999. The time of generations. *Time & Society*, 8(2), pp. 249–272.

Dayan, D. and Katz, E., 1992. *Media events: the live broadcasting of history*. Cambridge, MA and London: Harvard University Press.

Deacon, D. and Stanyer, S., 2014. Mediatization: key concept or conceptual bandwagon? *Media, Culture & Society*, 36(7), pp. 1032–1044.

Gumpert, G. and Cathcart, R., 1985. Media grammars, generations and media gaps'. *Critical Studies in Mass Communication*, 2(1), pp. 23–35.

Hepp, A., 2013. *Cultures of mediatization*. Cambridge, UK: Polity Press.

Hjarvard, S., 2013. *The mediatization of culture and society*. London: Routledge.

Jamison, A. and Eyerman, R., 1994. *Seeds of the sixties*. Berkeley, CA: University of California Press.

Kertzer, D. I., 1983. Generation as a sociological problem. *Annual Review of Sociology*, 9(1), pp. 25–149.

Landsberg, A., 1995. Prosthetic memory: total recall and blade runner. In: M. Featherstone and R. Burrows, eds. *Cyberspace/cyberbodies/cyberpunk: cultures of technological embodiment*. London: SAGE, pp. 175–190.

Lefebvre, H., 1991 [1974]. *The production of space*. Oxford and Cambridge, UK: Blackwell.

Lundby, K., ed., 2009. *Mediatization: concept, changes, consequences*. New York: Peter Lang.

Mannheim, K., 1952 [1928]. The problem of generations. In: K. Mannheim, ed. *Essays in the sociology of knowledge*. London: Routledge & Keegan Paul, pp. 276–320.

McLuhan, M., 1964. *Understanding media: the extensions of man*. New York: McGraw-Hill.

Mead, M., 1970. *Culture and commitment: a study of the generation gap*. Garden City, NY: Doubleday.

Opermann, S., 2014. *Generational use of news media in Estonia: media access, spatial orientations and discursive characteristics of the news media*. Huddinge, Sweden: Södertörn University.

Ortega y Gasset, J., 1931 [1923]. *The modern theme*. London: The C. W. Daniel Company.

Pilcher, J., 1998. *Women of their time: generation, gender issues and feminism*. Aldershot, UK: Ashgate.

Ricoeur, P., 1990 [1985]. *Time and narrative. Vol. 3*. Chicago, IL and London: The University of Chicago Press.

Rosa, H., 2013 [2005]. *Social acceleration: a new theory of modernity*. New York: Columbia University Press.

Siibak, A., and Vittadini, N., 2012. Introducing four empirical examples of the 'generationing' process. *Cyberpsychology*, 6(2), pp. 1–10.

Siibak, A., Vittadini, N. and Nimrod, G., 2014. Generations as media audiences: an introduction. *Participations*, 11(2), pp. 100–107.

Zukin, C., Keeter, S., Andolina, M., Jenkins, K. and Delli Carpini, M. X., 2006. *A new engagement?: political participation, civic life, and the changing American citizen*. New York: Oxford University Press.

4 Generational analysis of people's experience of ICTs

Leslie Haddon

Introduction

In the last 10 to 15 years, there has been revival of interest in generational analysis (Aroldi, 2011), including how it can be applied to the experience of information and communication technologies (ICTs). This chapter first outlines some of the different guises in which various types of generational and cohort research have appeared and then examines some of the general considerations that ICT research-ers might take into account if they consider using this perspective. It then looks at some examples of how generational analysis has been employed in relation to ICTs before demonstrating the dimensions researchers could explore through a case study of how cohort analysis was used in a study of those people who counted as being young elderly in the mid-90s.

The origins of generation and cohort analysis

Originating in the nineteenth century, the idea of a social generation referred to people born in the same age range who had similar cultural experiences. Social generation was used in the context of a generation experiencing a degree of change in society (e.g. industrialisation) or events (e.g. wars). The specific sociological origins of the term can be traced to Mannheim's essay 'The prob-lem of generations' (1952 [1923]). Mannheim, like some others had done in the nineteenth century, focused in particular on youth as a formative period, where experiences at this age stage could influence future social and political outlooks throughout life.

Anticipating this chapter's later discussions of the role of ICTs, it is worth add-ing a note about two developments of Mannheim's work. The first, picked up in a more recent revival of interest in generations, concerns generational conscious-ness, a sense of belonging to a generation and of having a 'common destiny'. For Mannheim, some generations could see themselves as being distinct in this sense. Later writers discuss whether a sense of generation informs political action, the most cited example being the 1968 student protests across Europe. But of inter-est in this chapter is the fact that these subsequent writers discuss in more detail the process of a generation gaining a sense of cultural identity, or becoming self-conscious as a generation, and the role of collective memory, institutionalised via shared rituals and memories (Edmunds and Turner, 2002, 2005; Eyerman and Turner, 1998; all discussed in Aroldi and Colombo, 2013). In fact, this issue of how people who live through the same circumstances become aware of themselves as being a generation, how they develop a 'we-sense' (Corsten, 2011) has become a topic in its own right, including, of relevance for ICT analysis, reflections on the different roles that media can play in this process (Aroldi, 2011).

The second development relates to discussions of whether processes of globalisation have created international generations, the first and perhaps main example of which is taken to be the 1960s generation. While this global consciousness of being a distinct generation has multiple causes, such as the ease of travel, and was experienced somewhat differently in different countries, one contributory factor cited is developments in communication and in particular, once again, the role of the media and mediated experiences (Edmunds and Turner, 2005).

In contrast to the concept of generation, the term cohort has its origins in demographics. As in the, more cited, literature on generations, as birth cohorts age, their members experience the same societal changes and events (e.g. economic change, social change, events such as wars), and as with generations, some of the analysts using the term cohort stress how these factors are more important in late adolescence/early adulthood. Apart from living through the same events, cohort members also experience the same social structures (e.g. the age of completing education, the nature of the labour market at a certain point in time; see Ryder, 1965). Some have even argued for using the word cohort rather than generation precisely because it avoids the element of generational consciousness that others embrace (Kertzer, 1983).

Contemporary generational analysis

Probably the most high-profile use of generational analysis in recent years was the literature, both popular and academic, contrasting the orientations of different cohorts in the post-war period. Most significant were the *Baby Boomers*, born in the 1940s–1960s, whose older members were youth during the 1960s. The subsequent generations were *Generation X* (born in the 1960s–1980s) and then *Millennials* (otherwise known as *Generation Y* – born in the 1980s–early 2000s). Older Western generations include the *Lost Generation* (born 1880s–1900s, many of whom fought in World War I), the *G.I. Generation* (born 1900s–1920s, who were young during the Great Depression and fought in World War II) and the *Silent Generation* (born 1920s–1940s, some of whom fought in World War II, Korea and Vietnam). These generations are broadly 20 years apart and so relate to family generations (e.g. parent-child). One typology even traces such generations back to the first US settlers (Strauss and Howe, 1991), according to which Generation X is the 13th generation. As with Mannheim's approach and that of cohort analysis, these more recent forms of generational analysis often posit that generations have particular shared social orientations, attitudes and beliefs. Some analyses emphasise the 'generation gap', i.e. the differences (and conflicts) between generations.

Generational/cohort analysis has been employed in a variety of disciplines, for example in politics where there is the issue of whether generational experiences affect socio-political orientation (e.g. Cutler, 1977, cited in Gilleard and Higgs, 2005; Putnam, 2000). In the sociology of work, the question has been posed as to whether there are generational differences in work values and attitudes between *Baby Boomers* and *Generation X-ers* (Smola and Sutton, 2002). Furthermore, in ageing studies, there is the issue of how generational experiences might affect the orientation to old age (Gilleard and Higgs, 2005). It is worth adding that outside of academia the concept of generations has been taken up (sometimes enthusiastically) by consultancies and in some media coverage, part of the attraction being that it has been used to explain consumer behaviour. Hence, this has been referred to (and criticised for its simplifications) as the 'generational marketing approach' (Colombo, 2011). In general, generational analysis has not necessarily been helped by more popular writings that make strong claims about generational influences of *Generation X-ers* and *Millennials*. This led some analysts to lament "Triumphant in popular culture, the cohort generation has been confined by experts to the shadow world of unproven hypothesis" (Strauss and Howe, 1991, cited in Giancola, 2006, p. 33).

Challenges for generation and cohort analysis

There are a number of difficulties in defining generations and in applying labels such as those above. For one thing, there is not necessarily an agreement on the start and end dates of these generations, e.g. the *Baby Boomer* generation has been reported by different researchers to start between 1940 and 1946. *Generation X-ers* start somewhere in the early 1960s, but according to different authors end in 1975, 1980, 1981 and 1982 (Smola and Sutton, 2002). Neither is there always agreement about what constitutes a generation, e.g. some see the *Swing Generation* (born 1934–1945) as being a subgroup of the *Silent Generation* (Mitchell, 2003). Other possible sub-generations from different researchers include *World War II-ers* (born 1902–1933), *Traditionals* (born 1909–1940) and *Matures* (born 1925–1942) (Smola and Sutton, 2002). Then there is the question of overlap between generations. Those born near the beginning or end of a particular generation can have more experiences akin to those in the next or previous generations (Wellner, 2000, cited in Giancola, 2006). One further problem is the generational interval is so wide that people within it may experience societal events differently. For example, although the *Baby Boomers* are often associated with late 1960s anti-Vietnam war protests, some of its young members were only in pre-school at that time (Hughs and Rand, 2005, in Giancola 2006). One last, but important, key issue is that the emphasis on what generations or cohorts share can underplay differences within them (e.g. in terms of class, gender, race). More careful writers note this heterogeneity (e.g. Ryder, 1965), but some writers do not.

Apart from these questions about definitional issues and the potential to overstress generations, there are also empirical challenges. For example, some research on work orientations found limited shared generation orientations and few generation gaps (Giancola, 2006; Mackay *et al.*, 2008). Other research comparing a whole range of different cohorts found it was difficult to say that they had unique values distinguishing them from each other (Noble and Schewe, 2003). Thus, generational differences may simply be greater for some generations than for others. For example, a study of sexual attitudes, personal responsibility, respect for parents and a range of other orientations found that the gap between *Baby Boomers* and their parents was greater than between *Baby Boomers* and their own children, leading some to talk about 'the vanishing generation gap' (Giancola, 2006).

While there are clearly challenges in conducting cohort or generational analysis, there are some studies that outline a more careful historical analysis. Gilleard and Higgs (2005) acknowledge the issues about drawing the boundaries around a generation, yet viewing these as a social construction, one can make an argument about where to draw them. Like some others, they make a link to Bourdieu's discussion of 'generational dispositions', which, according to Bourdieu, are 'habitus which have been produced by different modes of generation . . . which . . . can cause one group to experience as natural and reasonable practices or aspirations which another group finds unthinkable or scandalous' (1977, p. 78). Gilleard and Higgs note that people may vary in the degree to which they engage in such generational 'cultural fields' and some 'cultural fields' are more important than others, e.g. the 1950s/1960s youth culture. They argue that this youth culture was not just created by commercial interests, but involved an engagement by this cohort and their sense of generational identity. The authors then examine the circumstances of cohorts born from the 1880s and underline the continuities between them in contrast to those *Baby Boomers* who were involved in early youth culture as youths. In their analysis, Gilleard and Higgs observe the national differences between the US and the UK, and look at all experiences across the life course, not just when the *Baby Boomer* generation was young. They explore how the cohort now entering old age experienced this stage in their lives.

In sum, these authors are aware of the issues facing generational analysis but find merit in it. Differences between cohorts are sometimes more and sometimes less salient. The analysis is sensitive to national variation, gender differences and experiences after youth. Like the case study discussed later in this chapter, the authors focus on the cohort dimension as only part of the picture, given that they also look at this historical period through the lenses of class and changes in the experience of community.

Generations and ICTs

The various forms of cohort analysis noted above have had a limited amount to say about generational experiences of ICTs, one exception being Putnam's (2000) discussion of the decline in various forms of civic participation (voting, volunteering, religious observance) in the US since the 1950s. Although Putnam's main focus is on the difference between the values of the generation who lived through World War II and their successors, the *Baby Boomers*, he considers the role of factors such as suburbanisation and, of interest in this chapter, the widespread adoption of television that contributed to a move towards a more family-oriented, less communal, lifestyle.

One of the more prominent and controversial uses of cohort analysis has been in attempts to define a generation of children as being distinctive primarily by virtue of technological experiences. This was captured in discussions nearly 20 years ago of a 'Net Generation' (Tapscott, 1998) and of children as being 'digital natives' (Prensky, 2001) because they have grown up with ICTs as opposed to their parents, 'digital immigrants', who encountered them later in life.[1] For some of its critics, this discussion is seen as a step too far, one that simply gives too much weight to the influence of technology, and that is too technologically determinist (Buckingham, 2009). Just as in the critique of overstressing the role of generations in general, various writers have argued that referring to all children as being digital natives certainly does not do justice to the diversity among children in terms of technical capabilities and engagement with the digital world (boyd, 2014; Holmes, 2011). Thus, many commentators find the digital native claim to be an exaggeration (Selwyn, 2009), or an exotic representation of children that does not capture their mundane online practices (Stern, 2008). In general, it is a vast oversimplification that ignores many of the aspects of generational analysis discussed earlier (Aroldi, 2011). But such criticisms of the 'web generation discourse' (Hartmann, 2003) have not stopped Prensky especially, from being often cited within academic writings, being used by market researchers and appearing in the literature of organisations like the OECD (Aroldi, 2011).

The strong criticisms of these particular representations of a cohort of children (who by the time of writing this chapter would be young adults), does not mean that there is no place for considering the influence of ICTs in generational analysis. Taking a more cautious approach is the work that speculates about the extent to which there is a 'digital global generation'. In developing a theme explored in Edmunds and Turner (2005), Aroldi and Colombo (2013) return to the globalising influence of media, but taken a stage further by the rise of the internet. They stress both shared transnational experiences of the online world and the role of the internet itself in helping to create a generational consciousness, for example "bursting with websites and places dedicated to generational self-assertion" (Aroldi and Colombo, 2013, p. 185). However, the authors note that there might be limits to any shared international generational awareness, including citing an empirical study of Italian and Portuguese generational experiences that showed some shared generational consciousness across countries, but only among those with higher educational backgrounds (Aroldi and Ponte, 2012).

A case study

This last section considers other ways in which some of the themes from cohort or generational analysis can be used in the study of ICTs, by looking at a domestication research conducted in the 1990s, but which is still pertinent (Haddon and Silverstone, 1996). The concept of domestication was first formulated in the 1990s in the UK (Silverstone *et al.*, 1992; for its subsequent history see Haddon, 2016). Although there had been an empirical dimension to the original project in which the framework was developed, funding was found for an additional three years (1993–1996) to explore the processes of domestication in a variety of different circumstances, including teleworking and lone parent households. The third study in this three-year project was of the young elderly at that time, roughly defined as being 60–75 years old (hence born in 1920–1935). This group was chosen for a variety of reasons: as a strategic age group to explore the domestication of very early ICTs (e.g. early TV, the phone), to examine the longer-term careers of ICTs in households, to evaluate ageing effects on ICT use and adoption (e.g. declining mobility), and what cohort analysis could contribute to our understanding of ICT use. In terms of the generational typology, this group overlaps with what was called the *Silent Generation*, but since the cohort dimension was only one consideration among several, the choice of age range did not come from the writings about generations – if anything the ageing/age stage literature was more influential in this respect.

The young elderly research took place in 1994–1995 and involved interviews conducted in 20 households (both couples and singles). It mainly investigated how these people had domesticated a range of ICTs,[2] taking into account the past and current situation of the household. Classic domestication analysis tries to make sense of ICT experiences by asking about the social context in which these occur, which could include such elements as the financial context, social networks, values and aspirations. Over the years, researchers have added further elements of the social context that can be considered in domestication analysis, through empirical analysis but also through argument. For example, a study of domestication in China showed different ways in which the national context affects domestication processes (Lim, 2006). At the time of this research, the previous generational experience of this young elderly group was simply seen as being one more type of social context to consider in order to make sense of the group's behaviour and orientation. Although only the cohort aspects are reported here, generational analysis was clearly not the main aim and sole starting point of this study.

Financial circumstances and orientation to consumption

Turning now to the findings, apart from shaping attitudes towards technologies, the previous experiences of cohort members during their working life affected their later financial circumstances (e.g. pension) and hence ability to afford ICTs in later life. Those who were originally middle class or who had moved into middle-class jobs felt that they had become wealthier over the course of their lives, as did some working-class interviewees. But for some of this cohort, the lack of pension systems when they were younger had a bearing on the limited retirement income they had now.

Ray Englefield: You see, moving around so much when I was younger, I wasn't on a pension scheme. They didn't have pension schemes in those days so my pension was fairly small. So I don't have a great income now I've retired. I haven't enough money to indulge in some of the more fanciful aspects of retirement. So basically it's odd jobs, reading, occasional holidays, visiting people.

It has been noted elsewhere that the life experiences of cohorts can affect the development of their specific consumption habits (Aroldi, 2011). In this young elderly study, many participants whose early lives were lived in austerity felt that habits of careful spending stayed with them in later life. As young adults, some of this cohort had experienced social mobility and had earned more both during their working lives and later as pensioners. Because of that shared background, both working- and middle-class participants spontaneously referred to 'our generation' in the interview (i.e. in this respect they had a generational awareness) and talked about that cohort 'knowing the value of money'.

George Williams: I think probably our generation always needs to be able to justify. You know, even if you can afford something you think "Well, do I really need it?"

Dorothy Williams: So we've always been reasonably, as you say, cautious with money and you feel you've got to justify what you buy.

This was relevant for (and referred to by participants in) subsequent discussions of purchase decisions: a technology had to be seen as being useful to justify acquiring it. By implication, it was more difficult to acquire technologies and services that might involve experimentation to see if they were useful. Even when younger, these interviewees had not automatically embraced innovations simply because they were new. For example, many had gone to see what television looked like in someone else's house when the first sets appeared in order to help them decide if it was worthwhile for them to have one.

Joanne Englefield: I can always remember a colleague of yours had one and you arranged for you, me and [daughter] Christine to go down and have a look at it. Do you remember we sat there and solemnly looked at this television?

In fact, when discussing current ICTs generally, the age group often used the language of necessity: do we need something rather than do we desire it.

Vera Wellman: I'm sure, you know, that these things are wonderful for people of 20 who are coming up but quite honestly we've lived all our lives without them and I don't find they're necessary at all.

The relevance of ICTs and the timing of their appearance in relation to life stage

When looking at specific ICTs, few of these young elderly had been brought up in homes with telephones when they were themselves children. Most became familiar with phones (sometimes through work) and acquired landlines during adulthood. Some talked about the difficulty of getting used to phones at first, but after many years most were confident users. But some interviewees who had never needed to use a phone in their working lives still found it difficult to hold a phone conversation. In other words, early experiences, or in this case a lack of them, could have a bearing upon the extent to which people felt at ease when using technologies:

> *Eddy Evans:*   I can't hold a conversation [on the phone]. My sister gets on there [and I say], "Oh you want Gwen" [his wife], and that's it.

Some young elderly had by this stage in their lives acquired several handsets because they thought they were 'useful'; for example, with declining physical mobility it was a benefit to have a handset in each room. However, most had never used other services that had appeared over many years of their lives, often citing 'no need'.

> *Rosie Aldridge:*   I like the phone, you know . . . if I am in and lonely I have to get on the phone to someone . . . but other than that I wouldn't want to really go into anything more than just the phone.

Fewer than half of the participants used the phone memories and features such as re-dial even if they were present in the handset. Many said they could not be bothered to find out how they worked. And only 2 out of the 20 households had answering machines, one commenting on how they had wanted only a very basic machine.

> *Stuart Robbie:*   We just want something simple. Something the dog could work, you know.

At the time of the study, 1994–1995, no-one had a mobile phone. A few thought that this innovation might be useful for providing a sense of security when they were out of the home, but at the time of the interviews most considered these new mobile phones to be irrelevant.

As regards computers, for those in white-collar work office automation came into their lives late or not at all since they had retired by the time PCs arrived.[3] A few of the younger participants from this cohort had used PCs at work, but others had actively tried to avoid learning how to use computers so late in their working lives.

| *Roger Summers:* | The firm was [getting computerised] but I wasn't. I was still using my slide rule. I couldn't at that age assimilate it. It was completely foreign and quite beyond me. I wouldn't have known the first thing about them. |

And:

| *Ray Englefield:* | Yes, I was interested in the technicalities. I was quite intrigued as to how the thing worked . . . I could do a little bit of programming. I knew what they all meant but towards the end the pace of computerisation was quite fast and I was then in my 60s and I just couldn't be bothered to keep up with it. |
| *Joanne Englefield:* | Well I suppose if I had been that much younger and therefore thinking in terms of staying out at work that much longer and I really put my thoughts to it, I probably would [have managed to cope] . . . No . . . It's bad enough as you get older and find out all the things you can't do without trying to do new things and finding out you can't do those as well. |

In other words, one question one can ask in cohort analysis is about the circumstances of people at the time a certain technology appeared or became widespread. To take another example of this, one common route by which PCs entered the home from the mid-1980s was as a resource for children (Haddon and Skinner, 1991). However, the children of this cohort were the 'wrong' age when computers became popular. The children of many of these interviewees were either already adults or in their late teens when computers arrived in school or were first embraced enthusiastically for games-playing in the 1980s – mostly by slightly younger children than the children of this generation (Haddon, 1988). Of the two households that were exceptions – they had and used a PC in the mid-1990s – one husband was a technology enthusiast and had even built the first computer kits when they were introduced, and the other couple had younger teenage children at home in the 1980s (when they were in their mid-fifties).

Most had in the past not been able to see how a PC would be useful to them, and when interviewed in the 1990s they still could not:

| *Ray Englefield:* | We looked into it when Lawrence was at university. He was keen for us to have one . . . and I couldn't really think of a reason for having it . . . I remember my son saying: "Well you can keep your bank statements on it, Dad". I said: "Well I've got a bank to do that". |

As regards television, most of those interviewed used teletext and had done so for years before retirement. Most had VCRs – some had them before retirement, some had accepted them as gifts from children, or they were suggested by children.

Either way, the interviewees noted how at the time they could see how VCRs were useful innovations, i.e. they fitted in with that broader approach to consumption discussed earlier.

At the time of the study, morning TV had been launched, but most did not watch it – some referred to the fact that they had not watched TV at that time of day when they were younger and justified that decision as a habit carried over from their earlier lives. Although a few watched the recently arrived daytime TV, they also sometimes felt guilty about watching TV outside the traditional evening slot.

Earlier experiences and the perception of media

Some of the generational studies reviewed commented on the role of the media in helping to create a sense of generational identity, and television researchers had also noted the significance of reminiscing where TV touches on people's previous experiences (Willis, 1995) and connects with generational memory (Tulloch, 1989). For many of the young elderly interviewees in this research, TV programmes about the war period raised particular memories.

> *George Williams:*   It was mainly about how people lived in those days.
> *Dorothy Williams:*   Yes, well it was something we knew about because we'd done it, we were there, sort of attitude, and remember it. We were saying "Oh, do you remember we used to do this?" and we used to queue up at the Odeon, Leicester Square and things like that.

And:

> *Sam Waters:*   It's like *Dad's Army*.[4] I knew that. We knew about the Home Guard and one or two funny people like . . . similar to that. My father wouldn't let me join the Home Guard because I was only 17 or so.
> *LH:*   So when you see *Dad's Army*, it rings true to some extent?
> *Sam Waters:*   It's nostalgic and the officer in that, we knew a chap . . . he reminds us of him.

And:

> *Elsie Davey:*   I like war films. I think because we were in our teens it made a lasting impression. You used to go to the pictures and you used to get it on the news . . . like in the picture on the newsreel, wasn't it, all the soldiers . . . and I think when you're in your teens you're very impressionable.

Neither was it only programmes relating to the war that were particularly meaningful. Some young elderly also referred to historical dramas relating to the era of their childhood:

Muriel Cifonelli: I think that's partly because of the styles, it reminded us of childhood as well . . . the war films and the war programmes have been repeated so many times and they're so well documented. But things like the late 1920s, they're not so well documented. So just to see the fashions and the cars and go back to that kind of thing – the old-fashioned prams and things, that was more interesting.

The interviewees commented not only on the content but also the style of television. Previous writers have already noted elderly people's very critical reaction to sex, violence and bad language in the earlier TV viewing experience of this cohort (Bliese, 1986; Randall, 1995; Willis, 1995). The young elderly interviewees in this study frequently observed how TV had changed (mostly for the worse) since the TV they had first watched.

Solomon: There is a lot of violence (on TV now) and I don't like it. Perhaps in earlier times I never thought about it as violence.

Eva Solomon: I think the violence is different. The violence used to be much more of the western type.

LH: But how do you think the violence has changed? What's it like now?

Eva Solomon: More realistic, I think. The western was a remote sort of violence. Now it is the ordinary street violence. It's people doing things in our environment whereas the western is dressed up.

Sam Waters: The sexual act is something private and intimate between two people and it didn't ought to be displayed on the television for all to see. But it seems to me that every copper, whoever comes on the television, has to jump into bed with somebody. And they swear so much. I know in life they do swear quite a lot but I do believe that the television could do a great deal for the nation by stopping the swearing instead of making it the normal word.

Lucy Griffith compared current TV to when her daughter was young.

Lucy Griffith: Things were a bit different then. I can't remember having a programme on that I wouldn't let her watch. So, I think television was different then. The programmes you get on today there's such a lot of swearing and things like that. I mean I wouldn't let any child watch it.

Bernie Griffith: You turned it off one night, didn't you?

> *Lucy Griffith:*   Oh I turned it off. Oh dear, the language . . . I said "I've had enough of this". I said "My goodness! Good job it's late at night". It really was bad and, you know, I can't remember television (being) like that.

The above quotations show that earlier life experiences of a generation can affect not only how they adopt and use ICTs but also how they perceive them.

Dimensions of cohort analysis of ICTs

In sum, the case study shows a variety of different ways in which the earlier experiences of a cohort may affect their encounter with ICTs. The financial circumstances of earlier years can have a bearing not only on what ICTs people can afford but, perhaps more importantly, on their orientation to consumption in general. The evaluation of specific ICTs can reflect the timing of when they appeared in relation to their life stage, and have a bearing not only on decisions to acquire or not to acquire them but also on what facilities to use or not use on the equipment and services available. Furthermore, earlier experiences can have an influence on how at ease people feel in using particular technologies, how they feel some technologies, like television, have changed over the years, as well as how they appreciate the way specific content relates to generational identities.

Conclusions

There are some observations to be made about the case study. One concerns how these findings were derived. Some insights come from the young elderly as informants, explaining, for instance, the timing of office automation in their lives. However, the analyses are in part based on the background knowledge of the researcher, as in the example of the significance of the age of the participants' children when PCs first appeared. At other points, the potential cohort dimension appears in language used by the participants. For example, after the young elderly had commented on their general approach to consumption, the language of whether particular innovations were 'needed' or 'useful' (or not) spontaneously occurred again and again when discussing a range of ICTs. But it is also important to appreciate that whether overtly referring to the orientation of 'their generation' choosing what to talk about when accounting for their actions (not adopting PCs) or their preferences and perceptions (in relation to contemporary TV), the participants were themselves drawing on a form of generational analysis to explain their actions. In other words, they were making sense of their choices in terms of their past experiences, often with the implication that many of those experiences were shared by people of their age.

This particular case study is now old, so what those young elderly described was their behaviour and evaluations at that point in their lives, and in relation to ICTs that were sometimes only recently available. For example, at the time of the study, morning and daytime TV were relatively new and in terms of their lifestyle, a number of the participants engaged in alternative activities when many declined to watch these programmes. At the time they explained this decision in terms of older viewing habits. If interviewed now, 20 years later, when morning and daytime TV are more established, and when, as an older elderly cohort, their other activity options may have diminished in part because of declining mobility, they might watch TV outside of the evening slots. That does not mean that their justification of their behaviour by reference to habits from their earlier life was misleading. It just means that it is only a consideration, and if the social world (the establishment of morning and daytime) and personal circumstances change, so can habits.

While acknowledging that various factors relating to the period of the interview may have had a bearing on particular answers, the case study in this chapter is useful in terms of suggesting lines of investigation one could follow up if adding a cohort dimension to research. The review at the start of the chapter set the scene by outlining a range of generational studies, where the focus on the cohort is often the central form of analysis. In contrast, the aim of citing the case study of the young elderly and ICTs is somewhat different. It indicates how the generational dimension might be examined alongside other forms of analysis if the researcher suspects that previous shared experiences might have some bearing, among other factors, on how people adopt, use and perceive ICTs.

Notes

1 Subsequently a whole range of terms in a similar spirit have emerged to describe generations of children: Internet Generation, Nintendo Generation, Avatar Generation, N-gen, Wired Generation, Echo Boomers, Google Generation, the iPods, iGeneration, Facebook Generation, born digital, homo-zappiens and net-savvy youth (Colombo, 2011; Hardey, 2011; Selwyn, 2009)
2 This did not include the internet, which at that time was not widespread.
3 A simpler point is raised in a Swedish study by Hagberg, 2012.
4 A popular comedy programme in the 1990s about the Home Guard, a group of those too old and too young the serve in the army, whose role was mainly to act as a last line of defence in the case of invasion.

References

Aroldi, P., 2011. Generational belonging between media audiences and ICT users. In: F. Colombo and L. Fortunati, eds. *Broadband society and generational changes*. Frankfurt am Main, Germany: Peter Lang, pp. 51–67.

Aroldi, P. and Colombo, F., 2013. Questioning digital global generations: a critical approach. *Northern Lights*, 11, pp. 175–190.

Aroldi, P. and Ponte, C., 2012. Adolescents of the 1960s and 1970s: an Italian-Portuguese comparison between two generations of audiences. *Cyberpsychology: Journal of Psychosocial Research on Cyberspace*, 6(2). https://doi.org/10.5817/CP2012-2-3.

Bliese, N., 1986. Media in the rocking chair: media uses and functions among the elderly. In: G. Gumpert and R. Cathcart, R, eds. *Intermedia*. Oxford, UK: Oxford University Press, pp. 573–582.

Bourdieu, P., 1977. *Outline of a theory of practice*. Cambridge, UK: Cambridge University Press.

boyd, d., 2014. *It's complicated: the social lives of networked teens*. New Haven, CT: Yale University Press.

Buckingham, D., 2009. Introducing identity. In: D. Buckingham, ed. *Youth, identity and digital media*. Cambridge, MA: MIT Press, pp. 1–22.

Colombo, F., 2011. The long wave of generations. In: F. Colombo and L. Fortunati, eds. *Broadband society and generational changes*. Frankfurt am Main, Germany: Peter Lang, pp. 19–35.

Corsten, M., 2011. Media as the "historical new" for young generations. In: F. Colombo and L. Fortunati, eds. *Broadband society and generational changes*. Frankfurt am Main, Germany: Peter Lang, pp. 37–49.

Cutler, N., 1977. Political socialization research as generational analysis: the cohort approach versus the lineage approach. In: S. Renshon, ed. *Handbook of political socialization*. New York: Free Press, pp. 294–326.

Edmunds, J. and Turner, B. S., 2002. *Generations, culture and society*. Buckingham, UK and Philadelphia, PA: Open University Press.

Edmunds, J. and Turner, B. S., 2005. Global generations: social change in the twentieth century. *The British Journal of Sociology*, 56(4), pp. 559–577.

Eyerman, R. and Turner, B., 1998. Outline of a theory of generations. *European Journal of Social Theory*, 1(1), pp. 91–106.

Giancola, F., 2006. The generation gap: more myth than reality. *Human Resource Planning*, 24(4), pp. 32–37.

Gilleard, C. and Higgs, P., 2005. *Contexts of ageing: class, cohort and community*. Cambridge, UK: Polity Press.

Haddon, L., 1988. The home computer: the making of a consumer electronic. *Science as Culture*, 2, pp. 7–51. http://eprints.lse.ac.uk/64559/.

Haddon, L., 2016. Domestication and the media. In: P. Rössler, ed. *The international encyclopedia about media effects*. London: John Wiley and Sons. http://eprints.lse.ac.uk/64848/.

Haddon, L. and Silverstone, R., 1996. *Information and communication technologies and the young elderly*. University of Sussex, Falmer: SPRU/CICT Report Series. http://eprints.lse.ac.uk/62450/.

Haddon, L. and Skinner, D., 1991. The enigma of the micro: lessons from the British home computer boom. *Social Science Computer Review*, 9(3), pp. 435–449.

Hagberg, J.-E., 2012. Being the oldest old in a shifting technology landscape. In: E. Loos, L. Haddon and E. Mante-Meijer, eds. *Generational use of new media*. Aldershot, UK: Ashgate, pp. 89–106.

Hardey, M., 2011. ICTs and generations: constantly connected lives. In: F. Colombo and L. Fortunati, eds. *Broadband society and generational changes*. Frankfurt am Main, Germany: Peter Lang, pp. 97–108.

Hartmann, M., 2003. *The web generation? The (de)construction of users, morals and consumption*. Brussels: SMIT-VUB, Free University of Brussels.

Holmes, J., 2011. Cyberkids or divided generations? Characterising young people's internet use in the UK with generic, continuum or typological models. *New Media and Society*, 13(7), pp. 1104–1122.

Hughs, M. and Rand, A., 2005. The lives and times of the Baby Boomers. In: R. Farley and C. Haaga, eds. *The American people*. New York: Russell Sage Foundation, pp. 224–255.

Kertzer, D., 1983. Generation as a sociological problem. *Annual Review of Sociology*, 9, pp. 125–149.

Lim, S. S., 2006. From cultural to information revolution: ICT domestication by middle-class Chinese families. In: T. Berker, M. Hartmann, Y. Punie and K. Ward, eds. *Domestication of media and technologies*. Maidenhead, UK: Open University Press, pp. 185–204.

Mackay, K., Garden, D. and Forsyth, S., 2008. Generational differences at work: introduction and overview. *Journal of Managerial Psychology*, 23(8), pp. 857–861.

Mannheim, K., 1952 [1923]. The problem of generations. In: K. Mannheim, ed. *Essays on the sociology of knowledge*. London: Routledge and Kegan Paul, pp. 276–320.

Mitchell, S., 2003. *American generations: who they are, how they live, what they think.* Ithaca, NY: New Strategist Publications, Inc.

Noble, S. and Schewe, C., 2003. Cohort segmentation: an exploration of its validity. *Journal of Business Research*, 56(12), pp. 979–987.

Prensky, M., 2001. Digital natives, digital immigrants. *On the Horizon*, 9(5), pp. 1–6.

Putnam, R., 2000. *Bowling alone: the crumbling and revival of American community.* New York: Simon and Schuster.

Randall, E., 1995. Switching on at 60-plus. In: D. Petrie and J. Willis, eds. *Television and the household*. London: BFI, pp. 49–64.

Ryder, N., 1965. The cohort as a concept in the study of social change. *American Sociological Review*, 30(6), pp. 843–861.

Selwyn, N., 2009. The digital native – myth and reality. *Aslib proceedings: new information perspective*, 61(4), pp. 364–378.

Silverstone, R., Hirsch, E. and Morley, D., 1992. Information and communication technologies and the moral economy of the household. In: R. Silverstone and E. Hirsch, eds. *Consuming technologies*. London: Routledge, pp. 15–31.

Smola, K. and Sutton, C., 2002. Generational differences: revisiting generational work values for the new millennium. *Journal of Organizational Behavior*, 23(4), pp. 363–382.

Stern, S., 2008. Questioning the generational divide: technological exoticism and adult constructions of online youth identity. In: D. Buckingham, ed. *Youth, Identity and Digital Media*. Cambridge, MA: MIT Press, pp. 95–118.

Strauss, W. and Howe, N., 1991. *Generations: the history of America's future, 1584 to 2069*. New York: William Morrow and Company.

Tapscott, D., 1998. *Growing up digital: the rise of the Net Generation*. New York: McGraw-Hill.

Tulloch, J., 1989. Approaching the audience: the elderly, In: E. Seiter, H. Borchers, G. Kreutzner and E.-M. Warth, eds. *Remote control: television, audience and cultural power*. London: Routledge, pp. 180–203.

Wellner, A., 2000. Generation divide: are traditional methods of classifying in general still meaningful in a diverse and changing nation? *American Demographics*, 22(10), pp. 52–58.

Willis, J., 1995. Staying in touch: television and the over seventies. In: D. Petrie and J. Willis, eds. *Television and the household*. London: BFI, pp. 32–48.

Part II
Family generations and ICT

5 Mobile life of middle-aged employees

Fragmented time and softer schedules

Mia Tammelin and Timo Anttila

Technology and time-space compression: always online?

Technological innovations and information and communications technology (ICT) have many complex implications for social life. Technology changes the nature and meaning of everyday tasks and results in new cultural practices (Wajcman, 2008). One important aspect of ICT is that it changes the relation of time and place and has consequences for social relationships. In this chapter, we concentrate on patterns of ICT use among middle-aged employees in demanding knowledge work, i.e. workers with high levels of education working in expert positions. We discuss particularly how these people, aged 34–55, use ICTs to manage, coordinate and cope with the various schedules of family, work and free time. We show that regardless of belonging to the same broad social generation, they do not share the same patterns in their use of mobile technology; instead, their orientations to ICTs and practices vary. Therefore, it seems it is not generation as such that defines the use and orientation to ICT among this social group, but rather that there are differences between people, their work and family situations that influence ICT use.

The group in our focus, middle-aged employees, constantly have to confront the idea that time is a limited resource. Knowledge workers in particular experience hurriedness and have to synchronise their individual schedules and agendas both in work and within a family. Perhaps more than ever, people control and manage time (Adam, 1995; Hochschild, 1997) to obtain an increased agency on time (Daly, 2001). This is a result of modernisation, which has increased the pace of life and augmented the pressure to perform many tasks and roles simultaneously. This has created a new social problem: the lack of time (Garhammer, 2002; Southerton, 2003).

Wajcman (2008, 2015) links the sense of lack of time to the accelerating pace of technological change, as new ICTs heighten expectations on efficient use of time. Mobile technology is used to solve time-related problems, such as hurriedness, and to organise daily life, but it also seems to increase time fragmentation that can be a source of time-related problems. In addition, coordinating activities and time are essential aspects of everyday life, especially for families with children who have many schedules and activities tied together.

ICT plays a central role for and within time management strategies of middle-aged employees, and we propose that it changes their conception of time and scheduling of daily tasks such that time and schedules become fluid and flexible. Our focus on time and ICTs is based on the observation that time is a fundamental element of the orchestration and synchronisation of social life (Daly, 2001) and needs to be discussed along with ICTs. The main research questions of our study concerns the role of ICTs, particularly mobile communication technology, in organising daily schedules.

First, we analyse the role of ICTs in the accelerated pace of life and the possibilities portable technologies bring along for the middle-aged to deal with this faster pace. Second, we discuss if and how the conception of time is changing because of the widespread use of ICTs. We argue that middle-aged employees in demanding work form a generation with particular time management strategies characterised by increased fragmentation of time and the multiplication of time coordination practices. These time management strategies are being transformed with the affordances provided by ICTs, which add to fragmentation and enable the avoidance of time contamination. ICT also engenders new time management strategies, making it possible to multitask using technology. As a result, the conception of time changes among the study's group of middle-aged knowledge workers, and their ties to clock time and to societal rhythms loosen, although these ties do not disappear.

Accelerating pace of life and ICT-facilitated time strategies

Time is popularly identified with 'famine', 'squeeze' and accelerated ICT use (Hochschild, 1997; Robinson and Godbey, 1999; Florida, 2002; Garhammer, 2002; Rosa, 2003; Wajcman, 2015). Earlier studies indicate the lack of time as a common experience among the working population. On the one hand, hurriedness is explained by increasing requirements of work life (Green, 2006) and by the changing nature of work (Sennet, 1998). Along with the faster pace of paid work, the value of free time is emphasised and this leads to increasing consumer expectations (which take time) and consequent changes in the density of leisure time (Linder, 1970; Gershuny, 2005).

On the other hand, feelings of time scarcity or haste may relate to fast technological changes (Castells, 2000). The intervention of digital technologies is thought to speed up everyday life and the entire culture to an unprecedented degree (Lash, 2002). In addition, rapidly diffused new ICTs have shaped time-space relations in the realms of work and family in multiple ways. The time-space compression thesis (Harvey, 1989; Wajcman, 2015) is widely applied in the sociology of time and technology, to describe technology-driven transformations in time and space. Along with technological change, simultaneity and instantaneousness have increasingly become constitutive features of human activity. In mainstream sociology, Castells' (2000) concepts of timeless time and space of flows are widely utilised to describe transformations in the spatial-temporal organisation of everyday life.

In this chapter, we do not analyse hurriedness as such, but the accelerated pace of life serves as a background to this study in which we discuss the paradoxical nature of ICTs to time. We argue that ICT both fragments time through acceleration and serves as a tool to manage and coordinate time among middle-aged employees, who juggle with simultaneous time-demanding activities.

Data and method

We explore these themes using interview data from 21 employees in Finland (see Table 5.1). All interviewees are highly educated, are particularly prone to problems of hurriedness and use ICTs in their daily work. The interviewees work in both the public and private sectors in fields such as education, research and social services, and some are in supervisory positions. Interviewees are middle-aged, ranging between 34 and 55 years. Data were gathered in spring 2015 in various parts of Finland via 4 face-to-face interviews and 17 phone interviews. The semi-structured interviews included questions of work–life balance, time use and organisation of work.

We followed the principles of content analysis (Hsieh and Shannon, 2005) to systematically analyse the data. All interviews were read first from the view

Table 5.1 Characteristics of interviewees.

	Age	Occupation	Spouse	Children (No/yes, number & age)*
1	34	Specialist	Yes	No
2	35	Research manager	Yes	No
3	36	Educational designer	Yes	Yes, 2, both under school age
4	50	Civil servant	Yes	Yes, 3, one school age, two adults
5	53	Project coordinator	No	Yes, 4, one school age, three adults
6	42	Head of development	Yes	Yes, 2, both school age
7	40	Senior researcher	No	No
8	48	Civil servant	Yes	Yes, 3, two school age, one adult
9	47	Head of educational design	Yes	Yes, 2, both adult
10	35	NGO instructor	Yes	Yes, 2, both under school age
11	49	Head of design	Yes	Yes, 2, both school age
12	40	Project manager	Yes	Yes, 2, one under school age, one school age
13	39	Development designer	No	No
14	37	Researcher	Yes	Yes, 2, one under school age, one school age
15	55	Development designer	Yes	Yes, 5, one school age, 4 adults
16	53	Director	No	Yes, 2, both adults
17	40	Researcher	No	Yes, 2, one under school age, one school age
18	51	Programme director	No	Yes, 2, adults
19	55	Editor	Yes	Yes, 2, adults
20	43	Researcher	Yes	Yes, 2, both school age
21	47	Recreational instructor	Yes	Yes, 2, both under school age

Note: *Age of children: under school age (0–7 years), school age (7–17) and adult 18+ years.

of time, ICT and pace of life and then we analysed themes that occurred in the interviews. Some themes were theory-based, such as multitasking, time coordination and intergenerational relations, and others emerged from the interviews, such as the social costs of staying outside social media and the emphasis on synchronised communication.

The sample of our study was drawn from Finland, in which the feelings of hurriedness are considerably high. According to the European Working Conditions surveys (Parent-Thirion *et al.*, 2007) Finland is among the top countries where people, especially women, experience self-reported hurriedness. This is explained by full-time work practices for both men and women, while women still remain in charge of household duties. Hurriedness is not equally distributed but is most evident among highly educated, white-collar workers in Finland, as has been reported elsewhere (Anttila *et al.*, 2009). Our sample consists of highly educated employees working in knowledge work; therefore, we expect that these employees in particular would suffer from the accelerated pace of life. Overall, participants described being busy and having many schedules that needed to be tied together, yet busyness was mostly concentrated in the world of work compared to free time or time away from work. In presenting our analysis and results in the following sections, we use pseudonyms to ensure the anonymity of the interviewees.

Feeling hurried: example of the Eklund family

Next, we present an empirical example of the hurried family that illustrates demands of daily time management that stem from the need to reconcile multiple schedules. Susanna is in her late thirties and has a university degree. She works as project manager, and her work is characterised by unanticipated deadlines and a heavy workload. Still, for the most part, she has control over her work hours. Susanna typically works about eight hours a day, and she is active in non-governmental organisations (NGOs) that include evening and weekend activities. Her husband, Leo, does shift work with scattered hours. Susanna and Leo have a daughter, Emilia, age 4, and a son, Noel, age 11. Emilia is in the kindergarten, and Noel goes to school near their home.

In the interview, Susanna said that particularly life outside work is hurried. With her husband's irregular shift work, she is mostly responsible for the children but persists with her own hobbies as well. She says: "Like I said, I am active in various NGOs with responsibilities (I'm a treasurer and vice-president), but that is a hobby. This hobby requires a lot of foot work, but it motivates me because I can help other people".

When asked what hurriedness means to her, she replied with laughter: "Hurriedness is when you don't go to your sitting room for a week, although that is right next to the kitchen". Susanna explains further that now Noel is older and has hobbies, she feels hurried because they live in the countryside, which means that parents have to take children to their hobbies. Thus, commuting to work in the morning and to hobbies in the evening gives her many activities to take care of and a feeling of hurriedness.

Susanna has a very practical orientation to hurriedness which involves 'doing less' and relocating some domestic activities, such as having a meal, outside the house. She said:

> We only do what is necessary. That is, we go with minimal effort around the house, and we can take food with us, if we feel like it. Children can have their evening meal in the car . . . I feel that we have moved time elsewhere from the sitting room . . . You just need to plan everything carefully.

Her orientation to hurriedness is paradoxical. She first says that their life is busy and she has no time to do shopping, yet in the end she concludes that it is not hastened life but just 'life'. Susanna's strategy to cope with hurriedness involves very explicit orientation to using ICTs and resisting consumerism. She said:

> I order everything through internet. I have consciously reduced that time spent on shopping. There is no point in going shopping with your family. Children don't need that; they don't enjoy it. Once a year we can go to buy new shoes. Otherwise I order from the internet, and they are usually fine.

This illustrates that she is using ICTs to compress time and cope with hurriedness. In the following section, we describe time-related strategies related to ICTs.

Fragmentation increases time contamination: ICT both a reason and a solution

Wajcman and Bittman (2000) state that the contemporary view of increased time pressure may have more to do with the fragmentation of time than with any measurable reduction in primary leisure time. Hence, hurriedness appears as a result of more fragmented time. When time is fragmented, it is 'contaminated'. Roughly speaking, this means that time devoted to a single task is scarce; more and more activities penetrate a one single moment and we must constantly decide how to deal with them. This inevitably fragments time.

Fragmentation of time has many consequences. Wajcman (2008) notes that perpetual contact can disturb the boundary between the private and public realms, and she argues for the redefinition of 'public time' (or shared time) and 'private time' into 'on time' and 'off time'. Furthermore, Licoppe (2004) argues that 'connected presence' is blurring absence and presence for people. Before mobile technology, time was shared within families in face-to-face relationships, whereas now time also can be shared in technology-mediated communication. Social bonds are giving way to transient communication bonds that are immediate and accelerated, yet distant, forms of sociality (Wajcman, 2008).

Within families, women's free time is often fragmented due to distracting accompanying activities, such as preparing meals and caring for children. Women are found to have less free time, and what free time they have is often fragmented by other activities or the presence of children (Mattingly and Blanchi, 2003; Mattingly and Sayer, 2006).

We propose that ICT is one such source of time fragmentation, which is illustrated through the example of online parenting and time at work. Because of this fragmentation, individuals develop specific strategies to deal with the problem. Our analysis reveals that the interviewees use at least two ICT-related time strategies to manage time. Hence, first we discuss how technology increases the fragmentation of time but can be used to avoid it, and second, we discuss attempts to save time by multitasking.

Does online parenting contaminate time?

The working parents interviewed explained how parents take advantage of portable technologies to be in constant touch with their children. Online parenting might generate more time contamination, yet it is typical for working parents of young children who want to keep in touch with their school children while at work.

Brannen and colleagues (2013) argue that increased simultaneity – individuals occupying different social domains concurrently – is a constant in family life. For example, while parents (particularly mothers) are at work, they remain responsible for children. This means that time is even more fragmented; one's presence is torn between off- and online time. Ganito (2012) shows that women use mobile phones to coordinate and control their various roles – in many cases they are always 'on call' – and thus minimise temporal disorganisation (Southerton and Tomlinson, 2005). This creates a paradox in which mobile phones enable better coordination and lower anxiety, yet increase the need for multitasking and the emotional burden of managing multiple roles.

In our data, some parents show an explicit orientation to being available for children during work days. Anna, a mother of three children, said that "It might be that you are in a meeting when the child calls, but it does not matter. I think, children can call you whenever, if they need to. It does not disturb me". The same was repeated by a father of two who said that he and his wife had taught their children that they can always call their parents after school. Furthermore, another mother, Emma, said that work should not be so important that you cannot answer your child.

Yet not all parents believe family matters should be allowed to penetrate work. Those with teenage children said that they need to secure time for work and do not allow these interruptions that fragment time at work. These parents work as professionals where they have the possibility of being online but suffer from hurriedness. Therefore, as a strategy to control time at work, they only receive messages and get back to children when it suits their work schedule.

As family and life situations and orientation to online parenting differs, the different styles of maintaining intergenerational relations crash at the workplace. Some people, regardless of whether they are parents or not, feel there is no need to constantly communicate with children or spouses, while others like to maintain online relations while at work. Laura, who works in a small office space, said she finds constant phone calls disturbing and that they should be replaced with silent messaging. She explained:

> It is rare with my husband and children . . . One colleague here she/he calls with her children all the time. That disturbs me because then the phone rings here also. We have a small office here, like WhatsApp would be useful there, when questions are "Can I stay on the playground after school?", like they talk "Can I?", "No, you can't", and "Are you wearing a coat?", and these petty things. This continues into longer discussions, easily.

All in all, it seems portable technology fragments time as it is possible to stay in touch with family members regardless of where you are, and this potential is used unnecessarily. It is somewhat surprising that some parents are always online for their children while at work. This not only contaminates their time but that of others. Therefore, workplaces are melting pots for varying parenting practices because not all share the same orientation to the use of ICTs.

Avoidance of time contamination

It is also justified to ask if there are practices of time management and control that are used to resist time contamination that inevitably cause feelings of hurriedness. Our interviews show that people use various means to actively resist time contamination.

A central theme in the interviews was the use of strategies to avoid contamination of time at home. Because of pressures arising from work, many employees did work-related tasks at home. ICTs have made this possible, together with the changing nature of work; documents can be reached from home, and emails are read regardless of time and place. Consequently, some parents actively avoided work taking over home life, and interviewees described explicitly resisting technology to protect home time and space.

Maria, a mother of three, said that she decided not to get internet access at home so that time at home would not be fragmented. She further explained that as she had small children at home for almost a decade, she knows that sitting at the computer around the home is impossible. "Computers are tempting to children", she said. By not having an internet connection to be able to work at home, she is able to restrict work to the workplace and "to secure [a] hygienic home", as she explained. Time contamination at home is thus actively resisted.

Besides resigning oneself to not having the required technological devices, another strategy to resist contamination of time was refusing to use social media such as Facebook or LinkedIn. Social media in particular was seen as a polluter or time-eater to be avoided because of lack of available time. Silvia explained that "I feel that I don't have the time to update those. I try to avoid those kinds of time-eaters, and I feel that I have much more time".

Not being part of social media networks is a clear time-related strategy that has social costs, however (Raynes-Goldie, 2010). Anna explained the consequences of staying outside social media like this: "Social life suffers from it. I feel constantly that I should follow Facebook, I really should, but then – I don't have time. I feel like I have kind of mental peace when I only have this daily life here". Referring to not wanting to contaminate the time of daily life, she said that staying outside social media not only saves time but secures "a peace of mind".

This prevention of contamination leads to a lack of information and staying outside social relationships. Using Wajcman's (2008) conceptualisation, this is how we secure personal time off, rather than being online constantly. Silvia described friends and colleagues commenting on her desire to stay outside social media, asking her, for example, to check her Facebook once in a while to learn of the birth of babies in the work community or of previous colleagues. "People get upset when I dare to ask how is an old friend doing? . . . I admit that I miss out sometimes on baby news and such".

We expected to find discussion on the contamination of time and how ICTs affect it, yet it was somewhat surprising how explicitly informants told us of staying outside, the polluting effects of ICTs, and particularly that of social media. Due to hurriedness, they have to deal with time demands in one way or another so ICTs not only cause hurriedness but can serve as tools to deal with it. Another recurring time strategy related to ICTs was multitasking.

Mobile technology and multitasking

In addition to their constraining and time-fragmenting nature, ICTs may also have a time saving, controlling and coordinating role. In an attempt to control and save time, we perform many activities at the same time; that is to say, we multitask (Wajcman, 2015). In our analysis, we concentrated on the role of mobile technology. We do not discuss the role of so-called old technology, such as washing machines, which have – without question – enabled us to do things at the same time.

Portable phones and computers are tools for using social media applications, and based on our interviews as well as previous research (Rice and Hagen, 2010), it seems social media in particular are a central way to multitask and save time. Pauliina explained that the greatest benefit of social media and groups is that you do not have to be in touch with everyone separately but can reach everyone at the same time:

> I feel that what is best in WhatsApp and Facebook Messenger is that you can reach groups. That you don't have to individually contact everyone. That is the greatest benefit. When there is a big group of people, it is easier to do it this way, reach everyone at the same time.

Still, not everyone is part of the same social media application, so the possibilities to multitask may be lost because of the need to repeat the same activity through several channels. Eva in particular wondered if technology and social media groups cause duplicate messaging and, in the end, cause us to have more activities to perform. She also pointed out that part of the package of agreeing to social events with friends is to do it 'ridiculously' early. This implies that busy schedules require advanced planning and coordination of schedules. Eva explained like this:

> Those things that we organise with a big group we organise with Facebook and WhatsApp. With some friends, we have these Facebook groups. And then one group of friends to which I belong, it is funny; even when we have this Facebook group we still have a WhatsApp group. We use both. Then my mobile phone keeps vibrating when those WhatsApp messages come through. Typically it is like "Yes, we will meet in half a year in a summer cottage", or something. We have to plan really early in advance. It is ridiculous really.

In conclusion, the pace of life is accelerated because we have more to do and more feeds to deal with within a single moment. ICTs are both a cause and a solution for the contamination of time that follows from this change (see Rice and Hagen, 2010). We discussed online parenting as an example of these practices that cause fragmentation, which narrow the borders between various life spheres. Individuals have to decide whether they are online or offline. One strategy that interviewees used to deal with the fragmentation was to avoid it either at home or work or to avoid certain applications, such as social media networks. Another strategy was to do more at the same time; this was done especially using social media that enable more contacts at one time. Yet, social networks are not 'waterproof' as not everyone is part of the same applications, groups or networks. This results in doing the same activity repeatedly. These varying processes and ways of managing time led us to think: do ICTs change the conception of time?

Changing conception of time

One central element of everyday life is the coordination of various activities and time frames. Although time frames of social life might be loosening, there are still a great number of time institutions. Opening hours of shops and schools and hours at work, for example, define the schedules of family members. Integrating these schedules into family life and with the wider social network requires coordination. Mobile technology enables the coordination of such activities that are not fixed but can be done flexibly throughout the day. Ling's (2004; Ling and Lai, 2016) concept of micro-coordination best describes the ways the informants explained the relationship between mobile technology and scheduling activities (Townsend, 2000; Cooper *et al.*, 2002; Ling and Haddon, 2003). Research shows that mobile technologies are softening schedules; clear time markers of schedules are breaking down and the conception of time is changing.

Coordinating increasingly softer schedules

Technology-assisted coordination can be divided into micro- and hyper-coordination that differ in their nature (Ling and Yttri, 1999, 2002). Micro-coordinating refers to organising activities in time and space, i.e. for logistical purposes, whereas hyper-coordination refers to using technology as a means of self-presentation and personal expression. It has been suggested that mobile phones, in particular, are vital for performing coordinating activities, particularly micro-coordinating (Wajcman, 2015). Mobile technology was an important tool for one family in our study. Susan, a mother of two children, told how she and her partner micro-coordinate when fixing the daily routine. She explained:

> Yes, for example, today I just sent a message [to him] asking which child – or both – I should collect from care, and then he [her partner] said that he will take care of the son because of his practice, and then I will collect our daughter. And then he reminded me that we have to buy food [for] the day care centre, because it is a private crèche, therefore we take turns in buying food there. And then I replied that, good, this is good because now I have time to do this: first to pick up the list, second to go do the groceries and third to pick up our daughter.

Susan vividly explained the exchange of messages; there was not one but several messages between the partners that concerned organising family life and particularly the care of their children. This micro-coordination seems laborious but was not necessarily perceived as disturbing. "It is like [a] smooth exchange of information. Sometimes it might disturb the work day if it doesn't match your work schedules but better to know anyway". Others agreed that continuous messaging and micro-coordinating are laborious and fragment time.

Hyper-coordination means that technology is used for sharing emotions and social behaviour such as joking or showing emotional support. Our informants explained that hyper-coordination occurred between spouses or between a parent and a child. For example, Susanna said: "With my partner, we can tell [talk about] work-related news, or, for example, if you know that the other one has had an important presentation or something like that, then you can ask after that 'how was it'?"

Some explained that they used applications, particularly WhatsApp, to share their own emotions, saying, for example, "I had an inspiring meeting" or "I had a very difficult meeting". Furthermore, some used social media to cheer up their spouses, with no actual content but to get in touch with the other. Our data do not explain in more detail what the consequences of hyper-coordination are. In the interviews, we did not ask if there were misunderstandings, for example, or if hyper-coordination resulted in changing plans on how to use time.

Another theme that needs to be discussed is the way scheduling is transforming because of the possibility of a continuous online presence. It seems evident that mobile technologies have been softening schedules (Ling and Yttri, 2002). Softening schedules refers to schedule arrangements that are not fixed but agreed upon close to the activity itself. This amplifies coordination, or the work that is needed to order and arrange activities. Thus, ICTs are tools used to undertake the temporal and spatial arrangements (Ling, 2004).

Taking children to hobbies was a recurring theme among the interviewed that was related to time coordination. For example, Susanna explained they use online messaging with their son to coordinate commuting to hobbies. When she is ready to leave work to pick up her son for his hobby, they get in touch using WhatsApp. "Last year we started to use WhatsApp. There I might write to my son, that 'ten minutes to go', then he knows when to be ready". This quote is a good example of how schedules are softening and how, with the enabling features of technology, schedules are not fixed but left open to negotiation and reordering.

Softening schedules also have far-reaching consequences beyond changing scheduling; they also affect how we perceive schedules, time and activities. Our perspectives have become less rigid and are now subject to negotiation and reordering. Furthermore, it seems there is a paradox linked to softening schedules: to cope with softening schedules, interviewees said they returned to using old technology as messages can get lost in timeless time. Informants clearly favoured simultaneous communication through old technology, such as telephones, to make sure that the message has been received. For example, Matilda said that if there are changes to fixed schedules, she calls her partner rather than sending an email or using Facebook. This way she is sure that the message reaches her partner in time. But for activities that are further away and do not require immediate attention, communication can be done through email.

Discussion

This chapter draws from research concerned with how various forms of ICTs change the relation of time and implications for social relationships. The chapter began by noting the growing academic and public focus on ICTs as a fundamental domain of daily life that accelerates the pace of life and results in new forms of social interaction.

Our study focused particularly on questions of fragmentation of time and time coordination that are seen as key dilemmas in a modern society. The emergence of the 24/7 society has eroded collective temporal rhythms, and the spread of new ICTs has far-reaching implications in various spheres of life. Simultaneity and instantaneousness have become constitutive features of human activity and involve time strategies of doing things faster, multitasking or employing more detailed interpersonal time-planning. It seems that increasingly, more effort is needed to coordinate schedules and to maintain interpersonal relations. We are always online.

Demographic characteristics also can be proxies for families' time processes. Gender, life course and age of children represent constraints that shape differential temporal experiences. The need for time coordination varies especially with children's activities as the more activities and schedules they have, the more coordination is necessary. In addition, having small children requires more coordination to manage all family routines. Therefore, the importance of the life course is highlighted. Demanding work further underlines the challenge to juggle with simultaneous and instantaneous tasks and, at the same time, to think and manage the boundaries of public and private spheres. Our study does not support the idea that the strategies these middle-aged time jugglers employ are shared among the whole generation. Although their pressures from work and family life seem to be similar, we found distinct and partly controversial strategies to manage time.

ICTs also produce their own temporal demands, and we propose that it seems to change the way we orient ourselves to time and schedules. ICTs tend to colonise time slots and to take on habitual and routine forms. Many of our interviewees were conscious and worried of the time-eating routines produced by ICTs. We found distinct boundary management strategies to safeguard the home sphere and (children's) leisure from the contaminating and time-eating role of ICTs at home. Interviewees explicitly described their practices to resist technology.

Finally, another interesting conversion is taking place, that of softening schedules. This refers to the perception of how fixed scheduling is seen and performed. The orientation that it is always possible to rearrange, reallocate and redesign daily schedules transforms the process of scheduling into a fluid and transformative one. Mobile technology enables people to stay online and makes it possible to govern daily schedules in detail – waiting becomes a waste of mind.

The study brings up some new themes for further research. Our study concentrated only on highly educated knowledge workers. It would be interesting to gather more information on workers in different positions, such as blue-collar workers with more fixed working hours, for example. An interesting question is, does a fixed work schedule allow a softening of schedules?

As discussed in this chapter, our proposition is that technology is changing the conception of time, besides the actual use of time. This theme should be explored in more detail since some people seem to rely more on routines and fixed schedules, while others allow daily fluctuations and prefer softer schedules. It remains unanswered why these differences exist. Is it because of individual or family preferences, or are the explanations rooted in structural matters, such as schedules of work and hobbies? Another interesting topic is to analyse gender differences in this regard, and in particular among families with small children: can we identify conversions of gender roles – or do women's roles as coordinators prevail?

References

Adam, B., 1995. *Time watch. The Social Analysis of Time.* Cambridge, UK: Polity Press.

Anttila, T., Oinas, T. and Nätti, J., 2009. Predictors of time famine among Finnish employees: work, family or leisure? *Electronic International Journal of Time Use Research,* 6(1), pp. 73–91.

Brannen, J., O'Connell, R. and Mooney, A., 2013. Families, meals and synchronicity: eating together in British dual earner families. *Community, Work & Family,* 16(4), pp. 417–434.

Castells, M., 2000. *The rise of the network society. The information age: economy, society and culture.* Vol. I. Malden, MA: John Wiley & Sons.

Cooper, G., Green, N., Murtagh, G. and Harper, R., 2002. "Mobile society": technology, distance, and presence. In: S. Woolgar, ed. *Virtual society? Technology, cyberbole, reality.* Oxford, UK: Oxford University Press, pp. 286–301.

Daly, K. J., 2001. Deconstructing family time: from ideology to lived experience. *Journal of Marriage and Family*, 63(2), pp. 283–294.

Florida, R., 2002. *The rise of the creative class. And how it's transforming work, leisure, community and everyday life*. New York: Basic Books.

Ganito, C., 2012. Moving time and juggling spheres. *Feminist Media Studies*, 12(4), pp. 570–579.

Garhammer, M., 2002. Pace of life and enjoyment of life. *Journal of Happiness Studies*, 3(3), pp. 217–256.

Gershuny, J., 2005. Busyness as the badge of honor for the new superordinate working class. *Social Research*, 72(2), pp. 287–314.

Green, F., 2006. *Demanding work. The paradox of job quality in the affluent economy*. Princeton, NJ: Princeton University Press.

Harvey, D., 1989. *The condition of postmodernity*. Oxford, UK: Blackwell.

Hsieh, H-S. and Shannon, S., 2005. Three approaches to qualitative content analysis. *Qualitative Health Research*, 15(9), pp. 1277–1288.

Hochschild, A. R., 1997. *The time bind. When work becomes home and home becomes work*. New York: Metropolitan Books.

Lash, S., 2002. *Critique of information*. London: SAGE.

Licoppe, C., 2004. Connected presence: the emergence of a new repertoire for managing social relationships in a changing communication technospace. *Environment and Planning D: Society and Space*, 22(1), pp. 135–156.

Linder, S., 1970. *The harried leisure class*. New York: Columbia University Press.

Ling, R., 2004. *The mobile connection: the cell phone's impact on society*. San Francisco, CA: Morgan Kaufmann.

Ling, R. and Haddon, H., 2003. Mobile telephony, mobility, and the coordination of everyday life. In: J. Katz, ed. *Machines that become us: the social context of communication technology*. New Brunswick, NJ: Transaction Publishers, pp. 245–266.

Ling, R. and Lai, C.-H., 2016. Microcoordination 2.0: social coordination in the age of smartphones and messaging apps. *Journal of Communication*, 66(5), pp. 834–856.

Ling, R. and Yttri, B., 1999. *Nobody sits at home and waits for the telephone to ring: micro and hyper-coordination through the use of the mobile telephone*. Telenor Research and Development. Report 30/99.

Ling, R. and Yttri, B., 2002. Hyper-coordination via mobile phones in Norway. In: J. Katz and M. Aakhus, eds. *Perpetual contact: mobile communication, private talk, public performance*. Cambridge, UK: Cambridge University Press, pp. 139–169.

Mattingly, M. J. and Blanchi, S. M., 2003. Gender differences in the quantity and quality of free time: the U.S. experience. *Social Forces*, 81(3), pp. 999–1030.

Mattingly, M. J. and Sayer, L. C., 2006. Under pressure: gender differences in the relationship between free time and feeling rushed. *Journal of Marriage and Family*, 68(1), pp. 205–221.

Parent-Thirion, A., Fernández Macías, E., Hurley, J. and Vermeylen, G., 2007. *Fourth European Working Conditions survey*. Dublin: Office for Official Publications of the European Communities.

Raynes-Goldie, K., 2010. Aliases, creeping, and wall cleaning: Understanding privacy in the age of Facebook. *First Monday*, 15(1). https://doi.org/10.5210/fm.v15i1.2775.

Rice, R. and Hagen I., 2010. Young adults' perpetual contact, social connectivity, and social control through the internet and mobile phones. *Communication Yearbook 34*, 34. New York: Routledge, pp. 2–39.

Robinson, J. and Godbey, G., 1999. *Time for life: the surprising ways Americans use their time.* University Park, PA: The Pennsylvania State University Press.

Rosa, H., 2003. Social acceleration: ethical and political consequences of a desynchronised high-speed society. *Constellations*, 10(1), pp. 3–33.

Sennet, R., 1998. *The corrosion of character: the personal consequences of work in the new capitalism.* New York: W.W. Norton & Company.

Southerton, D., 2003. Squeezing time: allocating practices, coordinating networks and scheduling society. *Time & Society*, 12(1), pp. 5–25.

Southerton, D. and Tomlinson, M., 2005. "Pressed for time": the differential impacts of a "time squeeze". *The Sociological Review*, 53(2), pp. 215–239.

Townsend, A., 2000. Life in the real-time city: mobile telephones and urban metabolism. *Journal of Urban Technology*, 7(2), pp. 85–104.

Wajcman, J., 2008. Life in the fast lane? Towards a sociology of technology and time. *The British Journal of Sociology*, 59(1), pp. 59–77.

Wajcman, J., 2015. *Pressed for time: the acceleration of life in digital capitalism.* Chicago, IL: The University of Chicago Press.

Wajcman, J. and Bittman, M., 2000. The rush hour: the character of leisure time and gender equity. *Social Forces*, 79(1), pp. 165–189.

6 Intergenerational solidarity and ICT usage

Empirical insights from Finnish and Slovenian families

Sakari Taipale, Andraž Petrovčič and Vesna Dolničar

Introduction

Since the 1990s, it has been argued that social relations have individualised due to the increasing use of personal networking technologies (Rainie and Wellman, 2012). For instance, Kennedy and Wellman (2007) purport that individuals, rather than family solidarities, have become the principal unit of household connectivity as the daily agendas of family members diverge from one another. Supposedly, families are kept together ever more through ICT-mediated communication (Rainie and Wellman, 2012, p. 159). However, digital competencies and practices within families and between family generations may vary considerably, which makes it difficult to communicate similarly with all family members through ICTs. Also, states across Europe today enhance the importance of intergenerational solidarity within families rather than promote individualised lifestyle by providing publicly funded services and benefits (e.g. Hammarström, 2005; Garattini and Prendergast, 2015).

In this chapter, we suggest that recent advancements in the use of ICTs, on the one hand, and the life course perspective, on the other, can clarify these seemingly contradictory developments. For instance, while mobile phones transformed family communication from place-to-place to person-to-person (Rainie and Wellman, 2012, p. 164), at present smart phones and social media are making one-to-many communication within (and beyond) families possible (Hänninen *et al.*, forthcoming). We will also present here that such ICTs are differently engaged with and used in families across life stages, reflecting technological, personal and societal changes in a contemporary society (e.g. Haddon, 2011).

The chapter is inspired by the notion of intergenerational solidarity in the context of ICT use within contemporary families. The aim of the study is to investigate to what extent ICT usage is intertwined with different forms of intergenerational family solidarity. The families investigated are so-called (modified) extended families (Litwak, 1960) that consist of family members representing two or more generations, who may live in the same or different locations, and who stay in contact with one another by means of ICTs.

The chapter also investigates *potential country differences between Finland and Slovenia in terms of the relationship between the use of ICTs and forms of intergenerational family solidarity*. We anticipate that country differences in family makeup, housing arrangements and in the appropriation of ICTs in everyday life are reflected in the communication needs and practices of families and, thus, in the forms of family solidarity that are enhanced through the use of ICTs. For example, the percentage of multi-generational households (13.7 per cent vs. 0.6 per cent in 2007) (EuroStat, 2010) and of young adults (aged 18–34) living with their parents (60.8 per cent vs. 20.1 per cent) (EuroStat, 2016) is considerably higher in Slovenia in comparison with Finland. Although both countries rank highly in the ICT Development Index, Finland is a step further in terms of its population's ICT skills and access to the internet (ITU, 2015). Also, the difference in problem solving skills in technology-rich environments is considerable between the countries, Slovenia (23rd) ranking far behind Finland (3rd) in a recent comparison of 29 countries (OECD, 2016).

Theoretical background

Intergenerational family solidarity

Bengtson and Roberts (1991) presented the intergenerational solidarity model in the early 1990s. It stems from the assumption that the importance of intergenerational relations is primarily defined through its contribution to common social cohesion in the family (Lüscher *et al.*, 2015). Later, a large corpus of studies has built upon this model, investigating family relations between old parents, their adult children and grandchildren (Hammarström, 2005, p. 34). The model draws from the theories of social organisation, underlining the importance of group norms and functional independence in behaviour, while also being premised on socio-psychological theories of sentiments and interactions.

The model consists of six solidarity types, each representing a dialectic dimension. *Associational solidarity* (integration and isolation) refers to the frequency and patterns of interaction connecting members of a lineage to one another. The modes of interaction may vary from formal to informal, including both ritual and spontaneous communications. *Affectual solidarity* (intimacy and distance) alludes to sentiments exchanged in intergenerational family relationships, such as warmth, understanding, respect and trust. *Functional solidarity* (dependence and autonomy) refers to the idea of help exchange, covering a range of activities from financial assistance to immaterial help. *Normative solidarity* (familism and individualism) indicates the endorsement of familial obligations, while *consensual solidarity* (agreement and dissent) refers to the degree of consensus in beliefs, values or life orientations. The last dimension of the model is *structural solidarity* (opportunities and barriers) which implies the existence of an opportunity structure such as availability of family members that is reliant on physical proximity, morbidity, mortality and fecundity (Bengtson and Roberts, 1991; Bengtson *et al.*, 2002; Hammarström, 2005).

The model is most suitable for the study of 'idealistic' family relations (Bengtson and Roberts, 1991), and it captures the positive aspects of intergenerational relations and assumes the absence of conflicts between family generations (Bengtson *et al.*, 1996). In fact, the term solidarity in itself puts emphasis on consensus, rather than on conflict or ambivalence. Due to these limitations, the model was later extended to the idea of conflicts that coexist with solidarities both between and within generations (e.g. Bengtson *et al.*, 1996, 2002; Silverstein and Bengtson, 1997).

The concept of *intergenerational ambivalence* presented by Lüscher and Pillemer (1998) points out contradictions that exist between parents and their offspring but which cannot always be reconciled. They suggest that such contradictions stem from an individual's location in the social structure (structural ambivalence) and from an individual's sentiments when faced with structural ambivalence. Connidis and McMullin (2002) go further to claim that socially structured ambivalence is manifested in social interactions. Hence, agency, through which ambivalences are negotiated and privileged groups are formed, should be studied.

Confronted with criticism, Bengtson *et al.* (2002) conclude that the ambivalence approach complements and expands the family solidarity model rather than competes with it. They argue that the ambivalence brings into the discussion structural and institutional processes (e.g. policy, cultural, economy) that intersect with family life, and which are still a separate approach to family solidarity. In terms of methodology, Bengtson *et al.* (2002, p. 572) suggest that idiographic methods focusing on individual cases are perhaps more appropriate when studying negotiations that result in particular family forms and relations. Hence, qualitative methods might be more appropriate than nomothetic statistical approaches to investigate the ways in which various forms of intergenerational family solidarity are discussed vis-à-vis ICT usage and how possible contradictory expectations within families and between family generations are negotiated.

ICT and intergenerational family relations

ICTs contribute to domestic meta-work, such as managing schedules, availability and communication, as well as serving immaterial needs of families, ranging from entertainment and social networking to the feeling of security (e.g. Ling and Haddon, 2003; Madden, 2010; Zickuhr and Madden, 2012; Fortunati and Taipale, 2014; Zickuhr, 2014). Sayago *et al.* (2013) identified strategies that older people adopt in order to become successful ICT learners. These include linking learning to real-life needs (e.g. in order to be able to communicate with their children through Skype) and learning collaboratively.

The greatest motivator for older adults to get online and use social networking sites is communication with family and friends (Zickuhr and Madden, 2012; Zickuhr 2014). ICT equipment (e.g. tablet computer) are often gifted to them by younger family members (Piper *et al.*, 2016), who also help them to buy and set up a computer and go online (Selwyn, 2004; Zickuhr and Madden, 2012; Zickuhr, 2014). Previous studies show a rather consistent pattern of households with children being more likely to use and adopt computers, the internet and mobile phones than other household arrangements (Kennedy *et al.*, 2008; Mori and Harada, 2010; Lin *et al.*, 2012; Luijkx *et al.*, 2015).

Several survey studies explore ICT use and uptake in families by analysing the characteristics of individual family members, as more nuanced and knotty intra-family relationships are difficult to quantify (Eynon and Helsper, 2015). Another common feature in prior studies is that they contrast the concern over decreased family time with privatised solo use of new personal technologies (e.g. Livingstone, 2009; Oblak Črnič, 2009). Here we pay more attention to a range of new intergenerational relations of help, care and intimacy that take place in online environments and which are negotiated through ICTs (Valentine, 2006).

Research on the relationship between ICT use and intergenerational family relations is still scant in Finland and Slovenia. One of the few Finnish studies explored the associations between ICT use, and peer and parent relations among 10- to 13-year-old children in Finland (Punamäki *et al.*, 2007). It found that intensive ICT use for entertainment (digital games and internet surfing) and communication was related to poor parent–child relations. These relations were also gendered as digital gaming was specifically associated with poor mother–daughter and poor father–son relations. Another study investigated the use of old and new means of communication with a particular focus on geographical distance between grandchildren and their grandparents (Hurme *et al.*, 2010). It was found that there are fewer in-person, landline and mobile phone contacts between the two generations the farther away they live from each other. Conversely, the use of letters and/or cards increased with geographical distance. The social networks of older people, especially including grandchildren, play an essential role in their adoption and use of ICTs (Kilpeläinen and Seppänen, 2014; Rasi and Kilpeläinen, 2015). Some studies have also cast light on the use of ICT in families from the perspective of time use. Based on the data from Finnish time-use surveys, it is maintained that while computer and internet use are largely solitary activities in households, television programmes are still watched more with family members than with friends (Repo and Nätti, 2015).

Some relevant empirical studies were also conducted in Slovenia. The first analysed how the availability of emotional and social support is associated with proxy internet use. A survey study showed that internet non-users with larger social networks and stronger intergenerational support (e.g. a higher proportion of (grand)children in the social support network) are more likely to ask others to do things online for them (Dolničar *et al.*, 2013). The other study, based on interviews with parents and their children, shows that in Slovenian families the computer has several controversial roles depending on the generation that the user belongs to: from being 'an intruder', 'destroyer of personal relationships' or a 'comforter' to a 'multi-tool for every occasion'. While young people perceived computer technology as a bridge between various structures of everyday life, their parents often considered the same technology as a source of family disintegration (Oblak Črnič, 2009).

Method

Participants

Our empirical data consists of 45 student reports based on extended group interviews and observations collected from Finland and Slovenia.[1] College students served as key informants of the study. In Finland, the key informants were social sciences and communications studies students at the University of Jyväskylä, who completed the assignment between December 2014 and March 2015. The recruitment of the key informants was conducted through university emailing lists. The total number of informants in this study is 133, including the 22 key informants. Nineteen of the key informants are females and three males. Their ages range from 20 to 38, being 28 on average. The key informants interviewed and observed altogether were 61 female and 50 male family members, who geographically represent the whole country. On average, the interviewed mothers and fathers (N=36) lived 150 km, sisters and brothers 317 km (N=26) and grandmothers 239 km (N=10) away from the key informant.

In Slovenia, the key informants were students of the Social Informatics graduate programme at the University of Ljubljana. The students completed exactly the same assignment as the Finnish students, but as a compulsory course assignment between November and December 2014. The total number of Slovenian informants is 139, including the 23 key informants, of whom 15 were female and 8 male. The age of key informants varied between 23 and 30, being 28 on average just like in Finland. In Slovenia, the key informants interviewed and observed included, altogether, 61 female and 54 male family members. On average, the interviewed mothers and fathers (N=42) lived 58 km, sisters and brothers 141 km (N=27) and grandparents 90 km (N=22) away from the key informant.

Besides the longer geographical distances between family members in Finland, the main differences between the two countries' data relate to the age of interviewed family members. In Slovenia, the interviewed mothers were, on average, three years and grandparents four years younger than in Finland. In contrast, the siblings of the key informants interviewed for the study were about five years younger in Finland.

Procedure

The data collection method applied is called the *Extended Group Interview* (EGI) (Hänninen *et al.*, forthcoming). The EGI was designed to study intergenerational relations among a relatively large number of family members. The EGI is grounded on the collaborative nature of the ethnographic enquiry and new methodological ambitions concerning family group interviews (Reczek, 2014). 'Extended' refers to the many attributes of the method. First, it highlights that the method allows the study of (modified) extended families instead of nuclear families. Second, 'extended' refers to various methods of conducting interviews ranging from in-person to technology-mediated interviews (via phone, Skype, etc.), and third, the EGI allows us to reach a large number of family members by extending the interviews from one specific place and time into a series of interviews.

The combination of EGI and observation has a collaborative element between the key informants and the researcher, providing all family members with a possibility to express their own voice freely (Rappaport, 2008; Lassiter and Campbell, 2010). Also, dissenting voices were well reported by the key informants. Despite these strengths of the EGI, it is obvious that the preconceptions of key informants influence their observation and interviews (e.g. Marshall, 1996). Also, the double role as a researcher and as an informant may complicate key informants' interactions with other family members.

The key informants were given the assignment to observe ICT-related communication in their families for one week and then interview at least five of their family members on their ICT use. Based on the fieldwork, the key informants wrote three essays, with a minimum of 300 words each, in which they were asked to describe: (1) what ICT tools and applications were used to stay in touch with family members; (2) how the key informants consider their ICT skills in relation to one another; and (3) how ICT shapes the roles within their family. ICT was defined broadly as different kinds of digital communication devices or services that are used to stay in contact and communicate with family members (e.g. mobile phones, emails, Facebook, Twitter, WhatsApp, Instagram).

The key informants were instructed to interview at least one of their parents and one grandparent, if that was possible. They were free to determine the three remaining interviewees provided they were of different ages. Some key informants extended the interviews to their cousins, children and spouse's relatives. In addition to the reports, key informants gathered background information on each interviewee (e.g. gender, age, relationship with the key informant and the geographical distance if the key informant and the informant did not share a household). The modes of data collection used with different informants were also reported.

Analytical technique

The research material is analysed following the principles of a directed approach to qualitative content analysis (Hsieh and Shannon, 2005). Using the Bengtson and Roberts' (1991) model, we investigate the ways in which pre-determined solidarity dimensions are presented and discussed in the research material. Given that the solidarity model was not developed to study intergenerational solidarity in relation to ICT use specifically, it is possible that some categories are discussed less extensively than others, and the expressions of solidarity that match poorly with any or overlap with two or more categories can be identified. While reporting results, pseudonyms are used to guarantee the anonymity of the informants.

Results

Associational solidarity

The most salient observation from the key informants' reports is that ICTs facilitate intra-family communication, particularly in Finland. Social media applications in particular, such as WhatsApp, Facebook, Path and Instagram, have both increased and enriched interactions between family members. It is the possibility to use not only text and voice, both also photos, videos and voice messages that is considered enriching to family communication in Finland (e.g. key informants Teresa, Eva).

While none of the Slovenian reports discussed WhatsApp as a platform for family communication, two-thirds of the studied Finnish families had created a WhatsApp chat group for family. Sofia's brother Johan summarises the benefits of the group as follows: "Thanks to WhatsApp we write and communicated with one another more than before". Similarly, another Finnish key informant Emilia maintains that: "We are much more in touch with other family members after adopting WhatsApp". WhatsApp not only makes interaction more regular but it increases its volume and enables one-to-many communication.

> They [other family members] think that the group and its regular use have brought us closer. Now when everybody receives the same messages at the same time we can communicate with the family, and not only one-to-one. This is especially important for dad, since we otherwise call more to mom, but now communication within the family is more balanced.
>
> (Emma, Finland)

The above excerpt discloses another characteristic of associational solidarity in Finland. In particular, grandparents who do not use the same communication technologies as younger family members and often middle-aged fathers too, are either not included or they deliberately remain outside ICT-mediated family communication (e.g. Isabella's family). As Sara writes:

> I send most of my messages [in WhatsApp and Facebook] to my mom, just like my brother. Sometimes I send messages to my brother too, but often I prefer to make a call. To dad we seldom send messages by WhatsApp, as his internet connection is not always on, and he does not notice messages immediately.

Other reports further illustrate the limited communications with fathers in Finland. The sister of Isabella explains that she "counts . . . [on] her mother conveying the news from father". In some families, the feelings of exclusion are very explicitly described. Finnish key informant Julia writes that "Me and my sister have noticed that our father thinks that we continuously chat only with mom on the phone, and do not give him a ring nearly as often. Which is indeed partly true".

These excerpts reinforce the idea that mothers remain the main moderators of family communication in Finland. In some families, it was mother who proposed creating a WhatsApp chat group for the family (e.g. Emma's family). Teresa underlines the role of the mother in Finland, summarising that "WhatsApp is used in our family by mother and all children". Also, Finnish key informant Emilia writes that "Mom no longer needs to call once a week, asking [about] news from her offspring, as we exchange news everyday (via WhatsApp)". Besides WhatsApp, mothers are connected to their children through other social media such as Facebook and Instagram (e.g. Maria's family, Finland).

Conversely, family and multi-generational housing arrangements in Slovenia do not create a similar need for the use of digital technologies for family communication as in Finland. Consequently, ICTs support associational solidarity to a lesser degree, as Slovenian key informant Katarina elucidates:

> I communicate via my mobile phone with other members of my family because such means of communication is sufficient, since we live nearby and visit each other regularly, so there is no need to use Skype, Facebook, etc.

Occasionally when a family member travels abroad or a relative resides afar, Skype and social media are used to maintain contacts similarly in both countries (e.g. the families of Mia and Anton in Slovenia, and the families of Sara, Lucas, Maria and Emma in Finland). The geographical separation of families also makes older family members realise the associational capacity of new technologies. Katarina from Slovenia illustrates this as follows:

> Given the fact that my sister (29-year-old) lives in Rome (800 km away), they talk to her via the internet, i.e. Skype. Grandfather (82-year-old) has also learned how to use Skype in the last six years, as he wishes to communicate with his granddaughter, who comes to Slovenia only twice a year to visit.

In summary, country differences in the organisation of family and housing reflect in the ways informants describe the role of ICTs in family relationships. While geographically scattered extended families in Finland have found the exchange of short messages via WhatsApp and Facebook as a channel to perform family solidarity from afar, the physical propinquity of family members in Slovenia does not bestow a considerable role for the same ICTs in family communication.

Affectual solidarity

There is not much evidence that ICTs would particularly contribute to the exchange of positive or negative sentiments. However, the research material does reveal that good affectual relationships between children, parents and grandparents facilitate the uptake of new technologies in both countries. Intergenerational reassurance is considered in many families as a way to promote ICT usage among older family members. Other family members are encouraged "to try to find a solution on their own" when hands-on teaching in the adoption or use of ICT is not enough, as Marija from Slovenia writes. Another Slovenian key informant, Petra, writes that: "They [older family members] first need some encouragement".

Even if the practical and affectual support described above is at times considered a burden, younger family members appreciate that they are considered useful. In Slovenia, Jakob confirms this by writing: "If I may say so, those of us who help in such moments feel positive about ourselves because we feel useful and are happy to help". Likewise, in Finland, younger people try to advise their older relatives in the use of digital technologies. Simon puts it as follows: "I have noticed that I take a role in encouraging others in technology use. I am pleased to give advice and I try to motivate for instance my grandmother in the use of Skype".

The exclusion of certain family members from ICT-mediated family communication may also stem from the lack of affectual solidarity. This appears to be the case especially in Finland, where grown-up children consider their older relatives' comments on Facebook or Instagram posts embarrassing (e.g. Lisa, sister of Maria). Furthermore, the Finnish key informant Rita writes that as "phone calls with father are uncomfortable, I [would] rather send him text messages or talk face-to-face". The other side of the coin is that "in some more complicated relations, social media is a low threshold medium for expressing warm emotions that are difficult to express face-to-face or express in words", as Rita's fellow citizen Laura maintains. These contradictory examples illustrate well that social media and other digital technologies are used with careful consideration to serve the varied needs of families.

Consensual solidarity

By *consensual solidarity* we refer to the degree of agreement or dissent in beliefs, values or life orientations related to ICT use for family communication. In this regard, the key observation is that shared values and beliefs have not been established in the studied families, yet some are taking shape while parents follow their children's ICT use. Sometimes the gap between generations in their ICT-related skills is regarded as a barrier for the formation of consensual solidarity. Slovenian key informant Erika writes about this:

> He [father] was not always so confident and technologically educated, but with my help and because of my enthusiasm towards new technologies, he has become a sort of 'connoisseur' of ICT, although he still does not fully understand the scope of his knowledge, which can rival mine in some areas.

There is a greater agreement on the growing importance of ICT skills in families (e.g. Marija, Tia, Anton in Slovenia) and the consensus is built upon the idea that everyone should not even have exactly the same skills, but that skills can complement each other, making the family as a whole stronger. In Slovenia, Marija illustrates this as follows:

They [father, mother and aunt, all in their sixties or seventies] all stress the importance of communication skills, which are very important in everyday life, interpersonal interactions and in the use of ICT. They do not compare skills directly with each other, as they perceive them to be different categories of skills, incomparable with each other and which are intertwined, while emphasizing that they are all very important for successful and well-integrated functioning in everyday life and in the use of ICT tools.

The most obvious dissent, especially in Finland and to a lesser extent in Slovenian families, relates to what is considered as proper online communication. Younger family members are accustomed to open and straightforward online communication, while older people call for cautiousness and linguistic flawlessness. This disagreement between family generations is explicitly reported by Rita from Finland:

My parents are horrified about all that openness that my sister keeps on performing on Facebook and in her blog. In turn, my sister hasn't noticed that her openness on these platforms could cause harm for social relations or finding a job, for example.

Similarly, Finnish key informant Maria writes that: "My father thinks that parents associate some sort of formality to communication, everything is taken more seriously, each thing and saying is considered more carefully. Among the younger [generation] interaction is more easy-going and free". The Slovenian key informant Veronika also writes about disagreements between generations regarding the proper style of communication:

The younger generation also finds it unusual and slightly distracting that the older generation writes text messages in the proper register of Slovene. Most young people are accustomed to writing messages in colloquial language.

Despite some disagreements, the research material speaks about families' attempts to find consensus and overcome some generation stereotypes. For instance, the stepfather of Laura in Finland argues that: "There are 'jerks' in every generation" and he talks about "conflicts, and how it is easier to avoid them in social media by leaving the scene". Such consensus-seeking attitudes are reflected in the reports collected from both countries. Consensus is also associated with the idea of *democratic family*, in which everyone has an important, yet different role to play. Even if all informants do not agree that family have become democratised, family members seem to widely agree (e.g. Marija's family in Slovenia) that roles have somewhat changed. Even if parents may still have the final word, children are typically listened to and consulted in technology-related family decisions.

Functional solidarity

Two major themes emerge from the research material concerning functional solidarity with regard to ICT use. The first relates to the equity in the exchange of knowledge and resources over the life course. When children are young, parents teach them some basic ICT skills, like Marija from Slovenia writes: "When I first started using electronic banking a few years ago, my father had already been using it (he learned from my brother), and he helped me to learn how to use it, which I greatly appreciated". Sometimes parents and grandparents also teach their more mature children, for instance, about the use of domestic technologies which are not typically needed when young. Slovenian Veronika mentions an electronic blood glucose monitor or a digital meat temperature gauge as examples. Furthermore, it is generally agreed in both Slovenia and Finland that parents can deepen children's understanding on various issues owing to their life experiences (e.g. Karin in Finland and sister of Natalija in Slovenia). Parents can also teach patience in the use of ICTs (Sara and Mary in Finland) and help understand the line between formal and informal communication (Mary in Finland). Parents also give reminders about online risks and advise on wise ICT usage (e.g. Karin in Finland; niece of Tia in Slovenia). But when children grow up, the roles in teaching, especially technical matters, are typically reversed.

The second key observation pertains to the intergenerational provision of help by grandchildren. Contrary to Finland, where interaction between grandchildren and grandparents is typically limited to short calls and greetings via text messages (e.g. families of Sara and Emma), in Slovenia grandchildren have relatively close relations with their grandparents, which often means regular assistance in ICT use (e.g. families of Katarina, Franc, Veronika, Mia, Tina and Katja). The key informant Katarina describes this, revealing also the demands of such a relationship in the context of email use, as follows:

> It is a lengthy process and almost every Sunday when I visit him [grandfather]. I have to help him with something. I am also bothered by the fact that I often do not know what he needs help with . . . [if it is] for example, with the use of Outlook (formerly Hotmail), as a Gmail user I am unable to understand what he wants.

In Finland, young people do help their own parents in sorting out various technical problems, but they are less frequently and intensively in touch with grandparents than their Slovenian counterparts. A considerable part of this country difference is explained by the greater geographical distances between children, their parents and grandparents in Finland; providing assistance in technological matters from afar is really challenging, in particular when people in need of help are technologically less savvy.

Normative solidarity

The research material contains little concrete examples about the existence of family norms with regard to ICT usage. Nevertheless, concerning some specific issues like data security, family members in both countries seem to agree with one another. Like the brother of Finnish key informant Sofia argues: "Parents say:

'don't download this and that, even if they would be requisites [for the functioning of the programme or similar]'. I mostly do what they say". Similarly, in Slovenia Katarina writes about how her father "is very reticent to publish any personal posts and advocates and teaches others not to publish personal information on the web" and that her 25-year-old sister "is strongly aware of this, and posts only more general things". However, this norm is shared only by two in Katarina's family as others "do not post a lot of information online, and focus more on looking for information". In fact, it is not always clear how widely these norms are acknowledged, shared and/or complied with as there is much variation in ICT usage in families.

In both countries, there are some familial obligations that are entrusted to and typically well received by one person, to whom others turn to ask for help (e.g. the families of Isabella and Carla in Finland, and the families of Franc and Veronika in Slovenia). Borrowing the words of Bakardjieva (2005), these persons can be named as 'warm experts'; they are technically skilled and share the daily life of other family members. The latter makes them different from 'cold experts', external ICT professionals. The following excerpts from Finnish and Slovenian key informants, in respective order, illustrate this:

> My brother has the main responsibility with regards [to] the functioning of communication tools, applications and programmes. I feel it is self-evident that he sorts out the problems I detect in devices and programmes. I never hesitate to ask help from him either.
>
> (Karin, Finland)

> As for teaching others and introducing new ICT, my father (67), my mother (54) and my brother (35) unanimously agree that I am responsible for teaching others and ensuring the proper use of technology in our family.
>
> (Tia, Slovenia)

It is the regular provision of help between grandchildren and grandparents, which can be considered as a kind of filial duty or a cultural norm, that distinguishes Slovenia from Finland. What underscores the normative nature of such grandchild-grandparent ICT aid is that the interviewees oftentimes take it for granted. It is considered as a natural part of family life, as it turns out from the report of Slovenian key informant Petra: "Whenever family members need help, I am glad to help them no matter how busy I am. I feel a sense of duty because that is how I was raised". The Slovenian key informant Anja also writes that her grandfather often prefers contacting his grandchildren directly, as they know how to help.

What emerges from the Finnish data is the ambivalence of communication norms between different generations. For instance, Rita reports:

> My parents are, in turn, more dutiful and trustworthy as communicators than people of my age or younger. My parents always answer the phone, if they are not driving a car or taking a sauna. They also reply to all text messages they receive and read them immediately when incoming message beeps.

They also answer emails straightaway, when they have time to read them. With people of my age the culture of using mobile phones differs from that of fixed phones more clearly. . . . There is no need to always answer the phone, and you may switch it off completely, if you want to be alone.

This excerpt illustrates how the normative basis of use of ICT for communication has not been established in families yet. The disagreement concerning the proper uses of ICTs between generations seems to echo with more general normative expectations that separate younger from older people. Similarly, a relatively strong expectation concerning the provision of assistance from grandchildren to grandparents (or its absence, like in Finland) cannot be considered only specific to the use of ICT, but it certainly reflects more profound cultural values, prevailing housing arrangements and the integrity of the family that vary between Scandinavian and South European countries (e.g. Hank, 2007).

Structural solidarity

Structural solidarity refers to the opportunities and barriers to intergenerational family interaction via ICT. These structural factors shed light on many country differences discussed earlier in the chapter. While shorter geographical distances make possible regular in-person interaction between family members in Slovenia, longer distances in Finland create a demand for technology-mediated family communication from afar. The Slovenian key informant Tia notes: "I agree that our family has always spent a lot of time together, and the whole family lives relatively close, so in the time it takes to call someone you can simply find them and tell them in person" (also for Jakob and Angela in Slovenia).

On the contrary, Finnish interviewees highlight that regardless of different ICT preferences between younger and older generations, families are highly dependent on technology due to long distances keeping them apart. The key informant Emma writes: "As there are several hundred kilometres of physical distance, meeting face-to-face is not very often possible". Emma adds to this: "The utilisation of information technology makes it possible to maintain close relations with close ones even if there is lots of distance". Such comments are less frequent in Slovenia. However, the importance of ICT (e.g. email, Skype, Viber) for family communication and solidarity are recognised especially when a family member moves to another country (e.g. the families of Erika, Julija, Klara).

Health conditions and functional capabilities are other structural factors that influence the possibilities to enhance family solidarity via ICTs. Poor eye-sight and agility of hands are mentioned as factors reducing ICT use for family communication in both countries. For instance, in Finland, Emilia writes that "Grandfather's vision has worsened so much that he can barely read or write. He has also forgotten how all the equipment works, so he no longer uses other devices than the phone". In Slovenia, Petra writes about her parents and grandmother who use a feature phone, but find that "their fingers are 'too tough' and they do not have a lot of sensitivity in their finger pads" (also Marija and Aleksej in Slovenia).

Furthermore, comments show that health problems can make older people realise the benefits of ICTs. As Katarina from Slovenia writes: "Grandmother did not want a mobile phone, but she got one when she spent a longer period of time in the hospital for knee surgery". Both grandparents were "convinced to use ICT by the possibility of communicating with their granddaughters and great grandson".

Discussion and conclusions

In this chapter, we explored how the uses of ICT in extended families relate to family solidarity in Finland and Slovenia. Regarding our first aim, to what extent ICT usage is intertwined with different forms of intergenerational family solidarity, we showed that in spite of increasingly individualised networking, ICT use contributes to solidarity in extended families. However, this applies mainly to associational and functional solidarity, and is specific to life stages as well as reliant on prevailing housing arrangements and cultural values. Structural factors, such as long distances and physical ability to control ICT devices, influence the utilisation of ICTs for promoting associational and functional solidarity in families. We also revealed that normative, consensual and affectual forms of solidarity are manifested to a smaller degree in relation to ICT usage. This might be explained with increased individual networking, which presupposes less familial regulation for ICT use and may thus rather cause disagreements within families than add to its integrity.

Regarding our second aim, to investigate potential country differences between Finland and Slovenia in terms of the relationship between use of ICTs and forms of intergenerational family solidarity, we came across some obvious differences. It turned out that social media platforms have been particularly embraced in Finland to enable new micro-level (or nano-level, see Eranti and Lonkila, 2015) interactions between family members. A perpetual exchange of short messages, especially through WhatsApp, enhances associational solidarity between family members who live apart and have few occasions to meet in person. At its best, the use of one-to-many communication tools ties together many family members or the whole family. Unlike in Finland, the adoption and use of ICT in Slovenian families feeds functional solidarity between generations. Physical propinquity in intergenerational relations makes technological assistance – a new form of social support between grandchildren and grandparents – a common practice with positive consequences for family solidarity.

This result suggests that intergenerational assistance in ICT emerges not just from generational differences, but also pertains to life stages and country differences in the developmental stage of the information society. The higher use of social media for intra-family communication seems to account at least for the fact that young people live longer with their parents in the same household (EuroStat, 2016). Furthermore, in some life stages, a person is clearly more dependent on other family members when it comes to the use of ICTs (e.g. while a child learns to use ICT for the first time or an older adult tries to keep up with technological development). In light of the ICT Development Index, the need for intergenerational assistance in ICT use might be higher in Slovenia, where ICT skills and the share of individuals using the internet is somewhat lower than in Finland (ITU, 2015).

Some implications for further research can be drawn from this study. While many causal relations between various solidarity forms have been found earlier (e.g. Bengtson and Roberts, 1991; Grzywacz and Marks, 1999; Schwarz *et al.*, 2005; Hogerbrugge and Komter, 2012), our research indicates that ICT-mediated interaction may alter such associations. For instance, the lack of normative solidarity in family communication is perhaps not related to lower associational solidarity (cf. Bengtson and Roberts, 1991) as ICTs enable communication from afar and continuously. The research also pointed out some ways of measuring ICT-related family solidarity. In particular, intergenerational help with ICT use emerged as a potentially important indicator of functional support in Slovenia. Affectual solidarity, in turn, could be gauged through the level of encouragement contributing to ICT use among other family members. Having the same ICT tools and applications as other family members could work as an indicator of structural solidarity.

Finally, this study is also subject to certain limitations inherent to the EGI method (elaborated on earlier) and study design. It is obvious that the student key informants and their family members included in the sample are ethnically rather homogeneous. Including ethnic minorities and immigrants in the study could have revealed such practices of ICT use that enhance family solidarity but remained as yet undiscovered. It is also worth noting that even small age differences between the key informants and their interviewees may be reflected in the results. The fact that the key informants' mothers and grandparents were younger in Slovenia and the key informants' siblings were younger in Finland may be reflected in the distinct patterns of family interactions between countries, frequent in-person contacts being more typical for the former, and social media use for the latter.

Acknowledgements

This study was partly supported with the Academy of Finland research grant (no. 265986) and with networking grants for Short-term Scientific Missions provided by the COST Action IS1311 (www.interfasol.eu).

Note

1 The analysis here concentrates in these two countries, although data was also collected from Italy.

References

Bakardjieva, M., 2005. *Internet society: the internet in everyday life.* London: SAGE.
Bengtson, V. and Roberts, R. E., 1991. Intergenerational solidarity in aging families: an example of formal theory construction. *Journal of Marriage and the Family, 53*(4), pp. 856–870.

Bengtson, V., Giarrusso, R., Mabry, J. B. and Silverstein, M., 2002. Solidarity, conflict, and ambivalence: complementary or competing perspectives on intergenerational relationships? *Journal of Marriage and Family*, 64(3), pp. 568–576.

Bengtson, V., Rosenthal, C. and Burton, L., 1996. Paradoxes of families and aging. In: R. H. Binstock and L. George, eds. *Handbook of aging and the social sciences*. New York: Academic Press, pp. 253–282.

Connidis, I. A. and McMullin, J. A., 2002. Ambivalence, family ties, and doing sociology. *Journal of Marriage and Family*, 64(3), pp. 594–601.

Dolničar, V., Filipovič Hrast, M., Vehovar, V. and Petrovčič, A., 2013. Digital inequality and intergenerational solidarity: the role of social support in proxy internet use. In: *IR14: resistance + appropriation*. Denver, CO: Association of Internet Researchers.

Eranti, V. and Lonkila, M., 2015. The social significance of the Facebook Like button. *First Monday*, 20(6). http://firstmonday.org/ojs/index.php/fm/article/view/5505.

EuroStat, 2010. *Household structure in the EU*. Luxembourg: Publications Office of the European Union.

EuroStat, 2016. *Share of young adults aged 18–34 living with their parents by age and sex*. http://ec.europa.eu/eurostat/en/web/products-datasets/-/ILC_LVPS08.

Eynon, R. and Helsper, E., 2015. Family dynamics and internet use in Britain: what role do children play in adults' engagement with the internet? *Information, Communication & Society*, 18(2), pp. 156–171.

Fortunati, L. and Taipale, S., 2014. The advanced use of mobile phones in five European countries. *The British Journal of Sociology*, 65(2), pp. 317–337.

Garattini, C. and Prendergast, D., 2015. Critical reflections on ageing and technology in the twenty-first century. In: D. Prendergast and C. Garattini, eds. *Aging and the digital life course*. New York: Berg Hahn, pp. 1–15.

Grzywacz, J. G. and Marks, N. F., 1999. Family solidarity and health behaviors. *Journal of Family Issues*, 20(2), pp. 243–268.

Haddon, L., 2011. Domestication analysis, objects of study, and the centrality of technologies in everyday life. *Canadian Journal of Communication*, 36(2), pp. 311–323.

Hammarström, G., 2005. The construct of intergenerational solidarity in a lineage perspective: A discussion on underlying theoretical assumptions. *Journal of Aging Studies*, 19(1), pp. 33–51.

Hank, H., 2007. Proximity and contacts between older parents and their children: a European comparison. *Journal of Marriage and Family*, 69(1), pp. 157–173.

Hänninen, R., Taipale, S. and Korhonen, A., forthcoming. Refamilisation in the broadband society. The effects of ICTs on family solidarity in Finland.

Hogerbrugge, M. J. and Komter, A. E., 2012. Solidarity and ambivalence: comparing two perspectives on intergenerational relations using longitudinal panel data. *The Journals of Gerontology Series B: Psychological Sciences and Social Sciences*, 67(3), pp. 372–383.

Hsieh, H. F. and Shannon, S. E., 2005. Three approaches to qualitative content analysis. *Qualitative Health Research*, 15(9), pp. 1277–1288.

Hurme, H., Westerback, S. and Quadrello, T., 2010. Traditional and new forms of contact between grandparents and grandchildren. *Journal of Intergenerational Relationships*, 8(3), pp. 264–280.

ITU, 2015. *Measuring the Information Society Report 2015*. Geneva: ITU.

Kennedy, T. L. M. and Wellman, B., 2007. The networked household. *Information, Communication & Society*, 10(5), pp. 645–670.

Kennedy, T. L. M., Smith, A., Wells, A. T. and Wellman, B., 2008. *Networked families*. Washington, DC: Pew Internet & American Life Project.

Kilpeläinen, A. and Seppänen, M., 2014. Information technology and everyday life in ageing rural villages. *Journal of Rural studies*, 33(1), pp. 1–8.

Lassiter, L. E. and Campbell, E., 2010. What will we have ethnography do? *Qualitative Inquiry*, 16(9), pp. 757–767.

Lin, C. I. C., Tang, W.-H. and Kuo, F.-Y., 2012. "Mommy wants to learn the computer": How middle-aged and elderly women in Taiwan learn ICT through social support. *Adult Education Quarterly*, 62(1), pp. 73–90.

Ling, R. and Haddon, L., 2003. Mobile telephony, mobility, and the coordination of everyday life. In: J. Katz ed., *Machines that become us: The social context of personal communication technology*. New Brunswick, NJ: Transaction Publishers, pp. 245–265.

Litwak, E., 1960. Occupational mobility and extended family cohesion. *American Sociological Review*, 25(1), pp. 9–21.

Livingstone, S., 2009. *Children and the internet*. Cambridge, UK: Polity Press.

Luijkx, K., Peek, S. and Wouters, E., 2015. "Grandma, you should do it—it's cool": older adults and the role of family members in their acceptance of technology. *International Journal of Environmental Research and Public Health*, 12(12), pp. 15470–15485.

Lüscher, K. and Pillemer, K., 1998. Intergenerational ambivalence: A new approach to the study of parent-child relations in later life. *Journal of Marriage and the Family*, 60(2), pp. 413–425.

Lüscher, K., Hoff, A., Lamura, G., Renzi, M., Sánchez, M., Viry, G., Widmer, E., Klimczuk, A. and De Salles Oliveira, P., 2015. Generations, intergenerational relationships, generational policy, A multilingual compendium. www.kurtluescher.de/downloads/Luescher-Kompendium_7sprachig-komplett_online_15–10–2015.pdf.

Madden, M., 2010. Older adults and social media. www.pewinternet.org/files/old-media//Files/Reports/2010/Pew%20Internet%20-%20Older%20Adults%20and%20Social%20Media.pdf.

Marshall, M. N., 1996. The key informant technique. *Family Practice*, 13(1), pp. 92–97.

Mori, K. and Harada, E. T., 2010. Is learning a family matter? Experimental study of the influence of social environment on learning by older adults in the use of mobile phones. *Japanese Psychological Research*, 52(3), 244–255.

Oblak Črnič, T., 2009. Družinska (ne)harmonija ob računalniških zaslonih [Family (dis)harmony in front of the computer screen]. *Družboslovne razprave*, 25(61), pp. 41–58.

OECD, 2016. *Skills matter: further results from the survey of adult skills, OECD Skills Studies*. Paris: OECD Publishing.

Piper, A. M., Cornejo Garcia, R. and Brewer, R. N., 2016. Understanding the challenges and opportunities of smart mobile devices among the oldest old. *International Journal of Mobile Human Computer Interaction*, 8(2), pp. 83–98.

Punamäki, R. L., Wallenius, M., Nygård, C. H., Saarni, L. and Rimpelä, A., 2007. Use of information and communication technology (ICT) and perceived health in adolescence: the role of sleeping habits and waking-time tiredness. *Journal of Adolescence*, 30(4), pp. 569–585.

Rainie, L. and Wellman, B., 2012. *Networked. The new social operating system*. Cambridge, MA: MIT Press.

Rappaport, J., 2008. Beyond participant observation: collaborative ethnography as theoretical innovation. *Collaborative Anthropologies* 1, pp. 1–31.

Rasi, P. and Kilpeläinen, A., 2015. The digital competences and agency of older people living in rural villages in Finnish Lapland. *International Journal of Media, Technology & Lifelong Learning*, 11(2), pp. 149–160.

Reczek, C., 2014. Conducting a multi family member interview study. *Family Process*, 53(2), pp. 318–335.

Repo, K. and Nätti, J., 2015. Televisio ja tietokone lasten ja nuorten ajankäytön rytmittäjinä. In: A.-H. Anttila, T., Anttila, M., Liikkanen, M. and Pääkkönen, H. eds. *Ajassa kiinni ja irrallaan – yhteisölliset rytmit 2000-luvun Suomessa*. Helsinki: Statistics Finland, pp. 135–152.

Sayago, S., Forbes, P. and Blat, J., 2013. Older people becoming successful ICT learners over time: challenges and strategies through an ethnographical lens. *Educational Gerontology*, 39, pp. 527–544.

Schwarz, B., Trommsdorff, G., Albert, I. and Mayer, B., 2005. Adult parent–child relationships: relationship quality, support, and reciprocity. *Applied Psychology: An International Review*, 54(3), pp. 396–417.

Selwyn, N., 2004. The information aged: a qualitative study of older adults' use of information and communications technology. *Journal of Aging Studies*, 18(4), pp. 369–384.

Silverstein, M. and Bengtson, V. L., 1997. Intergenerational solidarity and the structure of adult child-parent relationships in American families. *American Journal of Sociology*, 103(2), pp. 429–460.

Valentine, G., 2006. Globalizing intimacy. The role of information and communication technologies in maintaining and creating relationships. *Women's Studies Quarterly*, 34(1/2), pp. 365–393.

Zickuhr, K., 2014. Older adults and technology. *JASA's Seminar on Advocacy and Volunteering in New Landscapes*. www.pewinternet.org/2014/04/29/older-adults-and-technology/.

Zickuhr, K. and Madden, M., 2012. Older adults and internet use. www.sainetz.at/dokumente/Older_adults_and_internet_use_2012.pdf.

7   Gendering the mobile phone

A life course approach

Carla Ganito

Introduction

The gender effect cannot be ignored in the design, development, innovation and communication of technological products (Cockburn, 1992). The 'technofeminism' theory proposes that technology is at the same time a cause and a consequence of gender relations (Wajcman, 2004). Wajcman (2007) defines technofeminism as opening new opportunities to studies focused on different groups of women and their response to diverse technologies. Technofeminism urges researchers to take into account women's agency and offers an approach to the gendering process which incorporates multiple contradictions.

This chapter aims to provide a broader picture of the relationship between women and technology through an inquiry into the role of the mobile phone in the lives of Portuguese women. The chapter takes on Wajcman's challenge and studies how different groups of Portuguese women encounter the mobile phone and incorporate it into their daily lives. The chapter is guided by one main question: What is the significance of the mobile phone in women's lives, at different life stages?

This chapter brings women to the forefront of the discussion of the usages and affordances of the mobile phone, and building on the concept of mobile communications (Goggin, 2008), it introduces the idea of feminist cultural studies as a conceptual lens through which to focus on mobile communication. Previous research on gender and technology widely argues that gender differences are less marked in younger populations (Ling, 2001b). However, there are also scholars who present that gender differences in technology usage are not only generational, but also shaped by socialisation processes (Grint and Gill, 1995; Wajcman, 2004). As Helsper notes: "Adults' behaviour in their current life stage might help predict their future online behaviour much better than studying young people's current behaviour" (Helsper, 2010, p. 353). According to this line of research, gender roles depend on the current stage of life, and thus gender differences will not just disappear as time goes by.

Mobile phones across life course: an egalitarian technology?

Although the mobile phone is currently one of the most pervasive communication technologies, only a few studies have approached it from a gender perspective and even fewer from a feminist viewpoint (Ganito, 2012). As many researchers point out, the usage rates and patterns between men and women are rather similar (Geser, 2006a, 2006b), but differences emerge when looking at the qualitative aspects of use; the purposes and nature of mobile use; and the discourses about the mobile phone (Geser, 2004; Lemish and Cohen, 2005a, 2005b).

Studies about gender and mobile phones can be divided into two categories: studies centred on the differences between men and women, and those that offer a more nuanced account of gender practices. Within the first category, there are plenty of quantitative studies mapping gender-related differences in which the mobile phone is described as an egalitarian technology, contrary to other technologies where the gender gap still persists, as is the case with the internet and computer usage. In Portugal, there seems to be no gender difference in people who own a mobile phone: ownership is split 50/50 between men and women (Cardoso *et al.*, 2007). After the first introduction phase where women and even girls lagged slightly behind, justified by men's positive attitude towards innovation, women, as in the telephone, soon became heavy users surpassing men in certain cultural contexts and uses (Ling, 2001a). In contrast to internet use, women exceeded males in all categories of mobile phone use (Rice and Katz, 2003) and seemed to favour written communication (Geser, 2006a, 2006b).

These and other statistical studies often offer a contradictory view to the second category of studies, claiming that the mobile phone, similarly to other domestic technologies, reinforces traditional roles (Lemish and Cohen, 2005a and 2005b; Ling, 2001a, 2001b; Lohan, 2001; Plant, 2001; Rakow and Navarro, 1993). These are also poorly aligned with studies that present the mobile phone as a tool that has levelled the playing field between men and women (Geser, 2006a, 2006b; Shade, 2007), and those that portray the mobile phone as a disruptive technology for gender roles (Lee, 2005; Skog, 2002). More recently, some studies have gone beyond the statistical duality of men and women, exploring the differences that take place among women (Fortunati, 2009; Fortunati and Taipale, 2012; Hjorth, 2005, 2007, 2009a, 2009b; Kurniawan, 2006).

Diverse lives of women: the life course approach

In this study, I follow the strand of research that explores differences among women, focusing on their life course:

> As a concept, the life course refers to the age-graded, socially embedded sequence of roles that connect the phases of life. As a paradigm, the life course refers to an imaginative framework comprised of a set of interrelated presuppositions, concepts, and methods that are used to study these age-graded, socially embedded roles.
>
> (Mortimer and Shanahan, 2004, p. xi)

A distinction should be made between life cycle and the life course. The first approach emphasises ages and life stages, while the second puts emphasis on the transitions into those stages (Allatt *et al.*, 1987). The life course approach enables the researcher to account for change and complexity. Castells (1996) describes how societies have to replace biological life cycle with a socio-biological one, and proposes that the network society is moving towards social arrhythmia. As societies become more complex, the use of the life cycle approach has to resort to a more flexible understanding of how different stages unfold.

Analysing the role women play at each life stage helps to better understand their relationship to technology, yet life stages no longer follow a sequential path or individual turning points (Hareven and Adams, 1982). Hence, an individual life course should be taken into consideration as well. The study thus analyses trajectories that are understood as sequences of roles and experiences incorporating social context and individual variation. I base the analysis of these trajectories on the principle of agency, where people construct their own life course through daily choices and practices within the limits and opportunities of given historical and social circumstances (Elder *et al.*, 2003).

Methodology

The findings are derived from qualitative data drawn from 36 in-depth interviews of Portuguese women. The list of women interviewed, their ages and main activities according to life stage are shown in Table 1 below.

Women interviewed were recruited through a 'snow-ball' method from a pool of urban heterosexual women. The interviews were carried out in 2011 and information was anonymised. The option was for semi-structured interviews, which allowed me to navigate the questions as befitted the flow of the conversation, and to pick up on interesting comments and follow them up more comprehensively, because the interest was in "thoughts and feelings that are often not articulated as stable opinions or preferences" (Turkle, 1984, p. 318), and these cannot be captured by more direct methods. The interviews were conducted in settings familiar to the interviewees: workplace, home or any other place of their choice where they would feel comfortable. There was no end time set for the interview; some lasted for three hours, others took more than six. The goal was to hear women speak freely about their lives and their relationship with technology in general and the mobile phone in particular, without limiting them.

The women in the study were aggregated into seven groups according to their life stage. The example of a Portuguese market research (Marktest, 2006), based on a sample of 10,093 structured interviews, was followed to define the 7 life stage groups. The Marktest study used 5 variables (marital status, age, occupation, number of people in the household, and number of children and teenagers in the household) to cover the entire life cycle of the Portuguese consumer constituted by 11 distinctive groups. For this research, the 11 categories were combined into seven to represent the different life stages of the women interviewed: single dependent, young independent, nesting, mothers, single mothers, mature independent and empty nesters.

Table 7.1 The interviewees, their ages and main activity according to life stage.

Single dependent

1   Constança, 23, university student, single
2   Joana, 20, university student, single
3   Raquel, 20, high-school student, single
4   Rita, 24, designer in an internship

Young independent

5   Carla B., 35, economist, single
6   Inês, 25, marketing manager, single
7   Nicole, 29, engineer, single

Nesting

8   Catarina, 31, teacher, married
9   Patrícia, 33, economist
10   Patrícia D., 36, marketing manager
11   Sandra A., 35, environment engineer
12   Sónia, 27, pharmacist
13   Vanda, 36, training technician

Mothers

14   Ana A., 34, web content producer, married, mother of an infant
15   Ana C., 34, journalist, mother of an infant
16   Ana D., 39, business owner, married, mother of two children
17   Carla D., 34, unemployed marketing manager, married, mother of a toddler
18   Margarida, 33, engineer, married, mother of two infants
19   Sara, 35, social worker, married, mother of two children
20   Sílvia, 29, nurse, married, mother of an infant

Mature independent

21   Ana, 56, assistant, single
22   Carla P., 30, tourism agent, separated
23   Estela, 36, communications manager, divorced
24   Marisa, 34, consultant, divorced
25   Susana, 36, engineer, single

Sole caregivers

26   Carmen, 40, secretary, divorced, mother of two
27   Cecilia, 46, human resource technician, divorced, mother of a teenage boy
28   Fatima 1, 52, unemployed administrative worker, divorced, living with her mother and niece. Her son as a military comes home on the weekends
29   Sofia, 47, human resource manager, divorced, mother of two teenage boys

Empty nesters

30   Deolinda, 51, hairdresser business owner, widow, now living in a new relationship
31   Fátima 2, 56, retired insurance professional, married, grandmother of one
32   Fernanda F., 52, computer manager, married
33   Fernanda R., 65, retired topographer, married, grandmother of two, caring for one of her grandchildren
34   Manuela, 56, pre-retired saleswoman, divorced, in a new relationship
35   Maria, 60, retired teacher, married, grandmother of three
36   Paula, 59, retired administrator, married, grandmother of two, caring for one of her grandsons

Women in the single dependent life stage are above 18 years old but still depend on their family financially and still live with them. In the next life stage, young women are financially independent, and although they may still live with their family, they are able to control purchase decisions. The nesting life stage is determined by the beginning of a co-habitation relationship that may or may not be formally constituted as a marriage. The next life stage is that of motherhood. Contrary to the Marktest (2006) study, women with children at different ages were aggregated, although I acknowledge some differences in the use of the mobile phone according to the age of the kids and if they are old enough to have a mobile phone of their own. Single mothers were either widows or single because they were divorced or separated from their partners. The interest was in analysing the effects of the absence of the masculine part of the couple in the relationships of women with technology. Women in the mature independent life stage are those that are around the age of 35, have no children and either have never been involved in a co-habitation relationship or have divorced or separated from their partners. Finally, empty nesters are women whose children have left home, who have retired or whose job has reached a plateau. This last stage is more complex to define as it presents much variation, including old pensioner, average retirees, fully abled elders, as well as elders with disabilities (Castells, 1996, p. 446).

Regarding the analytical strategy, that study is based on the ideal-type analysis. While in Weber's work ideal types are fictional constructions, in this research, following the sample of Turkle's (1984) study on computer cultures, real cases studies are used to serve the same end – to highlight particular aspects of the gendering of the mobile phone. The ideal-type analysis was conducted following the principles of Soulet (2002), who drew his ideas from Maxwell's (1999) proposal for an interactive approach to qualitative research.

This method of analysis is structured into two levels consisting of various steps. In the first level of local interpretation, each interview is analysed to construct particular life stories that help answer research questions. For this step, the researcher starts by writing a synopsis, which is a synthesis of the interview discourse. The following step is to write the inner history of the interview, providing a chronological reading from the point of view of the interviewee in relation to the problem being analysed. To complete the local level of interpretation, the researcher retrieves a message that we can define as what each person wanted to tell us. These three steps are conducted for every interview and then the researcher proceeds to the second level of global interpretation, a transversal of the individual stories. This interpretation helps identify the aggregated ideal types, which in the scope of this research are the seven life stages, and finally the overall story.

The analysis is informed by some major categories: identity, dependency, affectivity, norms and social fears, safety and control. The goal in analysing these categories is to identify the turning points[1] in women's lives that had an impact on their use of the mobile phone; to provide an account of their daily lives (technology uses, media diets, routines) and determine its impact on their technological intimacy; and to analyse mobile phone use, the affordances it allowed to women such as identity construction, affectivity, safety and control and how these affordances were translated into uses such as those of personalisation, micro-coordination, creativity and entertainment. The chapter presents main findings for each life stage, as a more detailed analysis would require a more extensive presentation.

Women's voices

The stories of women presented here illustrate the multiplicity of the facets of their emerging relationship with mobile phones, and how their life stories intersect with different uses of technology and the mobile phone in particular. For each life stage, one or more stories of individual women were chosen to provide a detailed account of women's lives as a whole.

Single dependent: autonomy and connectedness

The single dependent women interviewed are marked by their recent coming of age. They are at the stage where differences between men and women are less prominent and they still have not faced the challenges of entering the workforce and motherhood, which often constitute hurdles in women's lives in Portugal. For these women, the mobile phone is essentially a tool for social networking and autonomy. The device they choose is still a personal choice based only on self-expression, while they live in a highly complex media environment characterised by high internet use in which the mobile phone is only one piece of the puzzle but probably the most pervasive one. For them, the convergence of mobile phones and internet is only hampered by money constraints.

Raquel, a 20-year-old economics student is, like other young women in her life stage, searching for autonomy and independence, and technology is instrumental in that purpose. She feels the need to always be connected and mostly uses technology that satisfies this need and allows her autonomy from other family members that control activities such as television viewing: "I only see TV when I have nothing else to do on the computer. The TV is always on and my grandmother is always watching soap operas. Sometimes I keep her company but I don't care much about TV shows".

But all single dependent women felt that this always-connected culture has its flip side and that they sometimes feel the need to disconnect. But when they do disconnect there is a sense of guilt and peer and family pressure not to repeat the behaviour: "Not being available seems weird. I am always afraid something might happen to someone I love" (Rita, 24-year-old designer in an internship). This pressure builds up in the next life stage when professional demands are added to the equation.

Young independent: finding a place for femininity

The young independent are at the life stage where employment comes into the picture. Women at this stage have a genuine expectation to balance their professional and personal lives, but that does not mean barriers to professional success have fallen completely.

For young independent women, the mobile phone is a blend between a social networking and a professional tool, and their main concern is to project an independent and professional image, which oftentimes means a more masculine approach to what they wear or what they choose as technology. Inês is a vivid example of these women who struggle to find a balance between their female identity and their professional environment. Inês is a 25-year-old marketing manager who is also going through graduate school and for whom starting her first job was definitely a turning point. She was able to pursue the career she wanted and that made her feel very accomplished and fulfilled. But entering the job market brought with it increased responsibilities and commitments like "being forced to keep a schedule and limited vacation which was confusing for me at first".

Because of her job status, Inês is now forced to make concessions on her self-expression, like in the choice of clothing colours (Miller, 2004). When a researcher showed her a pink mobile phone, she immediately liked it but said she would never buy a pink phone:

> I would never buy a pink phone but I would buy a white one if it were an option for the Blackberry. Even in my notebook purchase that was a question. There was a pink, a white and a black one and my sister told me not to buy the pink one because I would not be taken seriously. Pink is a childish colour and because we tend to associate pink with a more feminine woman or more detail-oriented people might also think we are not professional and serious. I bought white because it is still a good colour for technology but is still a bit feminine. If I could choose I would choose pink. I still have lots of stuff that are girly and I like them a lot. In the mobile phone I could not choose so I have a black one.

To compensate for the masculine exterior, Inês personalises her mobile phone and her computer with images from a beach that she loves to go to, flowers and a pink screensaver, but she does not use ringtones because she is not interested in music. In addition, Inês feels so dependent on her mobile phone that she uses it to multitask and expresses dual feelings about it:

> On the one hand to be without the mobile phone would be great because I would have a less stressful life. I could enjoy things that now I cannot like simply staring at the landscape or be in silence. On the other hand, I would feel anxious. Even if I do not use it I need it to be there.

She never turns the mobile phone off even when staying with her family because the mobile phone is both a professional tool and a lifeline to the people she loves and cares about. This symbiosis between professional and private life makes her take the mobile phone with her even on vacation and to answer phone calls even if they are job related. Inês says: "It enables me to answer something in a few minutes and get that matter out of the way. I feel more in control and reassured that things are going smoothly". The changing routines and the feeling that time flies too fast intensify in the next life stage: the nesting phase.

Nesting: accommodating new routines

For nesting women, the mobile phone is an umbilical cord to friends and family that are now growing distant from their daily lives. Women are in the nesting phase when they share a house in a stable relationship that can range from the traditional marriage arrangement, as in the case of Catarina, to more unconventional living arrangements. When entering a more stable relationship, new routines settle in and for women that can also mean slipping into a more traditional gender role in household management and their relation to technology. Women also lose much of their prior focus for social networking as they become social coordinators for the couple, especially in what concerns family activities. The mobile phone becomes a nexus of social relations with now distant family and friends.

Catarina, 31 years old, has been married for four years and has no kids. As she is a teacher, she has irregular working hours and she brings a lot of work home. Technology serves a double need in her life – to support that flexible working arrangement and to keep track of her family and friends. As Catarina explains:

> I have to miss out on many dates with my friends because I end up having to work. And it is frequent to work on weekends because I was not able to organise myself during the week. I feel guilty about it but I cannot help myself.

Nesting women usually live in a new home where they do not have a landline phone, so the mobile becomes their main source of contact with friends and family for whom they have less face time than before. They blend professional and personal lives and they usually don't see the mobile phone as an intruder; these women do not feel anxious having the mobile phone around because it enables them to perform their tasks at a distance or solve problems quickly. Their levels of personalisation are very low and their option is for devices that project a professional look. Having a partner makes them transfer technology choices, an action they justify by their lack of interest or knowledge. Some of these women's practices will change in the next life stage and others will be reinforced; namely, the personalisation level increases as women have kids and start using the mobile phone as a portable photo album, which means placing a higher value on the camera features. Their dependency peaks with the constant need to be available for any problem their kids might have or because leisure time and social interaction are reduced dramatically.

Mothers: craving time

The mobile phone becomes the sole or main contact resource for women with children in Portugal. It is also employed as an electronic leash or a tool for remote mothering, replacing their physical presence by their kids. However, women's experiences as mothers vary according to the age of their kids. Carla D. represents the multiplicity of roles performed by mothers in Portugal.

Carla D. is a 34-year-old marketing manager who recently became unemployed for the second time in her career. She is also a recent mother of a baby girl. She is married and comes from a struggling family: "We feel the responsibilities in a whole different way: bills to pay and clothes to wash. The first months were really hard, so moving [in] together had a stronger impact on my life than getting married two years after". Now she is going through a second major shift with becoming a mother as her daily routines revolve around the baby: "The day no longer has days or nights, it's organised in periods of three or four hours".

Time pressure and time bind (Hochschild, 1997) are also part of Carla's life:

> I feel I have no time to myself, to go for a massage, or lay on the sofa whenever I want, or go out for a coffee whenever I feel like it. I miss working outside the house, being with other people and learning new things.

Carla tries to break her isolation using the mobile phone and the internet on a daily basis. She has also started to value the camera more to take photos of everything the baby does. She even thinks she uses the mobile phone more when she is at home, not only to keep in touch with other people but also as reassurance: "I always think something might happen so I don't leave home without it. I no longer have my own safety to think of. Nothing can happen because my daughter is there".

Since she started to work, Carla has had a mobile phone that she bought with her own salary. Now she has a Nokia that was her husband's: "The company gave him this Nokia but he wanted something better so he bought a Qtek for himself and I took his". But if she could choose she would have an iPhone because "it is modern and it gives you status. I wouldn't mind having a Diva either but most mobile phones targeted at women seem teenage like to me". She personalises her mobile with a photo of her daughter and she also uses a special case, some charms and a strap:

> I think the mobile phone can be a fashion accessory but I should need lots of money to have mobile phones in different colours or one to use during the day and another to go out at night. I think the mobile phone can be more attractive, have different colours like silver or gold, have a mirror or be branded, but for me its main benefit is to be able to talk wherever we are.

Although Carla is fashion oriented and is a heavy user, she places an emphasis on the communication function of the mobile phone and on efficiency features. She does not use the mobile phone for any service or leisure content like games, internet or music: "I don't like things to converge and so I browse the internet on my notebook and I have an iPod to listen to music".

Mothers are time-starved, stressed and sometimes unhappy with their mundane routine-driven life, and hence they look for solutions that help manage the complexities of their lives, lessen their stress and workload, as well as give them more time to focus on what they consider most important: spending time with their kids.

Sole caregivers: holding the world on their shoulders

Single mothers form a specific group of women who are financially even more constrained than other mothers, and suffer even more from the lack of time.

What they want is no frills and time-consuming technology. For them, the mobile phone is a tool for remote mothering and social networking. They need to keep track of their kids and, often, elderly members of the family, but they also want to keep track of their social networks. The mobile phone provides the opportunity to perform their gendered emotional labour in a more effective way.

Cecília is a good example of these women who are or have become sole caregivers through divorce or having become widows. Cecília is a 46-year-old divorced woman, mother of a 14-year-old son that spends half the week at her house and the other half at his father's. She is devoted to her career and her professional development, continually attending courses that improve her skills as a human resources manager.

Besides her son, and as most women her age in Portugal, Cecília has to take care of her parents. Her mother recently passed away after a long illness that was time-consuming for Cecília. Now she still feels the need to always be available for both her son and her father, and this is where the mobile phone plays its main role in Cecília's life. She no longer recalls the time when she first got a mobile phone. It started out for personal use, but it has become an important tool in her job:

> I would have more difficulty in giving up my mobile phone than my computer. It is where I have everything, my contact list, birthdays and it is the easiest way to reach me. I give out my mobile phone number to everyone. I give support to people that are sick at home and its easier for them to have a direct line to me and all my colleagues have my mobile phone but not all have my email.

Because accessibility is her main concern, the phone features Cecília values the most are ease of use, access to the internet and the agenda or calendar. For listening to radio, playing music and taking photos, she prefers to use other devices that perform better. She does not personalise her device either, but thinks that it is a highly personal device: "I would never touch someone else's mobile phone, let alone my boyfriend's or my son's. It is his space, a personal object".

Cecília is heavily dependent on her mobile:

> It is always with me. I never turn it off. I used to turn it off during the night but when my mother got sick I stopped doing it. I am afraid someone might need me. I had to spend a day without it and it was a bit hard, not being able to keep track of my son. When I am on vacation I don't like to be disturbed by phone calls but I can't turn it off either.

Regardless of these ambivalent feelings she describes the mobile phone as being a fundamental tool in her life that helps her keep track of her daily routines – both private and professional – and to keep in touch with her friends and family. This connection to the outside world of home is also important for mature independent women, like Carla P. and Ana, who are presented next.

Mature independent: back or still in the game

Carla P. and Ana are examples of the challenges mature independent women face when they find themselves back or still in the game for a romantic relationship. Mature independent women are those who live solo or have never been married. They may also be single through divorce, separation or because they have become widows and have no children. Mature independent women are presented here through two examples that represent two extremes in terms of age: Carla P. is a 30-year-old woman who ended an eight-year cohabiting relationship, and Ana is a 56-year-old woman who has never been married or had a long, stable, cohabiting relationship. Previous research from other countries points to a greater interest in single women purchasing and using new technology (Blumenthal, 2000). This comes out in the interviews with both Carla P. and Ana, whose mobile phones cater to their solo lifestyles by being social networking tools and providing safety to sustain their independence and freedom of movement.

Carla P. is single and lives alone; in this life stage, what is most important for her is making new friends and rebuilding the networks she lost or that are now scattered between Portugal and Germany, where she once lived. As for her mobile phone, she describes it as the most private technology she has. She had her first one at the age of 17 and it was a gift from her father for safety concerns: "I felt like a grown-up because I had a mobile phone which at the time was something only grow-ups had but pretty fast everybody started having one and it became a mundane thing to have". She is very self-conscious of being dependent on the mobile phone, which she tries to refrain from using in instances such as in a supermarket when she lost her friend for a second. However, she never turns the phone off, and carries the charger with her in case she runs out of battery.

Born years apart, the mobile phone has the same meaning for Ana D., a 56-year-old woman who lives alone with her cat. For her, safety was the trigger for getting a mobile phone:

> Once I got stuck on the highway and I could not reach a person. I felt I had to get something to talk with my dad. Before that I felt no one needed to know my whereabouts but we can also lie with the mobile phone.

Today she has two mobile phones: one for work and one personal. The personal mobile phone she chose because it took good pictures and because it is a clamshell model, "I am very distracted and I kept making calls by mistake". She uses the camera to take pictures of the cat but the main purpose of the mobile is to keep her company. The mobile phone is also an emotional reassurance tool for Ana D: "I keep all my messages and notes in there". If she could choose she would have an iPhone because she confesses to enjoying technology and would value internet and email access.

For Ana D., it would be hard to go without her mobile, "without noticing we pour our memory into it" and she feels calmer when she has it; emotional reassurance and freedom of movement are for her the main benefits. These are also important benefits for empty nesters like the women introduced next.

Empty nests: nests not so empty after all

Fátima and Maria show how empty nests are not so empty after all. Even after retirement, as in the case of Maria, many women in Portugal find themselves having to take care of their grandchildren or return to work to provide extra money for their families. For both of them, the mobile phone means safety and a connection with the outside world. They show high mobile usage, especially for leisure proposes and, when combined with low internet usage, a lack of internet skills. But the cases of Fátima and Maria also show how the place of a mobile phone within a wider personal media ecology shapes the use of a mobile phone.

Fátima is a 56-year-old retired insurance professional with low internet skills and who is profoundly dependent on her mobile phone: "I feel naked without it . . . it is always in my pocket and goes with me everywhere . . . It is how I keep in touch and it is safety, now even more", but Maria says she would rather use the computer. Companies often underestimate the interests of older women in mobile technology (Kurniawan, 2006). However, our interviewees showed that they are keen to understand, enthusiastic to learn and actually use some advanced features of mobile phones such as MMS (multimedia messaging services).

Maria is a 60-year-old retired school teacher who was obliged to take full-time care of two of her three grandchildren: a 9-year-old boy and a 3-year-old girl. She also looks after another granddaughter. The daily routine of taking care of three children leaves little time for leisure activities like listening to the radio or watching TV. But she does use the internet on a daily basis for everything from paying the bills to searching health topics related to the kids. Although she considers herself very proficient in the use of the computer, on the mobile phone she only uses voice calls and reads text messages, neglecting all other features, even personalisation. Her friend Fátima is at the opposite extreme.

Fátima also takes care of one grandson. She does embroidery as a hobby and runs a small business doing it. During the week, her life revolves around the television which is always on, "I have five TV sets, one for each room and I go around the house I always have one on and sometimes they are all turned on". But Fátima never uses the computer or the internet; and her husband performs all online activities. But it is completely different with the mobile phone, which she has possessed for many years, and now uses for voice calls and text messages to keep in touch with friends and family and to coordinate daily activities. Fátima explains that: "it [the mobile phone] keeps me company and it is also a way to feel safer. I once had a flat tyre in the middle of nowhere and I truly regretted not having a mobile phone". She even uses it to keep her small handicraft business running. Fátima also values having a camera feature and takes pictures of her grandchild to send to his mother and to reminisce about the moments with him afterwards.

Fátima never turns off her mobile phone and carries it everywhere. In fact, she was one of the few interviewees who kept her mobile phone on the table during the whole interview. Fátima is a good example of women who have no internet skills, but for whom a mobile phone provides a channel to communicate. The mobile phone allows them to keep in touch by sending text messages and conducting casual conversations with others.

Conclusions

The study reveals that in Portugal, the mobile phone has different roles and affordances throughout women's life courses. Instead of finding a dominant use that would be in line with other studies (cf. the theory of Apparatgeist, Katz, 2006), I found a nuanced relationship with the mobile phone that is continuously constructed across life stages. This study shows that Portuguese women value the mobile phone not for the device itself but because of the central role it plays in their lives, which is highly dependent on the life stage, as the role assigned to the mobile phone alters when women shift from one life stage to another. The interviewees reported a high degree of dependency across all life stages even while underlying reasons differed: for mothers, the main reasons relate to safety and control of their children; for single dependents, it is autonomy; for mature independents, accessibility; for single mothers, a combination of accessibility and control; and for empty nesters, the balance between autonomy and safety. Hence, the role of the mobile phone in the everyday lives of women cannot be reduced to mere socioeconomic factors, and the linear associations are often highlighted in statistical accounts.

Another striking finding is that the trajectory of the mobile phone across life stages does not have an expected evolution. If it is true that young women show a higher predisposition to a more diversified and intense use of the mobile phone, older women do not always correspond to the stereotype of lack of interest or skills. On the contrary, the mobile phone seems to play a very important role for empty nesters.

The methodological option for this study was to learn about women from women, to give them a voice, to gain insights from their discourse and thus the choice was for a qualitative design. However, it would be interesting to provide extensive analysis through a quantitative survey based on a life stage approach. This study is also limited to adult women, but it could prove insightful to apply the same methodology to younger and older women. The research, although situated in Portugal, opens avenues for cross-cultural analysis in the future.

Throughout their life stages, women face different challenges and needs that are expressed in different relationships with technology. It is related to their "situated knowledges" (Haraway, 1988) and specific locations. Each woman tells a different story, has a different voice. The question is if someone is listening. From a broader perspective, this study bears implications for product and service design by urging the mobile phone industry to use a life course approach to move from a functional perspective to a broader socio-cultural perspective that would enable the development of products that resonate with women's lives.

Note

1 Turning points can be defined as "traditional points in a person's life where daily rhythm and routine alter drastically due to a change in a person's role in society" (Helsper, 2010, p. 355).

References

Allatt, P., Keil, T., Bryman, A. and Bytheway, B., eds., 1987. W*omen and the life cycle. Transitions and turning-points*. London: Macmillan Press.

Blumenthal, D., 2000. *Targeting the single female consumer*. London: Reuters Business Insight.

Cardoso, G., Gomes, M. D. C., Espanha, R. and Araújo, V., 2007. *Mobile Portugal*. Lisbon, Portugal: Obercom.

Castells, M., 1996. *The rise of the network society*. Vol. 1. Cambridge, UK: Blackwell.

Cockburn, C., 1992. The circuit of technology: gender, identity and power. In: R. Silverstone and E. Hirsch, eds., *Consuming technologies: media and information in domestic spaces*. London: SAGE, pp. 32–48.

Elder, G. H., Johnson, M. K. and Crosnoe, R., 2003. The emergence and development of life course theory. In: J. T. Mortimer and M. J. Shanahan, eds. *Handbook of the life course*. New York: Kluwer Academic/Plenum Publishers, pp. 3–19

Fortunati, L., 2009. Gender and the mobile phone. In: G. Goggin and L. Hjorth, eds. *Mobile technologies: from telecommunications to media*. New York: Routledge, pp. 23–34.

Fortunati, L. and Taipale, S., 2012. Women's emotions towards the mobile phone. *Feminist Media Studies*, 12(4), pp. 538–549.

Ganito, C., 2012. Moving time and juggling spheres: (i)mobilities in the gendering of the mobile phone by adult Portuguese women. *Feminist Media Studies*, 12(4), pp. 570–579.

Geser, H., 2004. *Towards a sociological theory of the mobile phone*. http://socio.ch/mobile/t_geser1.pdf.

Geser, H., 2006a. *Are girls (even) more addicted? Some gender patterns of cell phone usage*. http://socio.ch/mobile/t_geser3.htm.

Geser, H., 2006b. *Pre-teen cell phone adoption: consequences for later patterns of phone usage and involvement*. http://socio.ch/mobile/t_geser2.htm.

Goggin, G., 2008. Cultural studies of mobile communication. In: J. Katz, ed., *Handbook of mobile communication studies*. Cambridge, MA: The MIT Press, pp. 353–366.

Grint, K. and Gill, R., eds., 1995. *The gender-technology relation: contemporary theory and research*. London: Taylor & Francis.

Haraway, D., 1988. Situated knowledges: the science question in feminism and the privilege of partial perspective. *Feminist Studies*, 14(3), pp. 575–599.

Hareven, T. K. and Adams, K. J., eds., 1982. *Ageing and life course transitions: an interdisciplinary perspective*. London: Guilford Press.

Helsper, E. J., 2010. Gendered internet use across generations and life stages. *Communication Research*, 37(3), pp. 352–374.

Hjorth, L., 2005. Postal presence: a case study of mobile customisation and gender in Melbourne. In P. Glotz, S. Bertschi and C. Locke, eds., *Thumb culture: the meaning of mobile phones for society*. New Brunswick, NJ: Transaction Publishers, pp. 53–67.

Hjorth, L., 2007. Snapshots of almost contact: the rise of camera phone practices and a case study in Seoul, Korea. *Continuum*, 21(2), pp. 227–238.

Hjorth, L., 2009a. *"It's complicated": a case study of women and mobile intimacy*. www.abs-center.si/gbccd/papers/P204.pdf.

Hjorth, L., 2009b. *Mobile media in the Asia-Pacific.* New York: Routledge.

Hochschild, A., 1997. *The time bind: when work becomes home and home becomes work.* New York: Metropolitan Books.

Katz, J., 2006. *Magic is in the air: mobile communication and the transformation of social life.* New Brunswick, NJ: Transaction Publishers.

Kurniawan, S., 2006. An exploratory study of how older women use mobile phones. In: P. Dourish and A. Friday, eds. *Ubicomp 2006: Ubiquitous Computing.* Berlin: Springer.

Lee, D., 2005. Women's creation of camera phone culture. *Fibreculture* 6. http://journal. fibreculture.org/issue6/issue6_donghoo.html.

Lemish, D. and Cohen, A., 2005a. On the gendered nature of mobile phone culture in Israel. *Sex Roles,* 52(7–8), pp. 511–521.

Lemish, D. and Cohen, A., 2005b. Tell me about your mobile and I'll tell you who you are: Israelis talk about themselves. In: R. Ling and P. E. Pedersen, eds. *Mobile communications: re-negotiation of the social sphere.* London: Springer, pp. 187–202.

Ling, R., 2001a. *Adolescent girls and young adult men: two sub-cultures of the mobile telephone.* Kjeller, Norway: Telenor R&D.

Ling, R., 2001b. "We release them little by little": maturation and gender identity as seen in the use of mobile telephony. *Personal and Ubiquitous Computing,* 5, pp. 123–136.

Lohan, M., 2001. Men, masculinities and "mundane" technologies: the domestic telephone. In: E. Green and A. Adam, eds. *Virtual gender: technology, consumption, and identity.* London and New York: Routledge, pp. 149–162.

Marktest, 2006. *O perfil do consumidor português* [The profile of the Portuguese consumer]. Lisbon: Marktest.

Maxwell, J. A., 1999. *La modélisation de la recherche qualitative: une approche interactive.* Paris: Editions Universitaires.

Miller, D., 2004. The little black dress is the solution, but what is the problem? In: K. Ekström and H. Brembeck, eds. *Elusive consumption.* Oxford, UK: Berg, pp 113–127.

Mortimer, J. T. and Shanahan, M. J., eds., 2004. *Handbook of the life course.* New York: Springer.

Plant, S., 2001. *On the mobile: the effects of mobile telephones on social and individual life.* London: Motorola.

Rakow, L. and Navarro, V., 1993. Remote mothering and the parallel shift: women meet the cellullar telephone. *Critical Studies in Mass Communication,* 20(3), pp. 144–157.

Rice, R. and Katz, J., 2003. Comparing internet and mobile phone usage: digital divides of usage, adoption, and dropouts. *Telecommunications Policy,* 27(8–9), pp. 597–623.

Shade, L. R., 2007. Feminizing the mobile: gender scripting of mobiles in North America. *Continuum: Journal of Media & Cultural Studies, 21*(2), pp. 179–189.

Skog, B., 2002. Mobiles and the Norwegian teen: identity, gender and class. In: J. Katz, ed. *Perpetual contact: mobile communications, private talk, public performance.* Cambridge, UK: Cambridge University Press.

Soulet, M.-H., 2002. *Gérer sa consommation. Drogues dures et enjeu de conventionnalité.* Fribourg, Switzerland: Editions Universitaires Fribourg Suisse.

Turkle, S., 1984. *The second self: computers and the human spirit.* London: Granada.

Wajcman, J., 2004. *Technofeminism.* Cambridge, UK: Polity Press.

Wajcman, J., 2007. From women and technology to gendered technoscience. *Information, Communication & Society,* 10(3), pp. 287–298.

8 How young people experience elderly people's use of digital technologies in everyday life

Leopoldina Fortunati

Introduction

The aim of this chapter is to investigate how young people experience the adoption and use of everyday life technologies, such as television, radio, mobile phones and computers, by their grandparents and by elderly people in general. Due to the rapid ageing of populations in contemporary societies, the relative importance of older people as a target of both academic studies and as technology users increases. According to the United Nations, there were 901 million people aged 60 or over, corresponding to 12 per cent of the global population, in 2015. The size of this age group is growing at a rate of 3.26 per cent per year, and although Europe has the highest percentage of 60+ population (24 per cent) in the world, rapid ageing is occurring in all continents save Africa (UN, 2015, p. 7).

The importance of the older population also relates to the fact that they have become healthier and wealthier than in the past (Piketty, 2014) with more education and more time to spend (Kearney, 2013). There is a burning need to better understand the magnitude of these changes in the nature of later life and the changing network of their family members who use various digital technologies to organise and maintain their everyday life. In this study, young people were key informants to examine older people's use of digital technologies in Italy. In Italy, the student key informants have a typically direct and immediate relationship with older members of their families. They are also widely considered as the experts on technology within their families (Schofield Clark, 2013), and hence are particularly suitable to give first-hand information on the use of technology by their aged family members.

Older people and digital technologies

Older people are probably the least-studied age group in respect to ICT use and adoption (Richardson *et al.*, 2011). Nowadays, the older population lives longer than before, and many will reach advanced old age (i.e. living well into their eighties and nineties). In many respects, they may even be in a better position than, for example, middle-aged adults today (Sarrica *et al.*, 2014; Petrovčič *et al.*, 2015). Thanks to the media and the internet, many can keep themselves updated and be informed about the latest innovations and news as well as stay in touch with friends and families through social media.

In Italy, the age group of 55–64 olds was the watershed in terms of internet use in 2014. In this age group, the share of internet users was 46 per cent. Among those older than 64 years of age, that figure drops to 12.5 per cent. These figures correspond to about 3.7 and 10.7 million internet non-users respectively (ISTAT, 2015a, 2015b). According to the same ISTAT data (2015a, 2015b), there is still a large gender difference in the use of the internet among those aged 65 years and older (31 per cent of men vs 17 per cent of women). As many as 40 per cent report the lack of knowledge about the internet as the main reason for their not using it, and this only increases with greater age.

These social changes in later life are interrelated with changes that affect other generations (Bolin, 2016). For example, the number of elderly people living alone has increased because their adult children live away from them (Chattopadhyay and Marsh, 1999). The dissolution of nuclear families (Gutmann, 1987) and the erosion of traditional social norms shape the lives of elderly people all around the world. For example, Cheung and Yui-Huen Kwan (2009) found that in China, where filial piety is one of the cultural bulwarks of society (Savelsberg, 2002), the material performance of intergenerational solidarity cannot but decrease as adult children take up jobs and live in places far away from their parents (Sheng and Settles, 2006; Ye *et al.*, 2014).

In this new context, the transmission of knowledge from one generation to another has changed direction. Young people are now the ones to teach their parents and grandparents how to use digital devices (Oksman, 2006; Correa, 2014; Lim, 2016). As a consequence of this change, young people have started to perform a certain amount of (digital) immaterial labour, and hence gain kudos inside the family. Kennedy *et al.* (2015) examined the gendered distribution of expertise in the performance of 'digital housekeeping' required to maintain a networked home. They showed how differential, gendered access to and use of ICTs is overcome inside the household, thanks to cooperation among family members. Such cooperation inside large families, between the older family members and the younger, technologically savant members may help mitigate generational digital divides (Vehovar *et al.*, 2006).

In this chapter, I argue that not only is the distribution of digital expertise in connection with digital housekeeping gendered, it is also organised intergenerationally within the family. Intergenerational digital housekeeping can be better understood and conceptualised by analysing the three characteristics of the social contract between parents and children. First of all, the 'social contract' established between parents and children is more deferred over time than that established between spouses. In the case of spouses, each contractor has to contribute to the wellbeing of the other on the basis of his/her material and immaterial capability. Spouses are expected to continuously verify the contract, and yet the high number of divorces today shows that the binding force of marriage and marital ties is also getting weaker.

Different conditions apply to the parent-child contract, which is expected to change over the life course. It is based on the hope that children will take care of their parents as their material (if necessary) and immaterial resources decline, as the parents grow old. While parents are clearly owners of their capacity of parental reproduction, children are so, only partially. For this reason, the exchange between parents and children is in part immediate and unaware and in part is deferred until the children grow up and become adults (Fortunati, 1981). Historically, countries have developed different welfare systems to collectively respond to this need for care and support (Esping-Andersen, 1990), and when these responses are insufficient, the responsibility falls to family members, especially in Southern Europe.

Second, the parent-child 'contract' is weakened by its compulsory nature. Paternal, maternal and filial labour cannot circulate as in the free market, but can do so only inside the family to which these individuals belong. This means that the family constitutes an obligatory market in which such labour must operate and collaborate. Due to the compulsory nature of the contract, parent-child relationships are particularly problematic because children do not decide to be born, neither do they choose their parents (or vice versa).

Third, the contract between parents and children contains many elements of uncertainty, because a series of social reasons might affect the performance of the reproductive labour by children (and in some cases, of the grandchildren) towards their parents (and grandparents). For example, increases in the intensity of work and the extension of the working day, increasing commuting time, children's residential mobility and children's family commitments, have resulted in unexpected social changes that in many cases have brought about an unequal distribution of public resources favouring the elderly. All these factors have become a serious impediment to honouring this contract of children taking care of their parents.

Bengtson and Oyama (2007, p. 9) have described the content of this contract by referring to the expression of "intergenerational solidarity" (cf. also Silverstein and Bengtson, 1997; Silverstein *et al.*, 2003). This construct is characterised by "the behavioural and emotional dimensions of interaction, cohesion, sentiment, and support between parents and children, grandparents and grandchildren, over the course of long-term relationships" (Bengtson and Oyama, 2007, p. 9). I would like to stress here the relevance of considering this process in the particular context of the immaterial labour carried out in the household. Digital housekeeping, which is necessary to maintain a networked home, is one of the domestic tasks that has now entered young people's agendas, extending the nature of what constitutes immaterial or 'reproductive' labour.

The aim of this chapter is to investigate how young people have experienced the use of technology by their elderly family members over the last four years. The theories to which I anchor the design of this study, but that I also challenge, are domestication theory (Silverstone and Haddon, 1996) and the diffusion of innovations theory (Rogers, 1995). Specific research questions guiding this study are: i) how do youth describe the relationship between older people and digital technologies? and ii) how do they perceive their own engagement with digital housekeeping towards their elderly relatives? The next section is devoted to the description of the methodology applied in this study. Then I illustrate the results of the study through the original words and expressions used by the young people who served as key informants. Finally, I end the chapter by discussing the results and providing some concluding remarks.

Method

In 2012, a group of undergraduates (N=23) studying for a Bachelor in Multimedia Sciences and Technologies at the University of Udine, Italy were asked to describe and reflect on their experiences of elderly people's use of digital technologies. In 2016, another group of 86 undergraduate students in the same course took part in the same study assignment. The majority of the students were males (61.5 per cent male; 38.5 per cent female). The age of the key informants ranged from 19 to 22 years. They represented two regions of North-East Italy: Friuli Venezia-Giulia and Veneto. The students were expected to be particularly sensitive to the issue of digital technologies, since understanding their features and functionality was part of their course syllabus.

Following a series of studies based on similar methods (Fortunati and Vincent, 2014; Taipale, 2014; Farinosi *et al.*, 2015; Fortunati *et al.*, 2015), the student key informants reported their observations and experiences in written form. They were asked to act as key informants, observe their grandparents' technology use and reflect upon older people's use of digital technologies in general. The students were also asked to describe their own engagement in digital housekeeping towards elderly members of their family. Some students felt it necessary to conduct brief interviews with the elderly people they observed. These key informants' reports should not be considered as windows to 'reality' but more as young people's articulations of their experiences of and attitudes towards older people. The reports can be seen as instruments that convey youth's perceptions of their grandparents and the older generation in general.

No specific instructions on how to write the reports were supplied, as the aim was to collect students' spontaneous thoughts and their everyday observations. The written reports obtained in this way allow for more self-expression and spontaneity of content than in a classical structured interview. However, students were requested to observe and describe how their grandparents used ICTs in everyday life in order to ensure students attended to the actual practices of use, and hence delivered more objective information. Epistemologically, this data collection method was motived by the will not to influence – if at all possible –the interaction between the key informants and the people who formed the focus of their study. The anonymity of the key informants and their family members was protected by reporting only the key informants' first names and the initial letter of their surnames.

Qualitative content analysis was applied to analyse the reports, which were first broken down into discursive frames that captured the most frequently recurring categories (Altheide, 1996). Categories with relatively low frequencies but possible importance for the clarification of some points of analysis were also retained and discussed, as Silverman (1997) advises. As the analysis progressed, at a certain point no new categories emerged indicating that informational redundancy had been reached. The main assets of this methodological tool consist in the fact that it gives us new food to revise concepts or ideas taken-for-granted in the literature related to the topic investigated, and enables us to formulate new lines of research for future quantitative studies with more representative samples from the elderly population.

Analysis of the reports

The results emerging from these reports concern the key aspects of the relationship between older people and digital technologies. The presentation of the results is organised according to the most frequently recurring categories representing the various discursive frames that emerged in these reports.

The long tail of domestication

In recent decades, many studies have adopted domestication theory as proposed by Silverstone and Haddon (1996) as a point of reference when exploring how users make sense of and appropriate new media. But then something happens to the domesticators once the domesticated technologies have become incorporated into the spaces and rhythms of their daily lives. In a personal communication in 2012, Maria Bakarijeva wondered: "Do activities, relationships and roles in the household remain fundamentally the same, or may be some cultural and even civilizational changes take hold? Does the private sphere retain its basic structure, or does it undergo a significant re-configuration?"

While these questions are more than appropriate to understand the post-domesticated world, in the case of the older population, they are not so timely. Many elderly people are still domesticating ICTs in their everyday life. This progress is under the eyes of all. The most recent EU-wide survey shows that the use of mobile phones among elderly people has increased at a very quick pace and that the use of personal computers and tablets is following close behind (Eurobarometer, 2016). However, many older people still seem to resist the adoption and use of new technologies. People aged 55 or more are less likely than younger age groups to embrace internet telephony, instant messaging, emails, social networks and even mobile telephony. Similarly, they consider online communications services and mobile internet less important than other, younger age groups. The key informant Valentina B. writes:

> My grandparents, who are between 80 and 90 years, after having purchased a mobile phone, have used it rarely and after a few attempts have not tried to use it anymore. They are not interested at all in domesticating the mobile phone.

These elderly people often have good reasons to resist digital technologies. They were not introduced to the new media until a later point in their lives, so their own life histories demonstrate that they can live successfully without digital technologies. When these technologies spread out in society, the patterns of older persons' personal, familiar and social behaviour and their everyday practices were already set and the ritualisation of their daily life was firmly established (Ling, 2008). In fact, many students report that their grandparents live very well without a computer and a smartphone since they do not perceive them as useful for their life. As Claudio L. maintains:

> My grandparents do not see the real utility of the new technologies and are convinced that having lived for most of their lives without these devices they can continue to do so. But when they have found themselves in a busy street with a broken car engine, they repented of not having the mobile phone.

Their weaker perception of (or engagement with) the *zeitgeist* of the times – that is the cultural, social and spiritual climax characterising any specific epoch – heavily influences the self-confident resistance of many elderly people. The research material indicates that the reduced energy and shorter time horizon of elderly people attenuate their ability to keep up with and even perceive the changes of the *zeitgeist*. Moreover, their ability to recognise these technological changes is often lowered, not least because the pace of social-technological change is in sharp contrast to their own rhythm of life, which is generally much slower. Further, their reduced awareness of these changes seems to be metabolised through a more general lack of interest. This lack of interest is often used as an (emotional) explanation for not embracing the digital technologies that are characteristics of the *zeitgeist*. Massimo D. R. captures this point when he notes that:

> My grandfather has had the same mobile phone for ten years. The technologies that the elderly have are old because they become old with them.

But there are of course many interesting exceptions like the following, as Simone C. explains:

> My grandmother is 96 and is a very lucid and intelligent person. She reads the newspaper every day, watches television, has had a mobile phone for years. Some months ago she asked me to teach her how to use a computer and the internet because she wants to keep up with the times.

In addition, generations employ different types of symbolisation. For young people and adults, the new technologies represent a 'window on the world'; a way to be in tune with the *zeitgeist*. In contrast, for some of the elderly people observed by the students, the new technologies seemed to represent a way of feeling young. For example, Chiara De P. reveals that:

> My grandparents have learnt quickly to use the mobile phone, maybe because they were really motivated or because they wanted to 'feel young'.

It is not surprising that elderly people feel young when using a mobile phone, since this device is deeply embedded in the narratives of modernisation, and its use is typically associated with a young or youthful lifestyle. However, the reports also reveal that many elderly people prefer not to look at the world through a technological window. This reluctance towards adopting digital technologies explains why the motivation to purchase and use these technologies is often quite weak in this age group. It also explains why older people often become owners and users of digital technologies, such as mobile phones, only when the devices are gifted to them by their children or grandchildren (cf. Piper *et al.*, 2016).

Another interesting issue that these reports describe is well-known to scholars who study the diffusion and adoption of ICTs: namely, that the ownership of a device does not always coincide with its use. Some elderly people formally own a device but do not use it, while others do not own but occasionally use that of their children or grandchildren. In this connection, Andrea F. reports:

> My grandmother is 92. Last month my brother went to Spain for an Erasmus exchange period. Thus, I set up a Skype call between us and him. Also, my grandmother participated. She was serious and excited as she was participating in a Skype conversation for the first time.

Erika F. states that her grandparents often ask her to go on Facebook in order to acquire information about relatives who live overseas and to see pictures of their great-grandchildren. Not only do grandparents ask for help, but sometimes so too do their elderly neighbours. Manuele D. M. reports that sometimes his 65-year-old neighbour asks him to download results of some medical tests. Since the results of the medical tests carried out in Italy are only available online, having a grandchild or a young neighbour becomes essential for those, such as older persons, who are not familiar with computer technology. In the reports, a clear distinction is often made between those elderly persons who became familiar with new technologies during their working life, and those who spent most of their lives without using any digital technology. Manuele D. M., for example, reports that the cousin of his grandfather, who is 91 years old, uses a computer to search for economic and financial information, given that he used to work in a bank. Sometimes elderly people can surprise youth with their skill and knowhow, as Stefano C. describes:

> My grandmother, having seen that I own a Nintendo DS console for playing videogames, asked me if she could try. She proposed some videogames I did not know and that she had discovered thanks to TV advertising.

However, in most of these reports, the elderly people depict more their ease with analogue technologies such as the old media (newspapers and radio) and older domestic appliances (such as washing machines, irons and ovens). What is problematic for many elderly people is the digital technologies and their interface. Unlike the analogue instruments that had few and very simple push key buttons, digital technologies require the user to follow a precise path of menus and touch

buttons to work properly. This shift, which entails a lack of push button imme-
diacy and increased complexity in use, is challenging for many elderly people.

Thus, it appears that for many older people, the problem is not the technology itself but the digital technologies and their interface. In many cases, they
tend to treat the digital technologies as if they were analogue devices operated
according to analogue rules. With their more limited skills and experiences,
older people often try to de-digitalise the device and make it simple to use. As
Piero M. explains:

> The problem with the elderly is that while they were all forced to switch to
> the DTT (digital terrestrial television), their use of the television continued to
> be exactly like in the analogue regime. They look at the same channels they
> used to see before, without taking any advantage from the digital.

The challenge of digital television for elderly people

As Eurobarometer (2016) reports, in every EU member state mobile telephony
is considered by far the most important communication device in people's daily
lives (74 per cent), followed by mobile internet (34 per cent) and fixed landline telephony (32 per cent). Similarly, internet connections (52 per cent) and
online communication services (46 per cent) are considered to be two of the most
important digital services. Regarding both these issues, there is a considerable
'generation gap'. In the case of older people, this also takes the form of a different
ranking of technologies that are considered important, when compared with the
rankings of other age groups. According to the study at hand, the most important
device for older people was neither the mobile phone nor the computer-internet,
but the television.

In elderly people's repertoire, the TV is the most essential of all technologies. This essentiality has made the digitalisation of the television, carried out
as a result of a European level political decision, a particular problem for many
elderly people. Whereas the modernisation of the landline telephone happened
outside the device itself, through the advent of the mobile phone, television
has been modernised by means of its digitalisation. In Italy, the landline phone
continues to be a well-established part of elderly people's lives and maybe is
still the most important channel through which family and social relationships
are maintained. With regard to the mobile phone, it may be said that they are
still domesticating it.

However, as social networks often narrow with age, the need for media that
entertains and keeps older people informed about the world increases – providing
also the mediated presence of other people on the other side of the screen. For
today's elderly population, television is a crucial device through which they organise and shape a large part of their social life. Now, digital television is at the core of
elderly people's media consumption and helps them to pass the time and get through
to the end of the day. Yet digital television poses many problems for those who have
managed to domesticate it with some degree of difficulty. As Chiara S. writes:

In my grandmother's life (96-year-old) the most important problem is the DTT. Sometimes it happens that the channel programming is bust because of the bad weather or some other difficulty in receiving a clean signal. Not being able to reprogram the television she cannot follow the programs in her favourite channels, such as Telechiara, RAI 1 and Channel 4.

To make this crucial technology – DTT – function for them, the students state that their grandparents often request their assistance in reprogramming the television and restoring their preferred channels.

Gender issues

Statistics on the diffusion and use of digital technologies show that gender is an important mediating influence that increases with age. Among younger generations, the differences in the use of digital devices between teenage boys and girls are smaller than those among older age groups, especially older people (e.g. Eurostat, 2013). In the case of the elderly population, the stringent power of social structures and normative expectations shapes the unequal gendered use of ICT more powerfully than among younger users. However, the students' reports analysed here reveal some interesting insights into their families, who mainly belong to a lower middle class. The key informants report gender differences concerning the propensity towards using different types of technology. Women, as expected, are more familiar and at ease with domestic appliances than men. Mariateresa M. writes:

> My maternal grandmother is 82 years old and has a good relationship with technology, especially for household appliances. She knows very well how to use the dishwasher, washing machine, microwave oven and vacuum cleaner.

Unexpectedly in this research, many men were reported to be less comfortable with digital technologies than women. This finding in a certain sense supports the line of discourse that conceptualises ICTs as tools for challenging tired gender roles and for pursuing women's empowerment (Ganito, 2010; Tacchi *et al.*, 2012). Probably many of the older men observed by the students had not been exposed to the use of ICTs in their working life. By contrast, women had had the experience and gained familiarity with domestic appliances and with landline phones, given that they usually had the principle communicative role to network with relatives and friends. For instance, Graziella E. F. notices that the grandmother of her friend makes calls via WhatsApp and also shares photos and videos. Stefano C. continues by writing:

> While my grandmother, although she has always worked as housewife, is capable and curious towards the communication tools, my grandfather, who is a retired bank employee is unprepared to use the new technologies.

Stefano C., whose grandmother's knowledge about the Nintendo console surprised him, also observed the gender difference between his grandmother and grandfather, writing that: "By contrast, my grandfather has a mobile phone but he does not use it, [and] has a computer but he often prefers to use a typewriter for making documents".

Morena C.'s report points in the same direction. She writes: "My grandfather interacts badly with technological innovations, while my grandmother tries her best to use them". These excerpts seem to lead to the conclusion that elderly women are generally more open towards digital technologies than men. Thus, they seem to confirm that the perception of the gendered competence of ICT use is often incorrectly stereotyped and does not correspond to the gendered skill levels observed in everyday life (Hargittai and Shafer, 2006).

Practices of digital housekeeping: the relationship between elderly and young people

The reports are replete with examples of digital housekeeping practices performed by young people in their families. Almost all the students report that they have taught grandparents to use DTT, mobile phones and the computer/internet. These warm experts, to use Bakardjieva's (2005) expression, have not only taught elderly family members how to use these devices but they report that they take care of these devices all the time, e.g. digital television needs to be reprogrammed, or the sound in the mobile needs to be reactivated, etc.

Given that, as we have already mentioned, younger family members are often considered the true experts on technology (Berg *et al.*, 2005), as they are the ones whose responsibility it is to patiently assist the elderly members of the family in their dealings with technology. The most frequent task for Matteo C. is:

> [t]o help retune the television or tune-up the mobile phone, check if it still has credit or if it has received messages or even to delete received messages. Other times the help is needed for the purchase or installation of new appliances that have become too complicated for an old person. More rarely I help my grandmother to look for something on the internet, such as recipes or information, or to purchase train tickets to go and find some sister who lives far away.

But how do elderly people themselves see young people's relationship with digital technologies? According to Adriano A., the three old ladies he interviewed stated that they were convinced that mobile phones, instead of keeping people in contact, create inopportune and impolite situations, such as making and receiving calls while eating. These ladies furthermore argued that:

> [n]ew technologies and above all social networks are creating quite a stir among the youth and are making them slaves of a virtual world in which you no longer need some good manners or have direct contact with their own kind.

Many reasons behind older people's resistance towards adopting the new technologies can be understood by analysing how they perceive the use of digital technologies by youth. The reports clearly revealed the elderly person's disapproval with youth's manner of using digital technologies. For instance, the 90-year-old grandmother of Daniele D. P. says that: "I like the new technologies but not the new generation, because I see many youth losing a lot of time to play with those devices, the mobile phones". Many elderly people see that their grandchildren are continuously distracted because of their constant engagement with their mobile phone and/or their computer. They also argue that these technologies do not increase the ability of their grandchildren to communicate but have the opposite effect. Daniele B. notices the elderly person's negative judgement on the effects that digital technology has on youth. He reports that his grandmother often says: "you guys are always fixed on the screen and you do not communicate with anyone".

Sara M. reports that her grandfather takes concrete measures against the use of the technologies by his children and grandchildren. Each time they go to visit him, he puts all their mobile phones in a drawer because he does not want them to interfere with their meetings. At other times, the key informants seemed to appreciate the elderly person's life style as they find it more authentic. For example, Elisa A., who has a 98-year-old grandfather, notices that:

> Although he shows disinterest towards the new technologies, my grandfather's life is much more 'true' and direct than that of her generation. Discussions were not interrupted by some telephone and nobody was hidden behind a screen. They look inside their eyes, weighing the words that they say.

But in some cases, there were very proactive reflections arising from the young key informants about the things that older people wanted from this technology. According to Paolo B.:

> The questions that my grandparents ask me most often are: "Which button do I press to make the writing on the TV go away?" Or "What buttons do I press to ensure that the light on the phone stops blinking?" Elderly people are not interested to find the cause of why something happens but they try to return everything to normal as soon as possible.
>
> For older people, it would be important to use intelligent voice functions that respond to the questions on the issues they have when they use a mobile phone. Another thing I really miss in technological products for [the] elderly are clear instructions that explain in a simple and understandable way the functions and that take as a reference the old user. A very trivial example would be the explanation of the functions of all the buttons on a remote control of a television set.

The digital housekeeping work of young people that combines digital competence, careful observation and the immediate experience of their own grandparents' attitudes and behaviours promises to become a significant resource for developing new technological innovations for older people, as well as a way of learning essential skills for using the devices and maintaining them.

Changes between 2012 and 2016

The reports from the two groups of students made possible a qualitative longitudinal inquiry into changes in the practices of ICT use by elderly people. However, the content of the reports collected in 2012 were not so different when compared with the reports collected most recently, in 2016. Perhaps the time span is relatively short; however, as the number of elderly people who have already engaged with new technologies in their adult life increases each year, I consider it important to analyse what kind of changes, if any, can be detected from the research material from the two cohorts of student informants.

The most notable difference is the increasing variety of digital media that is entering the technological ecology of elderly people in 2016. Andrea A. talks about the cordless phone that his 93-year-old grandmother uses normally. Davide A. reports that today it is not rare "to find elderly who, to keep pace with the times, send their best wishes on WhatsApp or 'Likes' a post in Facebook". Eleonora B. states that her grandmother asked for help regarding the use of WhatsApp. Adriano A. had interviewed two friends of his grandmother: the average age of all three ladies was 75 years. He was surprised to discover that two out of three had a smartphone, one had a computer and an email account, and two owned a flat screen TV with integrated digital receiver.

The presence of an increasing variety of digital media in elderly people's lives probably should be read as a kind of countermeasure. They are realising that given the current turmoil of mobility that has affected their children's lives, they often have to live far away from them. Likewise, their children in turn are often too busy in their everyday life (their work and their family) to have the possibility of being present in the lives of their parents with any degree of significant continuity. Thus, they are considering more seriously activating technologies that will enable them to continue living independently while staying in contact with their children and grandchildren. Elena B writes:

> I know, many young elderly (65 years) who are adapting to new technologies, so that they learnt to use a smartphone, Facebook, WhatsApp. Some also have an iPod and listen to music more modern than me (I listen mostly to 60s music strictly on CD).

Older people's use of the new media is not always appropriate, however, and they often behave like novices. As GianMarco A. observes:

> [h]aving discovered these technologies late in life they are not really aware of what they use. It often happens that they publish pictures of small children or private photos in their Facebook page naively, not knowing that it can be dangerous.

The elderly person's naivety (Livingstone and Bober, 2006) can be a problem because they approach the new media, as we saw before, with the same attitude they applied towards analogue technologies, which can have unpleasant consequences for them.

In 2016, several elderly people were reported to be attracted by online games. Generally, analogue card games had been more popular among elderly people in the past. Card games were considered good for memory and developing mental strategies important for the maintenance of cognitive abilities. Nowadays, playing online cards games and videogames are practices that are spreading rapidly among elderly people. Gloria N. reports that her 77-year-old grandmother, Gioia, has a Nintendo GameCube which she uses to play Super Mario and other games. Two years ago, the family gave her an iPad on which to play cards when alone, since gaming has been her passion. She enjoys this very much and is now climbing the world rankings in some games!

Discussion and final remarks

In the students' reports, there was little trace of generational consciousness in relation to new technology. Probably this stems from the social isolation in which many elderly persons live, which limits the possibility for them to feel any strong sense of belonging to or identifying with their own cohorts, or in creating a sense of identity with technology and a feeling of solidarity with their peers. This lack of reported generational consciousness may be also due to the fact that their peers remind them very vividly of the difficulties and the limits of the stage of life they are living – and instil caution about identifying too strongly with such an identity. While the construct of generation can create strength and closeness among youth who have a life ahead of them to build, among older people who, day after day, see their friends pass away, the same construct may not give them the same resources or provide the same support and sense of belonging. The peers of these grandfathers and grandmothers are relatively weak social agents, and probably any generational identity for them threatens ghettoisation and marginalisation rather than strength.

Many interesting points have emerged from this research regarding elderly people's life stage that have enabled me to offer some answers to my first research question: How do youth describe the relationship between the elderly and digital technologies? The domestication theory turned out to still be effective in understanding the gaze of youth on elderly people's engagement (or lack of) in the process of making sense and activating digital technologies. It enabled us to understand that the elderly practise domestication in a peculiar way and grasp domestication theory more profoundly. First, for the elderly the problem is not the technology itself, but rather the particular logic of digital technologies. As described above, among the digital technologies, the main concern is related to the digital television, since it is the most important technology for them but also the most difficult to manage. Second, the strategy they apply most frequently in the use of the new technologies is their de-digitalisation, that is, their attempt to make them more similar to the analogue technologies and thus simpler to use. Third, the process of domestication, which usually imposes a roadmap adhering to the dynamics of changes of the *zeitgeist*, is obliged to incorporate the much slower rhythm of the elderly, which is discordant with that typical of digital technologies. According to the students' reports, the elderly have a drastically different perception of *zeitgeist* in comparison with younger family members. Whereas the digital technologies have in their DNA a continuous updating and require a metacommunication strategy to learn how to use them, the elderly are used to a direct learning, which, once consolidated, tends to remain unchanged over time without requiring further learning. Fourth, the use of digital technologies is often carried out by the elderly through the devices of their children and grandchildren. This type of use probably escapes the large surveys, like those mentioned at the beginning of the chapter, on the diffusion and adoption of new technologies.

The analysed reports also provide interesting insights into the fact that elderly women appear much more curious and open to new technologies than men. This finding too remains somehow hidden in the large surveys on the diffusion and use of digital technologies, in which older women appear as the weakest users of technology. Furthermore, several important suggestions came from our respondents for improving the design of technologies, especially of the mobile phone, for the elderly. It also emerged that between 2012 and 2016, a higher degree of domestication was retrieved: new media, such as tablets and iPods, social networks like Facebook and mobile messenger applications like WhatsApp, have begun to arrive in the lives of the elderly. The larger variety of digital technologies present in the elderly's houses we investigated in 2016 shows that although de-digitalisation has remained the main strategy of domestication of the new technology, the elderly are now more available to encounter new languages and functions.

Regarding my second research question: How do youth perceive their own engagement in the digital housekeeping towards the elderly?, the *role of youth in the digital housekeeping of elderly people* emerged as quite serious and continuous. The students stated many times that they helped their grandparents to learn how to use these technologies by acting as warm, savant teachers and that any time their grandparents needed it, they provided support. Thus, my proposal that the distribution of digital expertise in connection to digital housekeeping is not only gendered but also intergenerational, finds support in this study. This finding resonates also with many quantitative studies, which found that the elderly who have grandchildren are the most skilful in technology and are technologically oriented (Hunt, 2012).

This finding also has implications on the diffusion of innovations theory (Rogers, 1995) since it sheds light on the specific mechanism of the transfer of innovation. For this theory, the laggards are the last to adopt an innovation, are generally focused on traditions and are typically in contact with only family and close friends. They arrive at the adoption through some communication channels that permit the transfer of information from one unit or group to another. The transfer of innovation from an individual or group to another is generally depicted as a linear phase, but the present study highlights how this process can be contradictory and thus obstruct the adoption of innovation. In this study, the elderly are clearly laggards as the time for them to adopt the digital technologies is quite long. The transfer of knowledge about new technologies comes, in this case, from their children and grandchildren, who are presumably innovators or early adopters. However, this transfer is ambivalent since, on the one hand, elderly people receive encouragement and support from their grandchildren regarding the adoption and use of the digital technologies. On the other, they are discouraged from approaching new technologies by the technological life style of their grandchildren of which they disapprove. The observation and evaluation of the practices of ICT use by their grandchildren and youth in general do not push them towards the appropriation of these technologies. The ambivalent meaning of the message that passes through the transfer is a factor that probably delays the elderly's adoption of digital technologies.

On the whole, these data suggest the need to redesign the questions in quantitative surveys regarding technology use in later life. First, the relationship between possession and use could be split in two; the role of elderly women, which needs to be investigated beyond the stereotypical assumptions with which we generally approach it; and second, the role of youth who 'take care' of their grandparents quite seriously (their digital housekeeping is a kind of domestic immaterial labour, which is never counted). More qualitative research on the relationship between elderly people and new technologies is needed in the future to better understand the unexpected findings that emerged in this study and the specific features that characterise this relationship, depending on whether elderly people are in their seventies, eighties or nineties. Further qualitative research is needed to better understand the limitations that such technologies possess in forging an intragenerational, rather than an intergenerational identity.

References

Altheide, D. L., 1996. *Qualitative media analysis*. Thousand Oaks, CA: SAGE.

Bakardjieva, M., 2005. *Internet society: the internet in everyday life*. London: SAGE.

Bengtson, V. L. and Oyama, P. S., 2007. Intergenerational solidarity: strengthening economic and social ties. New York: United Nations.

Berg, E., Mörtberg, C. and Jansson, M., 2005. Emphasizing technology: socio-technical implications. *Information Technology and People*, 18(4), pp. 343–358.

Bolin, G., 2016. *Media generations: experience, identity and mediatised social change*. New York: Routledge.

Chattopadhyay, A. and Marsh, R., 1999. Changes in living arrangement and familial support for the elderly in Taiwan: 1963–1991. *Journal of Comparative Family Studies*, 30(3), pp. 523–537.

Cheung, C.-K. and Kwan A. Y.-H., 2009. The erosion of filial piety by modernisation in Chinese cities. *Ageing & Society*, 29(2), pp. 179–198.

Correa, T., 2014. Bottom-up technology transmission within families: exploring how youths influence their parents' digital media use with dyadic data. *Journal of Communication*, 64(1), pp. 103–124.

Esping-Andersen, G., 1990. The three worlds of welfare capitalism. Princeton, NJ: Princeton University Press.

Eurobarometer, 2016. *E-communications and the digital single market*. Special Eurobarometer 438. www.eena.org/download.asp?item_id=177.

Eurostat, 2013. Devices used for mobile connection to the internet. Special module 2012: mobile connection to the internet. http://ec.europa. eu/eurostat/web/products-datasets/-/isoc_cimobi_dev.

Farinosi, M., Lim, C. and Roll, J., 2015. Book or screen, pen or keyboard? A cross-cultural sociological analysis of writing and reading habits basing on Germany, Italy and the UK. *Telematics & Informatics*, 33(2), p. 410–421

Fortunati, L., 1981. *L'arcano della riproduzione: casalinghe, prostitute, operaie e capital*. Venice, Italy: Marsilio.

Fortunati, L. and Vincent, J., 2014. Sociological insights on the comparison of writing/reading on paper with writing/reading digitally. *Telematics & Informatics*, 31(1), pp. 39–51.

Fortunati, L., Taipale, S. and Farinosi, M., 2015. Print and online newspapers as material artefacts. *Journalism*, 16(6), pp. 830–846.

Ganito, C., 2010. Women on the move: the mobile phone as a gender technology. *Comunicação & Cultura*, 9, pp. 77–88.

Gutmann, D., 1987. *Reclaimed powers: toward a new psychology of men and women in later life*. Chicago, IL: Northwestern University Press.

Hargittai, E. and Shafer, S., 2006. Differences in actual and perceived online skills: the role of gender. *Social Science Quarterly*, 87(2), 432–448.

Hunt, D. M., 2012. *Technology and the grandparent-grandchild relationship: learning and interaction*. Master's thesis. The University of Toledo, Ohio, USA.

ISTAT, 2015a. *Internet@Italia 2014. L'uso di internet da parte di cittadini e imprese*. Rome: ISTAT.

ISTAT, 2015b. *Italia in cifre*. Rome: ISTAT.

Kearney, A. T., 2013. Understanding the needs and consequences of the ageing consumer. The Consumer Goods Forum, Korea. www.theconsumergoodsforum.com/files/Publications/ageing_consumer_report.pdf.

Kennedy, J., Nansen, B., Arnold, M., Wilken, R. and Gibbs, M., 2015. Digital housekeepers and domestic expertise in the networked home. *Convergence*, 21(4), pp. 408–422.

Lim, S. S., ed., 2016. *Mobile communication and the family*. Dordrecht, The Netherlands: Springer.

Ling, R., 2008. The elderly and texting. *The Information Society*, 24(5), pp. 334–341.

Livingstone, S. and Bober, M., 2006. Regulating the internet at home: contrasting the perspectives of children and parents. In: D. Buckingham and R. Willett, eds. *Digital generations: children, young people and new media*. Mahwah, NJ: Lawrence Erlbaum, pp. 93–113.

Oksman, V., 2006. Young people and seniors in Finnish "mobile information society". *Journal of Interactive Media in Education*, 2. http://doi.org/10.5334/2006-3.

Petrovčič, A., Fortunati, L., Vehovar, V., Kavčič, M. and Dolničar, V., 2015. Mobile phone communication in social support networks of older adults in Slovenia. *Telematics and Informatics*, 32(4), pp. 642–655.

Piketty, T., 2014. *Capital in the twenty-first century*. Cambridge, MA: Harvard University Press.

Piper, A. M., Cornejo Garcia, R. and Brewer, R. N., 2016. Understanding the challenges and opportunities of smart mobile devices among the oldest old. *International Journal of Mobile Human Computer Interaction*, 8(2), pp. 83–98.

Richardson, M., Zorn, T. E. and Weaver, C. K., 2011. Older people and new communication technologies: narratives from the literature. In: C. T. Salmon, ed. *Communication Yearbook 35*. London: Taylor & Francis, pp. 121–154.

Rogers, E., 1995. *Diffusion of innovations*. New York: The Free Press.

Sarrica, M., Fortunati, L. and Contarello, A., 2014. New technologies, ageing and social well-being in a South-Italian context. In: T. Denison, M. Sarrica and L. Stillman, eds. *Theories, practices and examples for community and social informatics*. Melbourne, Australia: Monash University Publishing, pp. 19–44.

Savelsberg, J. J., 2002. Dialectics of norms in modernization. *Sociological Quarterly*, 43(2), pp. 277–305.

Schofield Clark, L., 2013. *The parent app: understanding families in the digital age*. New York: Oxford University Press.

Sheng, X. and Settles, B. H., 2006. Intergenerational relationships and elderly care in China: a global perspective. *Current Sociology*, 54(2), pp. 293–313.

Silverman, D., ed., 1997. *Doing qualitative research: theory, method, and practice*. London: SAGE.

Silverstein, M. and Bengtson, V. L., 1997. Intergenerational solidarity and the structure of adult-child parent relationships in American families. *American Journal of Sociology*, 103(2), pp. 429–460.

Silverstein, M., Bengtson, V. L. and Litwak, E., 2003. Theoretical approaches to problems of families, aging, and social support in the context of modernization. In: S. Biggs, A. Lowenstein and J. Hendricks, eds. *The need for theory: critical approaches to social gerontology*. Amityville, NY: Baywood, pp. 181–199.

Silverstone, R. and Haddon, L., 1996. Design and the domestication of information and communication technologies: technical change and everyday life. In: R. Mansell and R. Silverstone, eds. *Communication by design: the politics of information and communication technologies*. Oxford, UK: Oxford University Press, pp. 44–74.

Tacchi, J., Kitner, K. R. and Crawford, K., 2012. Meaningful mobility: gender, development and mobile phones. *Feminist Media Studies*, 12(4), 528–537.

Taipale, S., 2014. The affordances of reading/writing on paper and digitally in Finland. *Telematics & Informatics*, 31(4), pp. 532–542.

UN, 2015. World population prospects: the 2015 revision, key findings and advance tables. Working Paper No. ESA/P/WP.241. https://esa.un.org/unpd/wpp/publications/files/key_findings_wpp_2015.pdf.

Vehovar, V., Sicherl, P., Hüsing, T. and Dolničar, V., 2006. Methodological challenges of digital divide measurements. *The Information Society*, 22(5), pp. 279–290.

Ye, W., Sarrica, M. and Fortunati, L., 2014. A study on Chinese bulletin board system forums: how internet users contribute to set up contemporary notions of family and marriage. *Information, Communication & Society*, 17(7), pp. 889–905.

9 ICTs and client trust in the care of old people in Finland

Helena Hirvonen

Introduction

As one of the Nordic welfare states, Finland offers some of the world's longest-established universal provision of health and social care services for its elderly citizens. However, these support systems have come under financial pressure in recent decades. Scarcity of public resources and efforts to increase efficiency now motivate the development of welfare services. Technology is a key factor influencing public policy-making in Finland, among other postindustrial countries (UN E-government, 2014) and, as a result, the knowledge economy and technology-assisted control and regulation of services are increasingly seen as solutions to the crises of the public service economy. The Finnish government emphasises digitalisation of public services as one of its strategic priorities (Strategic Government Programme, 2016). Strong optimism and hopes of more flexible and efficient service production, better civic participation, improved transparency, documentation, quality and comparability of service outputs validate digitalisation (Ministry of Social Affairs and Health, 2015). Due to growing service demand and the fiscal crisis, more is now expected of family members as carers of old people, while information and communication technologies (ICTs) and digitalisation of services are highlighted as solutions to improve public service performance (Jolanki *et al.*, 2013).

Yet, digitalisation is not only a technological transformation for public service organisations and workplaces, but also a *cultural* and *social* one. On the one hand, care professionals are key actors in reasserting citizens' trust, while on the other, the rather hidden role of (un)paid family carers as primary care takers of older relatives has come to the fore in recent years. As intergenerational help and care is mostly provided between dispersed households, ICTs provide an important tool for coordinating between informal and formal care and help. There is a vast literature on the adoption and use of ICTs in different organisational settings of care work and on the co-construction of new technologies and the body (Haddon *et al.*, 2008). However, the question of how implementation of ICTs affects the formation of trust between participants in these relationships, and between them and the care service system, has not been studied in depth.

Trust is an important vehicle to reduce and deal with complexity in technological societies, and the digitalisation of welfare services poses specific challenges in the formation of trust in health and social care work. Care involves technical and medical expertise, but also more intangible aspects of personal service, bodywork and emotional orientation to the needs of another human being (Tronto, 1993). These cannot always be captured or replaced with ICT. Following Luhmann (1979), the trust that welfare service users develop towards the welfare state and its service system ultimately depends on individual encounters and the personal trust that is created between service users and care professionals in face-to-face encounters. To date, research about professional–citizen relations strongly shows that face-to-face-encounters are very important for the emergence of trust in these relations (Hirvonen, 2014). Meanwhile, expert knowledge of care professionals is increasingly questioned in contemporary knowledge societies (Santiago and Carvalho, 2015), obliging professionals to use a growing amount of ICT-mediated accountability work, such as reporting and registering of tasks and activities in various electronic databases.

What does the (at least partial) substitution of face-to-face encounters by digital encounters mean for trust in the context of formal and informal elderly care? This chapter aims to gain insight into this question. It analyses cultural and social transformation brought on by the use of ICTs (namely mobile phones and computers) in the care of old people. The analysis is based on qualitative data collected from caring family members of old people (n=12) and elder care professionals (n=12). The chapter strives to answer the question of how the growing use of ICT affects trust in care relationships. The system level trust – citizens' confidence in the competence of public services – has remained high in Finland (Kouvo *et al.*, 2012). However, a recent survey suggests that only half of the people in the 75–89 age group trust getting help and care from the public service sector, while nearly 80 per cent trust getting help and care from family members and next of kin (Aging and Housing, 2012; Jolanki *et al.*, 2013). This is contrary to previous research claiming that trust tends to increase with age (on the ageing effect, see Robinson and Jackson, 2001).

The decline in the overall level of trust (the period effect) could partly result from the paradigm shift in Finnish elder care policies. In light of these changes, it is important to study if, how and to what end ICTs mediate trust in the care of elderly people. The great variation within the old age cohorts in terms of individuals' cognitive capacities, quality of kinship ties and ICT readiness can further increase inequality in old people's opportunities for a good quality of life. The chapter begins with an introduction of the context of elderly care in Finland, and the conceptual framework applied in the study. It then introduces the data and methods, followed by results and concluding remarks.

ICT and the care of old people in Finland

I use a broad definition of ICTs in this chapter, with an emphasis on conventional technologies, such as mobile phones, computers and the internet. The definition follows from descriptions used by the informants in the two data sets used in this study. In the case of care professionals, ICTs were described as software and devices, such as computers, hand-held devices and mobile phones. With almost 80 per cent of elderly people in Finland owning a mobile phone (Intosalmi *et al.*, 2013), the market for so-called assistive technologies for old people living at home is rapidly growing. In line with these statistics, the ICT described and used the most by caring family members in this study was the mobile phone.

Following Kröger and Leinonen (2011), care of older people in Finland can best be described as a loosely coordinated web formed by actors in four realms: informal, public, private and voluntary. The focus in this study is on the informal and public provision of help and care, representing the two main ways of organising elder care. Informal care and help by family members is the most general and often the only source of help for old people (Kröger and Leinonen, 2011). While there are more expectations than before, especially on the involvement of adult children in the care of their old parents, most family members assist their relatives while themselves remaining in the labour market full time. Importantly, there is no legal obligation on families to provide care or financial support to older people in Finland.

In official policy, the role of family members remains complementary to local municipalities who are responsible for forming public welfare policies and providing care services (Kröger and Leinonen, 2011). The coverage and the contents of care services have changed rather dramatically in Finland since the 1990s. Before that, almost all institutional and home care services were organised and provided as public services by municipalities, but since the mid-1990s marketisation of care services has been a strong trend in Finland (Anttonen and Häikiö, 2011). Today, care of old people involves various actors, including municipal home care services, private and non-profit service providers, as well as family members. The changes represent erosion of the idea of universalism. Meanwhile, living at home in advanced age has become an important welfare policy goal in the twenty-first century (Kröger and Leinonen, 2011; Aging and Housing, 2012). However, an increase in the number of older people in poor condition as well as the scarcity of resources have led many municipalities to tighten the criteria for home care service eligibility. Provision of elder care services is now based on individual needs assessments, which prioritise home care and avoid institutional care as much as possible. There is a growing focus on assisted living at home, while service users are forced to purchase supportive services – previously provided by the municipality – from the market.

The uses of ICTs in mediating trust in the care of old people

Trust is an important vehicle to reduce and deal with complexity in increasingly technological societies. When defining trust in any relationship, the complicated social, cultural and psychological networks underlying the relationship deeply affect the systems and individuals involved. For the care of old people, ICTs are a vehicle that has the potential to induce communication and to generate trust between old people, their family members and professional carers. However, the context of elderly care is also special in terms of communication.

The communicative actors it encompasses are old and their communicational capabilities can be limited, which highlights the importance of physical closeness in the help and care of old people (Jaava, 2006). The more limited the cognitive capacities of the person in question, the more the communication happens through speech, touch and small gestures that one learns to interpret through accumulating knowledge of the other person.

Such a context poses challenges to ICTs. Proximity between individuals has traditionally been an essential requirement for the execution of corporeal and social practices of care that transfer the feeling of being in good hands (Tronto, 1993). Consequently, the growing use of ICT affects the mechanisms through which trust can be generated and reasserted. Previous studies suggest that the use of ICT does not self-evidently facilitate formal or informal care relationships, but it may even inhibit good communication and interaction in care relationships by expanding the physical distance between the parties involved (Di Luzio, 2006). The negative impacts of ICT partly derive from the disregard of the value of verbal and non-verbal communication in face-to-face interaction and in the formation of client trust (Brown and Calnan, 2011; Van Wynsberghe, 2011).

Regarding the potential of ICTs in terms of their availability and attitudes of old people as ICT users, there are great differences among the age cohort 75–89 in Finland. In 2015, a third of people in this cohort had used the internet within the last three months and 13 per cent of the age group used it regularly (Statistics Finland, 2015). The diversity in the life situations of the people in the age cohort greatly affects individuals' capacities to use ICTs. For one, internet user rate rises with the old people's occupational status, level of education and the number of next of kin and social networks they have (Rasi and Kilpeläinen, 2016). The same goes for mobile phones, which are the most common ICT device used by people aged 75–89. Over 80 per cent of this age group own a mobile phone, though the user rate declines with rising age, and lower occupational and educational status (Intosalmi *et al.*, 2013). People's distinct lifestyles, identities, interests and culture may also shape ICT use, especially in more rural areas (Hakkarainen, 2012).

In this study, the role of ICTs in the care of old people is analysed from the point of view of sociological theorisation on trust (Luhmann, 1979; Kuhlmann, 2006) on two levels: on 'the system level' as citizens' trust towards the welfare service system, and on 'the personal level' as trust towards care professionals and other carers. Luhmann (1979) emphasises that system level trust ultimately depends on personal trust created between individuals, in this case the old people and their family members and/or care professionals. Therefore, the personal trust that is created in everyday encounters between workers, service users and family members can have far-reaching consequences on trust in the system level between citizens and the welfare state in general.

Data and methods

In the context of health and social care provision, empirical research has mainly studied trust from the point of view of patients/service users. The focus in this study, however, is on the ICT use of family members and care professionals as mediators of help and care of old people. The study focused on two aspects of elder care: first, on how ICTs mediate care workers' multiple accountabilities (their organisational and professional trust) in the context of formal care service work, and second, on how ICTs mediate family members' activities in the context of informal care. These two realms of care – formal care by professionals and informal care by family members – are interrelated in elder care provision and can thereby be studied in relation to one another.

The data comprises two separate sets of qualitative interview data. The first is a focus group interview data (n=12) collected in Finland in 2013 from women involved in the care of an older family member.[1] The interviewees were aged between 40 and 59, apart from one who was under 30 and 2 that were aged 60+. All of the women participated in working life and had an elderly family member they helped regularly. Most of the interviewees represent the typical example of a caring family member in Finland who provides informal care to their older relative (in most cases their parent/parents) in the age group 75–89. Apart from one respondent, the interviewees did not share the same household with the relative whom they helped. Following the typology of Byrne *et al.* (2009), the women's descriptions suggest their elderly relatives had some capacity to manage Activity of Daily Living tasks. In most cases, the women assisted their relative with Instrumental Activity of Daily Living tasks. The women thus offered more 'help' than 'care', as is often the case in countries with wide-ranging provision of public services (Brandt *et al.*, 2009).

The focus group interviews dealt with the women's life situations, their experiences in combining work and care responsibilities, and their role in the help and care of their older relative. The respondents' experience in using ICTs was not explicitly taken up during the interviews, but it turned out to be central to their accounts. Based on information given in a background questionnaire the informants completed, the majority of them are active ICT users, namely well-educated adults who live in a large or middle-sized municipality, and who work and have children (e.g. Fortunati and Taipale, 2012; Taipale, 2013).

The second set of data includes interviews (n=12) collected in 2007–2009 from health and social care workers in Finland by using snowball sampling and by recruiting interviewees through adverts posted in welfare service facilities. The interviewees worked in municipal home care services or supported service housing, which are the main forms of public elder care services in Finland. The interviewees were between 25 and 61 years old. In terms of the ICT usage described by the respondents, the focus of the interviews was mostly on patient information systems and various computer software programs the interviewees used as part of their work. The interview themes focused on the nature of the participants' jobs and their relationships with co-workers and clients, as well as the changes they had experienced in their work. Overall, the aim was to map the respondents' accounts of organisational life and work practices in various locales within the contemporary public service sector.

The interviews in both data sets were semi-structured and were recorded and manually transcribed. The focus group interviews with caring family members lasted approximately two and a half hours, while individual interviews with care professionals lasted approximately one and a half hours each. In both cases, specific themes were introduced using key questions and prompts when necessary. Both data sets only include female respondents, which should be taken into consideration in the interpretation of the results. Furthermore, since the data from care professionals were collected in the period 2007–2009, it does not reflect the most recent turns in technology-mediated practices of professional care. However, because this is an exploratory study on ICTs and trust in the context of elder care, the results should be taken as a preliminary investigation into the field that requires further research.

The analysis was carried out by reading and re-analysing as a methodological tool (Dampier, 2008) in light of Luhmann's (1979) idea of personal and system level trust. In the first-order analysis, the focus was on finding the parts containing informants' descriptions of ICTs and their use in everyday activities of care and help. In the second-order analysis, these accounts were further organised and analysed based on the concepts of personal trust and system level trust. The results are organised under two sub-sections. The first recalls informal carers' accounts of ICT use. The second sub-section presents the results from the data collected from care professionals.

Results

The role of mobile phones in informal care and help of older people

Policy-making regarding old people's help and care needs at home can be divided into two discourses, in parallel with Higgs and Gilleard's (2015) discourse of the third and fourth age: the third age sees old people as active seniors with financial resources, making independent choices according to their lifestyle and preferences. The fourth age discourse reflects the negativity and otherness that are presumed characteristics of the 'old' old age where frail old people's living arrangements and care needs are dictated by their deteriorating physical and cognitive state of health and resulting dependence on family members and/or care professionals. In the majority of interviews that I conducted with caring family members, the discourse resembled the more negative one, that of the 'fourth age'. A woman who gave help to her mother who lived by herself gave a typical description of a caring family member's situation among the interviewees:

> I have these two sisters. We all work and they also have young kids, and a bit more stable routine in terms of working times and lifestyles. So, I have become a kind of a carer for our mother, I take care of all things, financial and medical, I make check-up phone calls every day and drive to her if needed. And it wouldn't be that tough if it wasn't for her memory disease [dementia]. The disease makes everything so unpredictable: has something happened or not, is she lying to me on the phone, and so on. She lives at home alone and has become sort of a hermit, and now I try to take care of her from afar.

Respecting the autonomy of a mother who suffers from dementia is not easily combined with trusting that she is doing well. The description of the interviewee brings out the complexity and somewhat unsettled nature of the care and help of old people. In Finland, it is not common for adult family members of different generations to share a household, and adult children often live a significant distance from their old parents. As this was the case for many of the interviewees, mobile phones were the key device for coordinating activities of care and help. In some cases, the role of mobile phones was mainly sociable, whereas in others, it had become an irreplaceable lifeline between the interviewee and their elderly relative, as for one of the interviewees who described the situation of her late father as follows:

> I was the only relative to my father who suffered from cancer and lived 200 km from here. Towards the end, he was suicidal and in a lot of pain. So, I told at work that I have my mobile phone in my pocket, although we're not supposed to carry them during work, and I felt that it made it easier that he could contact me and talk to me, and it always did . . . those calls were really tough during workdays and at home, too. But the physical distance, which we've talked about, I understand well what it feels like when you can't just take a bicycle and go to him, but he lives somewhere far away. And in my case, you can't send anyone to him because he won't open the door to anyone . . . The distances these days, it makes me think it's the elderly who should move closer to their children (laughter), so it would be easier!

Where possible, workplace cultures have adapted to employees' use of personal mobile phones. While such practices can ease the anxiety of both caring family members and their old relatives, having a mobile phone within one's reach all day can also become a burden, as one of the interviewees recalled:

> What made it so straining was that this spring, mom would first call my sister seven to thirty times a day – mom has a panic disorder. She is so insecure, although she gets home care service, and we visit often . . . So my sister was very tired with the situation, and if mom couldn't get a hold of her, mom would call me. I have my phone on me all the time. Well, she didn't call at night so much, but during the day and so on.

For the women in this study, the constant availability through their mobile phone had both positive and negative consequences. On the one hand, it eased their feelings of helplessness and guilt over the old relative's wellbeing when they could not be physically close to them. On the other, being available 24/7 was also a source of stress and anxiety. Recent surveys from Finland suggest that the health, life experiences, needs and wishes of people in the age group 75+ are much more diverse than those of people in younger cohorts (Aging and Housing, 2012). The variables behind the diversity include socio-economic status, family relations and health. In line with these findings, the results in this study suggest that the accumulation of various resources throughout one's life course greatly affects one's capacity for relatively independent living at home. The results also point to the complexities with family members' attempts to respect the older relative's decision-making autonomy regarding his or her capacity for independent living at home.

Providing help and care to an older family member is often a balancing act between three issues, as Kunk (2010) suggests: taking responsibility for the relative's care, respecting their autonomy and placing a limit on one's own involvement. The tension between autonomy and responsibility can at times create particular difficulties in terms of family members' involvement in the help and care of an older relative. Many of the women interviewed for this study made special efforts to set both practical and emotional boundaries between themselves and their older relative. Considering the widespread use of mobile phones and the associated expectation of one's constant availability, drawing these boundaries is not always easy.

In terms of trust that is mediated in care and help through mobile phones, many of the interviewees emphasised how they could not fully trust the accuracy of information on their elderly relative's condition received via phone calls. One thing in common with all of the interviewees was their general reservation towards the idea of extensive use of ICTs in the help and care of their old family members, especially in cases where the cognitive capacities of their elderly family member were impaired. This was the case with a woman whose mother was diagnosed with dementia and who continued to live on her own:

> She takes her own temperature thirty times and then calls and asks me "what does this mean?", and I respond: "36.4 means no fever". Eventually, it got to the point where she was taking her temperature, checking her blood glucose level and blood pressure, all with using a single device! And there I am, trying to stay calm, when she calls and I ask her what (device) she has used to take these measurements, and she says "It says Omron on this", and I respond, "Yes, well, that's the thermometer".

Typically, old people evaluate the 'worth' and value of technology based on how it supports their ability to carry out everyday activities and chores, and to manage their health and wellbeing (Leikas and Saariluoma, 2008). Users need to have confidence and skills to use these technologies, and understanding of the processes of ageing and the lifestyles of old people is therefore crucial for the successful use of technologies. Ideally, products and services are designed so that they increase people's experiences of wellbeing, so that they don't cause harm or become excluded from society (Leikas and Saariluoma, 2008).

Apart from devices and surveillance technologies that did not require active usership and skills, such as security bracelets, all interviewees were sceptical about the introduction of new technologies in the help and care of their elderly family members. Importantly, it is precisely family members who are the primary helpers of old relatives who, in practice, can encourage or discourage the introduction of any new technologies into the lives of old people. Old people in Finland are rather willing to make financial investments in technology and changes to their everyday lives at home (Intosalmi *et al.*, 2013; Kilpeläinen and Seppänen, 2014), and even to accept the use of social robots in health care (Taipale *et al.*, 2015) if they see that it improves their quality of life at home. The distributed competencies within families to help and support old people in using ICTs are crucial in this respect (Rasi and Kilpeläinen, 2016). A lack of sufficient information about the possible uses of new technologies, and also the negative attitudes among caring family members can stand in the way of ICT use in the care of old people who live at home. Although the women in this study represent the age groups and socio-economic groups of skillful, active users of new technologies, their know-how does not necessarily extend or transfer into willingness or expertise in assessing if and how new technologies could be used in the help and care of their old family members.

ICTs mediating professional help and care of old people: a balancing act

In contrast to the position of caring family members as private citizens, the choice to adopt or not adopt ICTs in professional care is not so much an individual one. As end-users of ICTs in the formal care sector, all health and social care personnel in Finland have computer skills, ability to read and document patient information, and access to the internet (Hyppönen *et al.*, 2015). However, especially in social services, the use of digital communication between professionals and citizens is still in its early stages, and electronic information exchange between workers and service users in home care service work remains rare. While workers believe that technology has a positive effect on service users' sense of safety, they see unreliability of technology as its greatest disadvantage. Implementation of new technologies thereby requires training for both professionals and service users.

In professional care, the social dynamics of ICT use are subject to micro level and meso level influences (Loos, 2008). On the meso level, interaction within the organisational environment (e.g. service users and managers) drives professionals' adaptation of ICTs that are supposed to enhance the effectiveness and efficiency of work and communication processes. Particularly at the micro level, however, employees do not greet all innovations enthusiastically. This applies especially to managerial technologies that do not directly facilitate patient work. Care professionals devote a significant proportion of their working time to ICT-related tasks of recording and reporting, and therefore also assess the sensibility of their time use carefully, as a home care service worker described:

We've recently begun to also report all the indirect tasks that are not part of our official job descriptions, such as phone calls and references. But I'm not convinced that this is a good use of our time and skills . . . Then again, if I don't have the time to go to the electronic patient record to read the patient files, it seems crazy to go into the clients' homes because then I can only do the necessary basic tasks. I don't always have the time, but when I do, I try to read their files the day before, to check who I'm supposed to see the next day, to go through their medical history and their life history, to get an overall picture. It feels meaningful to be able to piece together their life situations. It allows me to help them the best way I can, so that it's not just separate tasks I do here and there.

The excerpt shows that the purposefulness of accountability work with regard to the core tasks of care is important for the acceptance of technology-assisted management practices. These practices affect workers'accountabilities and have consequences for client work and the ways in which client trust is enhanced. When directly related to client work, ICTs can benefit workers' professional development and client relations in line with normative value systems and the ethics of care work, such as in the case of familiarising oneself with clients' histories through electronic patient records.

However, care work is also increasingly framed by practices of accountability that entail assessment, reporting, budgeting and administrative tasks (Dahl and Rasmussen, 2012; Hirvonen, 2014). This accountability work by care professionals is closely related to the question of personal and system level trust. System level trust towards elder care service ultimately depends on the inclination towards risks being kept under control by service providers. Service users' confidence in the functionality of care services builds on their continual, affirmative experiences in using these services (Jaava, 2006). Thus, minimising risks and making care work more transparent with the help of ICTs can help improve citizens' trust towards care service provision at the system level.

In elder care work, this kind of risk management work by professionals requires not only appropriate managerial tools and technologies but also more immaterial resources such as time. In fact, some interviewees suggested that ICT-assisted accountability work could reduce rather than increase professionals' opportunities to engage in patient work:

One thing I've noticed in home care work is that we don't have enough staff. Yet, we need to take care of all our clients. And when we have to hurry, we make more mistakes that the worker in the next shift will have to deal with. We forget to give them their medicine, give them wrong medication or forget to order in the medication we need . . . So the time goes into correcting these mistakes, making safety incident reports online, sending and printing them and dealing with them in the unit. The mistakes build up, it's not just about correcting them, but reporting, dealing with and planning how to prevent them in the future. It's kind of a funny cycle.

More often than not, technology-mediated practices of care do not contribute directly to increasing time for face-to-face work with clients, but rather to the growing transparency of the service system. The irony in this is that for many care professionals, the rewarding aspect of elder care is precisely in the face-to-face contact with service users (Laine *et al.*, 2011; Hirvonen, 2014). Previous studies show how the growing use of ICTs by care professionals for managerial purposes often means a depersonalisation of social contact and a reduction in the autonomy of the workers' decision-making (Loos, 2008; Eriksson-Lidman *et al.*, 2012). For one, Calnan and Rowe (2008) suggest that we can no longer assume professional trust to be embodied in the professional. Instead, this trust has to be earned through careful, explicit documentation of daily work that Kuhlmann (2006) describes as 'checking-based trust'. In line with these studies, the results here suggest that although the task of 'leaving visible markers' of one's work is now a central feature of care work, the human service aspect of care work continues to be valued by both care professionals and service users, as one of the interviewees explained:

> I like it when many of my clients say that "it's nice that you're here, you do the job so well". It tells me I've managed to gain their trust. So, they trust me and are happy and give feedback . . . They're more relaxed, because sometimes old people can be very specific about certain issues, so they don't go and check that I've done everything I was supposed to. So, they know when I'm there, the job gets done.

The excerpt highlights how trust in the context of elder care is ultimately founded on a personal relationship that evolves over time in face-to-face encounters. This suggests that earning a service user's trust at the personal level, and temporal resources for such engagement, can be important for building trust in the context of professional care work. To connect this issue with the question of old people's agency, ICTs and telecare devices have proven to be useful for giving patients control of their own care, improving their autonomy and increasing the amount of information available for both service users and professionals (Pols, 2012). However, old people's capacities for such engagement varies tremendously. Opportunities to reassert personal trust in terms of face-to-face encounters between service users and care professionals therefore remain necessary for ensuring service users' equal access to good care, and also for the meaningfulness of work for care professionals.

Conclusions: the complex construction of trust in the care of old people

A growing number of old people live in their own homes at a late age, receiving both informal and formal help and care. Assuring elderly citizens that they are in good hands is a key component of a good quality of life at home. At the policy level, respect for old people's autonomy and a simultaneous assumption of their capabilities to make choices regarding their own care go hand in hand with the logic of consumer choice, which has become prominent in health and social care services in recent decades (Anttonen and Häikiö, 2011). In this chapter I have tried to demonstrate the role of ICTs from the point of view of personal level and system level trust. It would be wrong to assume that the introduction of novel ICTs into care services for old people is 'a magic bullet' that will cure all ills and automatically improve their sense of security. Rather, it seems that the enthusiasm for technologisation of care simply overlooks some crucial aspects of elder care.

First of all, the availability and acceptance of the use of ICTs among the age group 75+ varies greatly, based on an individual's life situation, their location (rural vs. urban), differences in their cognitive capacities and socio-economic and social resources (Intosalmi *et al.*, 2013; Kilpeläinen and Seppänen, 2014). In terms of using ICTs as a part of help and care, mobile phones and the possibility for 24/7 contact and communication is one of the most crucial aspects of the care of old people who continue to live in their own home. Second, family members are in a key position to introduce new devices to their elderly relatives. The social and socio-economic resources of old people and their family members, as well as the distance between family members and their elderly relatives, influence the ways in which technology is used.

The question of how best to cater for the care and help needs of a growing number of old people is an acute one. In Finland, more e-health services are now provided directly to citizens than ever before. Nevertheless, electronic information exchange between patients and health care personnel is still not widely used. According to Hyppönen *et al.* (2015), the challenge is to make e-services user-friendly and show their added value to citizens (and professionals) so as to encourage their use. This, of course, requires a renewal of service processes. In 2014, citizens' use of online e-health and e-welfare services through electronic patient records was still modest (12 per cent). The top services citizens wanted to use electronically were access to information, such as laboratory test results, and online renewal of prescriptions. Apart from prescription renewals, however, a strong belief remains that contact with care professionals cannot be replaced by e-services. This is by far the most important barrier to citizens' uptake and use of e-health and e-welfare services (Hyppönen *et al.*, 2015).

The results suggest that in ageing societies, a growing number of service users need help and assistance that require embodied, personal care (Hirvonen, 2014). Yet, the work of care professionals is not being articulated any more consciously than before, because the world of policy-making – where problems are presented in abstract, neutral terms – is a disembodied one. Hence, the outcome of the research is that apart from managerial purposes, ICT use in professional care does not necessarily contribute to client trust at the personal level, and that the use of the mobile phone as a vehicle for communication between professionals and service users remains rare in home care service work. Regarding formal care and help of old people, the growing use of managerial technology is therefore a double-edged sword. On the one hand, it enables better transparency and organisational accountability of care services. This can help in securing citizens' trust towards the care services at the system level and, ultimately, help secure the legitimacy of the welfare state. On the other, widespread managerial use of technology does not necessarily contribute to service users' sense of personal trust. Verbal and non-verbal communication between care professionals and service users remains an integral element to service users' sense of personal trust and care professionals' sense of meaningfulness of work. To improve service users' sense of personal trust, it seems that public elder care service provision has yet to take advantage of old people's growing use of mobile phones and the internet, which could provide a cost-effective and user-friendly means to reassert care relationships and service users' personal trust towards service providers.

Although only one-third of people aged 75+ currently have access to the internet in Finland, the proportion will rise with younger cohorts. The frequency of mobile phone ownership among old people therefore gives a promising example of how technology can be of great help when the distance between old people and their family members is great, as the results in this study suggest. Yet, this is so only if caring family members and old people themselves have access and the ability to use this technology. Those in the oldest age groups with low socio-economic status and with few or no next of kin are in the most precarious position in this regard. This is alarming because once they become users of ICTs, people in the age group 75–89 find that ICTs, and mobile phones in particular, increase their sense of security (Blazun, 2013; Intosalmi *et al.*, 2013). The dispersed access and ability to use technology among old people can therefore add to existing disparities in the quality of life of old people.

As a conclusion, the chapter suggests that ICT use in the care of old people needs to be assessed from a sociological point of view, with a focus on the consequences of digitalisation on both personal and system level trust, which are both essential for the legitimacy of the service system. Attention should also be paid to the great differences in the life course accumulation of social, cultural and economic capitals within old age cohorts. Attention to these resources brings about differences in individuals' cognitive, social and socio-economic capacities that greatly affect how ICTs can improve people's abilities to live independently at home and, ultimately, their quality of life.

Note

1 The data were originally collected as part of the cross-national comparative project *FLOWS - Impact of local welfare systems on female labour force participation* (EC, FP7, 2011–2014, www.flows-eu.eu).

References

Aging and Housing, 2012. Ikääntyminen ja asuminen. 75–89-vuotiaiden näkemyksiä asumisesta ja ikääntymisestä. KÄKÄTE-project Publications. Helsinki, Finland: Vanhustyön keskusliitto ja Vanhus- ja lähimmäispalvelun liitto.

Anttonen, A. and Häikiö, L., 2011. Care "going market": Finnish elderly-care policies in transition. *Nordic Journal of Social Research*, 2(2), pp. 1–21.

Blazun, H., 2013. Elderly people's quality of life with information and communication technology (ICT): toward a model of adaptation to ICT in old age. PhD Dissertation in Social Sciences and Business Studies, no 59. University of Eastern Finland.

Brandt, M., Haberkern, K. and Szydlik, M., 2009. Intergenerational help and care in Europe. *European Sociological Review*, 25(5), pp. 585–601.

Brown, P. R. and Calnan, M., 2011. The civilizing process of trust: developing quality mechanisms which are local, professional-led and thus legitimate. *Social Policy & Administration*, 45(1), pp. 19–34.

Byrne, D., Goeree, M. S., Hiedemann, B. and Stern, S., 2009. Formal home health care, informal care, and family decision making. *International Economic Review*, 54(4), pp. 1205–1242.

Calnan, M. and Rowe, R., 2008. Trust relations in a changing health service. *Journal of Health Service Research & Policy*, 13(3), pp. 97–103.

Dahl, H. M. and Rasmussen, B., 2012. Paradoxes in elderly care: the Nordic model. In: A. Kamp and H. Hvid, eds. *Elderly care in transition. Management, meaning and indentity at work: a Scandinavian perspective*. Copenhagen, Denmark: Copenhagen Business School Press.

Dampier, H., 2008. Re-reading as a methodology: the case of Boer women's testimonies. *Qualitative Research*, 8(3), pp. 367–377.

Di Luzio, G., 2006. A sociological concept of client trust. *Current Sociology*, 54(4), pp. 549–564.

Eriksson-Lidman, E., Norberg, A., Persson, B. and Strandberg, G., 2012. Healthcare personnel's experiences of situations in municipal elderly care that generate troubled conscience. *Scandinavian Journal of Caring Sciences*, 27(2), pp. 215–223.

Fortunati, L. and Taipale, S., 2012. Organization of the social sphere and typology of the residential setting in Europe: how sociability affects the adoption of the mobile phone in rural and urban locations. *Technology in Society*, 34(1), pp. 33–43.

Haddon, L., Mante-Meijer, E. and Loos, E., 2008. Introduction. In: L. Haddon, E. Mante-Meijer and E. Loos, eds. *The social dynamics of information and communication technology*. Aldershot, UK: Routledge, pp. 15–22.

Hakkarainen, P., 2012. "No good for shovelling snow and carrying firewood": social representations of computers and the internet by elderly Finnish non-users. *New Media and Society*, 14(7), pp. 1198–1215.

Higgs, P. and Gilleard, C., 2015. *Rethinking old age: theorising the fourth age*. London: Palgrave.

Hirvonen, H., 2014. From embodied to disembodied professionalism? Discussing the implications of medico-managerial management in welfare service work. *Social Policy & Administration*, 48(5), pp. 576–593.

Hyppönen, H., Hämäläinen, P. and Reponen, J., 2015. *eHealth and eWelfare of Finland: checkpoint 2015*. Helsinki, Finland: National Institute for Health and Welfare.

Intosalmi, H., Nykänen, J. and Stenberg, L., 2013. Teknologian käyttö ja asenteet 75–89-vuotiailla. Raportti kyselytutkimuksesta. KÄKÄTE-projekti. Helsinki, Finland: Vanhustyön keskusliitto ja Vanhus- ja lähimmäispalvelun liitto.

Jaava, J., 2006. Trust as a decision: the problems and functions of trust in Luhmannian systems theory. PhD Dissertation. University of Helsinki.

Jolanki, O., Szebehely, M. and Kauppinen, K., 2013. Family rediscovered? Working carers of older people in Finland and Sweden. In: T. Kröger and S. Yeandle, eds. *Combining paid work and family care: policies and experiences in international perspective*. Bristol, UK: Policy Press, pp. 53–69.

Kilpeläinen, A. and Seppänen, M., 2014. Information technology and everyday life in ageing rural villages. *Journal of Rural Studies*, 33, pp. 1–8.

Kouvo, A., Kankainen, T. and Niemelä, M., 2012. Welfare benefits and generalized trust in Finland and Europe. In: H. Ervasti, J. G. Andersen, T. Fridberg and K. Ringdal, eds. *The future of the welfare state: social policy attitudes and social capital in Europe*. Cheltenham, UK: Edward Elgar Publishing, pp. 296–328.

Kröger, T. and Leinonen, A., 2011. Home care in Finland. In: T. Rostgaard, C. Glendinning, C. Gori, T. Kröger, A. Österle, M. Szebehely, H. Theobald, V. Timonen and M. Vabø, eds. *Livindhome: living independently at home: reforms in home care in 9 European countries*. Copenhagen, Denmark: SFI – Danish National Centre for Social Research, pp. 117–138.

Kuhlmann, E., 2006. Traces of doubt and sources of trust: health professions in an uncertain society. *Current Sociology*, 54(4), pp. 607–620.

Kunk, L. M., 2010. Prioritizing parental autonomy: adult children's accounts of feeling responsible and supporting aging parents. *Journal of Aging Studies*, 24(1), pp. 57–64.

Laine, M., Kokkinen, L., Kaarlela-Tuomaala, A., Valtanen, E., Elovainio, M., Suomi, R. and Keinänen, M., 2011. *Sosiaali- ja terveysalan työolot 2010. Kahden vuosikymmenen kehityskulku.* Helsinki, Finland: Työterveyslaitos.

Leikas, J. and Saariluoma, P., 2008. "Worth" and mental contents in designing for ageing citizens' form of life. *Gerontechnology*, 7(3), pp. 305–318.

Loos, E., 2008. Using ICT in human service organisations: an enabling constraint? Social workers, new technology and their organisation. In: L. Haddon, E. Mante-Meijer and E. Loos, eds. *The social dynamics of information and communication technology*. Aldershot, UK: Routledge, pp. 119–132.

Luhmann, N., 1979. *Trust and power*. Chichester, UK: Wiley.

Ministry of Social Affairs and Health, 2015. *Information to support well-being and service renewal: eHealth and eSocial strategy 2020*. Helsinki, Finland: Ministry of Social Affairs and Health.

Pols, J., 2012. *Care at a distance: on the closeness of technology*. Amsterdam: Amsterdam University Press.

Rasi, P. and Kilpeläinen, A., 2016. Older people's use of learning of new media: a case study on remote rural villages in Finnish Lapland. In: J. Zhou and G. Salvenrdy, eds. *Human aspects of it for the aged population. Healthy and active aging, PART II*, Second International Conference, ITAP 2016 Proceedings. Switzerland: Springer International Publishing, pp. 239–247.

Robinson, R. and Jackson, E., 2001. Is trust in others declining in America? An age-period-cohort analysis. *Social Science Research*, 30(1), pp. 117–145.

Santiago, R. and Carvalho, T., 2015. Towards changes in professions and professionalism: academics, doctors and nurses. In: T. Carvalho and R. Santiago, eds. *Professionalism, managerialism and the health services.* Basingstoke, UK: Palgrave, pp. 1–12.

Statistics Finland, 2015. Use of information and communication technology by individuals. www.stat.fi/til/sutivi/2015/sutivi_2015_2015-11-26_tie_001_en.html.

Strategic Government Programme, 2016. *Action plan for the implementation of the key projects and reforms defined in the Strategic Government Programme.* Finnish Government Publications 1/2016. Helsinki: Prime Minister's Office.

Taipale, S., 2013. The dimensions of mobilities: the spatial relationships between corporeal and digital mobilities. *Social Science Research*, 43, pp. 157–167.

Taipale, S., De Luca, F., Sarrica, M. and Fortunati, L., 2015. Robot shift from industrial production to social reproduction. In: J. Vincent, S. Taipale, B. Sapio, L. Fortunati and G. Lugano, eds. *Social robots from a human perspective*. London: Springer, pp. 11–24.

Tronto, J., 1993. *Moral boundaries: a political argument for an ethic of care*. New York: Routledge.

UN E-government Survey, 2014. United Nations Department of Economic and Social Affairs. New York: United Nations.

Van Wynsberghe, A., 2011. Designing robots for care: care centered value-sensitive design. *Science Engineering Ethics*, 19(2), pp. 407–433.

10 Mobile phone use and social generations in rural India

Sirpa Tenhunen

Introduction

Mannheim (1952) introduced the concept of social generation – people who were born during the same date range and share similar cultural experiences – and it has since been developed to include human agency and social divisions, such as gender, class and race (Aboim and Vasconcelos, 2014; Woodman and Wyn, 2015). In its sense of kinship descent, the concept of generation has a long tradition in social anthropology (Kertzer, 1983). However, the notion of social generation has mostly been applied to Western countries, whereas, particularly, anthropological scholarship of India has examined social relationships mainly through the concepts of gender, kinship and caste. My earlier research revealed how positions in the kinship system influence mobile phone use patterns in rural India and, in turn, how phone use mediates changes in family and kinship (Tenhunen, 2014). Nevertheless, rural India has experienced numerous social changes that have influenced different generations in distinct ways. In this chapter, I explore these generational differences in the appropriation of mobile phones in rural India.

Broad changes such as the decline of agriculture, changes in caste and gender relationships, and rising levels of education that have influenced rural West Bengal where I carried out my research, are also prevalent in other parts of rural India (Kumar, 2016; Otten and Simpson, 2016). In fact, much of my motivation to carry out long-term ethnographic fieldwork in rural West Bengal is based on my interest in these changes. Every visit has revealed new and interesting developments, and mobile telephony was just one of the many changes I witnessed during my fieldwork.

Demographic changes make crucial contributions to the formation of social generations; consequently, I start by briefly exploring demographic trends in India and more specifically in rural West Bengal. Next, I describe ongoing social changes in the region – the decline of agriculture, changes in caste and gender relationships, and rising levels of education – to examine how the changes that resulted in the formation of social generations influenced different age groups. Thereafter, I analyse how social generations use phones in distinct ways as part of local hierarchies. My identification of different mobile phone user groups reveals that it is especially the groups whose structural position has undergone changes that use mobile phones to negotiate their positions in local hierarchies. These groups are youth, high caste women and low caste people. I also demonstrate that social generations do not evolve or use new media in isolation from each other; instead the younger generation plays an important role in helping the elder generation use calling functions of mobile phones as well as to access the internet.

My fieldwork site, Janta, is a multi-caste village in the eastern state of West Bengal with 2,441 inhabitants (Census of India, 2011a), the majority of whom earn their livelihood from paddy cultivation and vegetable farming. This chapter is based on interviews, observation and survey data on the use of mobile phones in 2005, 2007–2008, 2010 and 2012–2013. I also draw from my earlier work in Janta in 1999–2000 and 2003–2004.[1]

Age groups formed an important context for both the diffusion and appropriation of mobile phones in Janta. When I searched for phone owners in Janta, I was usually introduced to young men. However, the very first phone in the village was acquired by an elderly woman's sons for her. Her sons had emigrated from the village and the phone helped them stay in touch with their mother. The first group of mobile phone buyers were adult men: micro entrepreneurs as well as car and tractor drivers who found phones useful for staying in touch with customers and calling for help if they experienced problems on the road. As mobile phones became associated with communicating with kin, it became common for women to receive mobile phones as gifts from their fathers, brothers or husbands.

When inexpensive smart phones became available around 2011, it was again time for the young men to express their technological agency by pioneering the use of smart phones – if their older models were still working, they were kept in the house and used by the rest of the family, particularly by women, who usually stay at home more than men do. At the same time, women who moved outside the home for work or study started to acquire personal phones. Young women also preferred smart phones and expressed their technological agency and aspirations for change by readily discussing the multiple functions of these phones and demonstrating their ability to use them. The following discussion begins with a description of demographic trends in the village before moving to explore the social changes that contributed to the abovementioned generational differences in mobile phone use.

Social changes

The population in Janta is predominantly young and the village has a skewed male-female ratio (see Figure 10.1). Both these striking demographic trends are in line with broader trends in India. India has the largest youth population – 356 million 10- to 24-year-olds – as well as one of the world's most skewed gender ratios (The UNFPA Report, 2014). According to the 2011 census, the ratio of female children in the age group 0–6 years had decreased from 945 to 914 per 1,000 male children, the lowest level since India's independence. The imbalance is explained by girls receiving poorer nutrition and health care than boys, as well as the higher rate of abortion of female foetuses. In particular, wealthy urban Indians influence the sex ratio by ascertaining the sex of their unborn child with ultrasound tests and aborting female foetuses, even though this is illegal in India. There are also

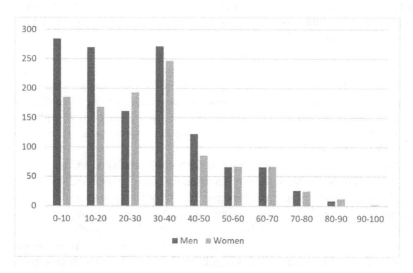

Figure 10.1 Age groups according to gender in Janta.

significantly fewer girls than boys in Janta, which may indicate the neglect of female children, as I did not find any evidence of villagers determining the sex of unborn children with ultrasound.

The quintessential Janta village scene of cows and goats and a cluster of small brick and mud houses connected by dirt roads and paths, hides the fact that the village experienced diverse social upheavals. Land reforms and the increase in agricultural productivity due to the introduction of new farming technologies improved the living conditions of small farmers and landless labourers after India's independence in 1948 and during the communist party (CPI(M)) rule of the state of West Bengal (1977–2011). Extreme poverty, which manifested itself as occasional food scarcity, disappeared from Janta in the 1990s, reflecting the decrease in poverty[2] in the entire state from 73 per cent to 32 per cent during 1977–2000 (Banerjee *et al.*, 2002). In Janta, affluent houses have television sets, motorcycles, tractors, jeeps and, from 2003 onwards, mobile phones. However, for most villagers, the rise in living standards has meant small but important improvements in their quality of life. Daily labourers have prospered in that they can now afford a more balanced diet, better quality clothing, soap and oil. The villagers' understanding of the essentials of the standard of living is summed up by the Bengali expression *khaua–makha–pora*, which literally means eating, anointing the skin with oil, and clothing.

Since the economic liberalisation in the 1990s, small farms have, however, become less profitable due to increases in farming costs and decreases in the prices of agricultural products. Only large-scale farmers have continued to make profits, thanks to the greater volume of their production and investments in side businesses. Smaller farmers' main coping strategy has thus been to send young men to work as paid labourers, mainly in the southern and western parts of India.

Class crucially overlaps with caste in Janta, and the village is divided into caste neighbourhoods. The dominant caste, both numerically and in terms of land ownership in Janta, is the Tilis (50 per cent). Other major caste groups are the Bagdis (15 per cent) and Casas (16 per cent). Most Tilis and Casas own land, while most Bagdis, who are classified as a scheduled caste, earn their livelihood by means of daily labour, mainly agricultural work or work in the brick factories. In Janta, 87 per cent of Bagdis are landless, whereas 59 per cent of Tilis are landowners. Villagers know one another's caste identity, while strangers' caste identity is assessed on the basis of their dialect and behaviour, or directly inquired, unlike in the cities, where it is no longer such an appropriate topic for conversation with strangers.

Caste is a social institution that evolved from Hindu religious thinking during the Veda epoch (1000–600 BC), which defines the cosmic order into four hierarchically organised categories, or varnas, based on purity: the Brahmins, the highest group, are in charge of religious rules, speech and prayers; the Kshatriyas, the warrior caste, maintain and conserve the sacred order (dharma); and the Vaishyas, as merchant caste, create prosperity. The Shudras, the lowest caste, serve the upper castes with their manual labour (Stern, 1993, p. 55). The varna classification of the religious texts does not, however, reflect how caste is classified in everyday life in India, as only the Brahmins are labelled by their varna title. Other castes are called by their local jati names – jati is a wide-spread local term for caste. Hierarchical standing of numerous jati groups is locally determined, but in relation to the varna hierarchy and its principles. The higher the caste, the purer it is held to be. The concepts of purity are not associated with hygiene, but with the distance from biological processes like birth, death and refuse. For example, the skinning of animals, fishing, cleaning, cremation and laundering are impure professions. The impurity is transmitted when a person touches one who is purer, or when the purer one enjoys food or drink prepared by someone who is considered ritually less pure.

Whereas small farmers experienced a sharp rise in their standards of living in the 1990s and their position has become increasingly precarious, landless and scheduled caste labourers have prospered since 2000. Bagdis, the lowest caste groups of the village, benefit from their caste status in that they have traditionally worked at the tile factories in the region. As work at the brick kilns is not available during the rainy season, Bagdis also work as agricultural labourers. The Rural Employment Guarantee Programme (NREGA), which officially guarantees at least 100 days of paid unskilled manual work annually, has increased job opportunities for casual work. Although in practice people obtain less work than is guaranteed, the NREGA has diversified their sources of income. Moreover, government quotas have given scheduled castes real possibilities for class mobility, as almost half of the jobs in India's central government and seats of education have been reserved for scheduled castes and tribes (Varshney, 2000). Even if quotas have only helped a few Bagdis in the village to obtain salaried jobs, these exceptional career paths are important tangible examples of emerging new opportunities.

There are signs of the lessening of caste discrimination, as low castes are no longer dependent on the few large landowners of the dominant caste. In addition, opportunities for inter-caste socialising, which starts in primary schools where children of all castes have their central government-sponsored midday meal together, have increased. Yet, caste groups still live and interact in their own neighbourhoods, and inter-caste marriages are rare. Higher castes seldom visit lower caste neighbourhoods and lower castes enter higher caste neighbourhood as day labourers, to sell fish and vegetables, or just to chat with higher castes. When lower castes do visit the homes of higher castes, they usually stand or sit in the yard – they do not enter the house. Lower caste labourers have their meals on the veranda as part of their payment, but they never enter the higher caste house, and higher castes do not eat food prepared in lower caste houses.

Despite the continuity of caste discrimination, Bagdis are not particularly motivated to organise themselves in order to change their position as a caste group, neither have the scheduled castes in the entire state of West Bengal joined the Dalit movement through which scheduled castes have organised, particularly in the western parts of India. The lower castes in Janta talk about imitating the upper strata of village society in terms of consumption, of being able to eat and dress so well that they can no longer be recognised as low, thereby circumventing the purity criteria for social ascent by striving for a new identity through consumption.

Another major change in India – and in Janta – is the increase in the levels of education. Literacy rates have improved in India during the last decade by 9 percentage points, and the improvement among women has been more pronounced than among men. Primary school enrolment at the age of six has become nearly universal, although the dropout rate remains high (Rustagi, 2009). In 2011, 74 per cent of men and 58 per cent of women in Janta were literate (Census of India, 2011a). The same figures for India are 82 per cent for men and 65 per cent for women (Census of India, 2011b). As Figure 10.2 shows, in Janta the decline in illiteracy has been most dramatic among higher caste females, for example the age group 11–15 is fully literate. This is the highest rate in any age group, and is also higher than the literacy of high caste boys in the same age group. High caste women have thus caught up with men in terms of literacy, and the younger age groups in the low castes are catching up with the high castes, but the gap between the literacy levels of low and high castes is still wide. Both upper and low caste women have experienced significant improvements in education in comparison to upper caste men. As a result, upper caste men have been losing their relative advantage in education.

Women were allocated quotas in the local governing organs, *panchayats*, in 1993. During the CPI(M) rule of West Bengal (1977–2011), women of all castes joined *mahila samiti*s (women's committees) and regularly attended meetings. The women's committees focused on raising women's consciousness about their rights and motivating women to participate in *panchayat* led programs. The first female panchayat representative from Janta, Tapati Kundu, arranged income earning opportunities and a literacy program for women. According to her (Kundu, 2000), women should identify and protest against cultural practices that are harmful to them. She advocated the protection of the kinship-related morality by protesting against women's mistreatment and demanding that men should fulfil their duties as breadwinners. However, Kundu also demanded changes in central

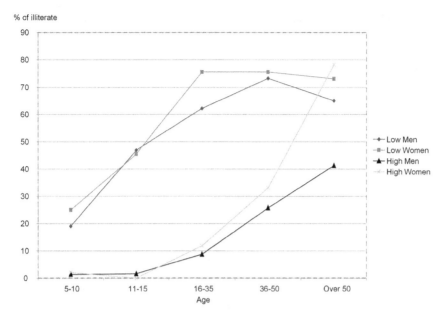

% of illiterate

Figure 10.2 Illiteracy rate according to gender and caste status in Janta.

cultural institutions including the marriage system, by advocating women's rights to divorce, to earn an income and for the eradication of the dowry system.

Even if female representatives have taken active political roles, the scope of the panchayats' powers is limited, and state policies towards women have been ambiguous. While involving women in its activities and state administration, the ruling CPI(M) party carried out land reform without considering women as land owners until most of the land had been distributed (Basu, 1992). In India, land mainly gets passed by inheritance through the male line, and ideas of the home as the women's place prevent women from participating in market activities such as running small-scale businesses. Only a few middle-class women have benefitted from women's rights economically, as these discourses encouraged them to obtain college education, which qualifies them for public sector jobs. The first upper caste girls (Tilis and Brahmins) of Janta graduated from college in the 1990s, and two of them found white-collar jobs (one as a teacher and the other in public administration) soon after. Like middle-class women, only a few upper caste women have followed these occupational footsteps in the subsequent decades.

Mobile phone user generations

Based on the abovementioned changes, I delineate three age groups in relation to mobile phone use. These groups also form social generations due to their experiences of different social changes. Those in the age group 40+ are illiterate or have a low level of education. Consequently, they are unable to browse the internet. I frequently witnessed how many could not even make a phone call without help. Most people in this age group know numbers as written in Bengali script. Mobile telephones with Bengali script were initially available, but in 2012 I no longer saw these around; most people had switched to using Chinese phones, which use the English alphabet. Therefore, most people in this age group can answer a phone, but are unable to read and type numbers written in English script. The reason for this age group's inability to learn English is that in 1981, the state's former ruling Marxist government banned the study of English in schools up to class 5; however, English was re-introduced from class 2 in 1999.[3]

A technical ability to use a phone matters; nevertheless, the inability to read English numbers and text does not exclude anyone from calling, because phones are shared and people are helped to use a phone. I witnessed both young men and women acting as phone use experts in their families. Consequently, intergenerational relationships give the elder generation access to digital media similarly to rural China, where Oreglia (2014) discovered unlikely ICT users in older women who maintained relationships and accessed online entertainment after receiving training from their children. Similar kinds of assistance relationships have been observed in many locations, both in developing and developed countries. Based on her research on internet users in North America, Bakardjieva (2005) established the concept of a 'warm expert' to refer to the local technical expert who is sympathetic to those who need help and support with ICTs and who has knowledge about the people s/he helps. Many people worldwide are also involved in proxy internet use, defined as using the internet on somebody else's behalf or relying on others to access the internet (Selwyn *et al.*, 2016).

The importance of education for mobile phone use was highlighted when I observed a 12-year-old girl effortlessly learning to browse English language information from the internet by means of a smart phone while the older, less educated generation in the same family needed help to just type in a number. Since mobile phones are not considered private, children play an important role in enabling the elder generation's phone use by helping them manage the phone's functions. A wealth of studies (Fortunati, 2001; Kasesniemi and Rautiainen, 2002; Wilska, 2003; Höflich and Hartmann, 2006; Ito *et al.*, 2006; Yoon, 2006a, 2006b) demonstrate that teens and children use digital media to construct identity and fine-tune social relationships, especially in Western countries. In Janta, the generational divide differs from that in most Western countries, since children and teens in rural India still rarely have a chance to independently use digital media. Most people simply cannot afford to allow their children to make regular phone calls. Although children are not perceived as consumers with a certain degree of autonomy, as in Western countries, in Janta both girls and boys are skilled at operating phones, even smartphones, which they use to play games and listen to music.

Like children, the age group 25–40 is better educated than the older generation, and most of the first college-educated people in the village belong to this cohort. Consequently, this generation has the ability to use phones independently. In addition, they are the first generation to grow up experiencing the decrease in the

importance of farming, and young men in this group, considered the main opera-
tors and owners of household phones, are more motivated to use their phones to
build networks outside the village than older generations. The majority of phone
owners mentioned calling relatives as the main reason for obtaining their phone.
However, in practice, men call their friends more than their relatives.

Women in this age group of 25–40 are influenced by the women's movement
in India. The most important function of mobile phones for young married women
is to better connect with their natal families, as for most women, natal families
are a major source of support in times of difficulties. Women appreciate how
mobile phones offer them the possibility to move away so that fewer people are
within hearing distance, although it is seldom possible to make a call in complete
privacy. For instance, young daughters-in-law told me that they usually call their
natal homes when the in-laws are not at home. Another example is a mother I
observed advising her daughter over the phone to disobey the mother-in-law. Her
daughter had married into a well-to-do family, where the daughter was expected
to take responsibility for all housework, while the mother-in-law did very little.
Although the villagers considered the daughter as happily married because she
had married into a wealthy family, the division of work between the women of
the household was not considered fair. The woman's mother saw that the only
solution was that her daughter should express her view and refuse the excessive
work in her in-law's house. Without the phone, the chances for this conversation
would have been limited because the mother would usually only meet her daughter surrounded by the daughter's in-laws. As Lim (2016) argues, based on studies
of diasporic families in Asia, families are actively 'done', shaped and reshaped,
through mobile communication.

Whereas in many parts of India women's mobile phone use has been experienced as a threat to the marriage system (Grodzins Gold, 2009; Doron, 2012;
Jouhki, 2013; Kärki, 2013), in rural West Bengal the marriage system and the
ensuing hierarchical relationships between kin groups encourage and legitimise
women's mobile phone use. The old practice of maintaining relationships with the
in-laws has continued, with a new emphasis on women as initiators of contact. It
is tangible proof of the change that it has become common practice for newlywed
wives to stay in touch with their parents over the phone right after their marriage, whereas just a decade ago I observed that contact between kin groups was
avoided for a year after the marriage. Mobile phones help women to cultivate the
matrilineal tendencies in the kinship system and thereby challenge male domi-
nance. Furthermore, women's increasing access to mobile phones influences the
kinship code of conduct and kinship hierarchies within families and between kin
groups. Motivated by women's rights discourses and political activism, women
use phones to realise their goals of widening the domestic sphere.

Mobile phones are a double-edged sword in that they undermine the author-
ity structure of joint families, which could contribute to conflicts and make young
women vulnerable. However, since women who call their parents often receive
money for their calls from their husbands, women's calling does not lead to conflicts
with husbands, which long visits to women's natal families could. A husband who

provides money for his wife's calls strengthens his relationship with his wife and loosens the grip of the joint family on the couple's relationship. Moreover, women calling their natal families serves to reduce the distance between the kin groups, which can have unintended consequences for the meaning of all kin relationships.

Generations within local hierarchies

The concept of social generation has appealed to market researchers in their quest to understand generational differences in consumption through such notions as Generation Y, which has mostly been used to refer to young and adventurous consumers mainly in Western countries, but also in India. For example, Jain and Pant (2015) identify Generation Y as those born between 1980 and 2000, from three Indian metropolises. Nevertheless, their description focuses clearly on upper class youth since they are the ones who can afford to access multiple media simultaneously. In rural West Bengal, class and caste crucially influence the above discussed age groups' experiences and phone use. The biggest barrier for both men's and women's phone use is the cost of calling. Low-income families share the understanding that phones need to be used sparingly, thus reflecting their financial means, whereas the upper classes can spend generously on phone calls. I will next discuss how local hierarchies influence the meaning of new media within generations.

Considering the difficulties many villagers face in using even basic phones for calling, I was surprised to discover in 2012 that most households had a Chinese-made smartphone. I was told that nowadays Bagdis (the lowest caste) have acquired fancy phones. These inexpensive Chinese smartphones cost around INR 700 (€9.5),[4] which equals approximately one week of a daily labourer's salary, and they are internet ready. Most people in the scheduled caste neighbourhood of the village did not own a television when they purchased a Chinese smartphone. When I told my upper caste friends in the town of Vishnupur about the popularity of smartphones among the Bagdis, they commented that common people's use of phones as entertainment centres entails the misuse of phones, which should be used for making calls. The low castes and classes' use of mobile phones for entertainment stirred controversy, because their new ability to possess such advanced technological gadgets was deemed as disruptive of local hierarchies – apparently, a Bagdi caste person owning a smartphone challenges upper castes' views of lower castes as backward. Although Bagdis did not buy branded phones, their smartphones are a similar statement of identity that confirms their relative improvement in relation to the upper, land owning castes in the village. Smartphones represent Bagdis' services and consumer products from which they had been excluded. This exclusion, in turn, had contributed to their social standing in neo-liberal India where media images have delineated the urban middle classes as the consumers of not just the newly available commodities but also of the new India produced through the meanings of these commodities (Fernandes, 2000).

Even though most households now own smartphones, only a few people used their personal phones to browse the internet in the village. Those who accessed the internet with their personal phones all had college education and therefore belong to a minority. In 2012–13, I found 33 villagers (1.4 per cent of the population of the village, the total population of which was 2,441 in 2011) who either had a college degree or were studying in college. Two sisters had used a service provider's free trial period to access the internet via their mobile phone, but had not continued after this period had expired. Two young men, both of whom had service jobs, occasionally used search engines to browse the internet after the free trial period. They also accessed Facebook through their mobile phones. Others used the internet to download music and films, find out about prices, products, jobs and exam results, as well as to send email and access study sources. Since the screens of low-cost smartphones are small, browsing the internet with a phone is difficult; consequently, even people who are able to use search engines to browse the internet with their phones often preferred to use internet shops to, for example, access exam questions and results.

Smartphone owners who did not have a college education found that the phone's most interesting feature was it could be used for leisure activities. They preferred to use their internet-ready phones for listening to music, taking and storing photos, and watching movies. Instead of browsing the internet directly through their smart phones, most people use the internet indirectly on their phones. They buy music, videos and pictures, which are downloaded on the phone's memory chip. The usual package sold in the downloading shop in Janta includes popular Hindi and Bengali songs and films, devotional music, pictures of scenery, women, film stars, and gods and goddesses.

The availability of internet-ready phones in Janta has not, regardless of class and education, caused people to become internet users. Grasping the textual content of the internet requires more than the average level of education in the village and thus, only those with a college education can use search engines to browse the internet. Like mobile calls, internet use is considered expensive: the lowest monthly fee was INR 98 (€1.3) in 2013, which only offers a limited number of gigabytes and a slow connection. Most people preferred to spend this amount on cable television instead of internet connection as it is possible to get more than 100 television channels for INR 100 per month.

As Donner (2015, p. 153) argues, practitioners, theorists and policymakers should be wary of proclaiming that the digital divide between developed and developing countries has been bridged thanks to smartphones. Access to the internet by means of smartphones does not provide the same affordances as a broadband connection by means of a desktop or laptop computer. In addition to the difficulties of reading on a small screen, it is hard to use smartphones to author internet content, which is one of the key affordances of the internet, as compared to printed text. Moreover, when every click on the internet costs money, users are likely to conserve airtime and their data bundles' balance carefully.

Conclusions

My exploration of social generations in rural India highlights how people's positions in hierarchical social structures shape the formation of social generations as well as how the generations use new media. Moreover, in Janta village, the generational divide in mobile phone use is different from most Western countries since children and teens in rural India still rarely have a chance to use digital media autonomously. Most children and youth do not possess their own personal phones and therefore cannot use mobile phones and social media to strengthen ties with their peers, as youth in many parts of the world do. Nevertheless, they play an important role in making mobile telephony accessible for the elder generation: in rural West Bengal, the 'soft expert' is usually the younger family member rather than a peer or friend. The situation in Janta also differs from many other locations (Bakardjieva, 2005; Oreglia, 2014) in that people rely not only on others for using the internet but also for using the calling functions of the phones. By taking an expert role with regard to the mundane use of mobile phones, children and young adults are able to introduce subtle changes in family hierarchies, which is customarily based on seniority. The younger generation, understood broadly as people who are in junior positions in their families, therefore use mobile phones to contest family hierarchies and build networks outside the family, more than the elder generation who are able to use mobile phones only with the help of an intermediary.

Much of the anthropological research on the use of mobile phones has an emphasis on the way technologies tend to reinforce existing structures and, especially, adherence to kinship patterns (Horst and Miller, 2006; Barendregt, 2008; Archambault, 2011; Doron, 2012; Jouhki, 2013; Lipset, 2013). Applying the concept of generation helps to shift attention to how phones are used as part of social changes. The identification of different mobile phone user groups reveals that it is especially the groups whose structural position has undergone changes that use mobile phones to negotiate local hierarchies: youth, high caste women and low caste people. Therefore, not only do social generations reflect objective social changes, they also provide opportunities for agency, which in turn crucially shape generational experiences.

Notes

1 My earlier research in Janta focused on gender, politics, and exchange relationships (Tenhunen, 2003, 2008, 2011).
2 The official poverty line in India was calculated based on the minimum energy requirements until 2011, when a new poverty line based on a cost of living was introduced.
3 Primary education from class 1 to 10 in India is for children aged 6 to 14 years old.
4 In 2013, the minimum payment for daily workers according to the standards set by the government work scheme NREGA in India was INR 174.

References

Aboim, S. and Vasconcelos, P., 2014. From political to social generations: a critical reappraisal of Mannheim's classical approach. *European Journal of Social Theory*, 17(2), pp. 165–183.

Archambault, J., 2011. Breaking up 'because of the phone' and the transformative potential of information in Southern Mozambique. *New Media and Society* 13, pp. 444–456.

Bakardjieva, M., 2005. *Internet society: the internet in everyday life*. London: SAGE.

Banerjee, A., Pranab, B., Basu, K., Datta, M., Chaudhury, M. D., Ghatak, M., Guha, A. S., Majumdar, M., Mookherjee, D. and Ray, D., 2002. Strategy for economic reform in West Bengal. *Economic and Political Weekly*, 37(41), pp. 4203–4218.

Barendregt, B., 2008. Sex, cannibals, and the language of cool, Indonesian tales of the phone and modernity. *The Information Society*, 24(3), pp. 160–170.

Basu, A., 1992. *Two faces of protest: contrasting modes of women's activism in India*. Berkeley, CA: University of California Press.

Census of India, 2011a. *Primary census abstracts*. West Bengal, New Delhi: Office of the Registrar General and Census Commissioner.

Census of India, 2011b. Provisional population totals [online] www.censusindia.gov.in/2011-prov-results/indiaatglance.html.

Donner, J., 2015. *After access: inclusion, development, and a more mobile internet*. Cambridge, MA: The MIT Press.

Doron, A., 2012. Mobile persons, cell phones, gender and the self in North India. *The Asia Pacific Journal of Anthropology*, 13(5), pp. 414–433.

Fernandes, L., 2000. Nationalizing 'the global', media images, cultural politics and the middle class in India. *Media, Culture and Society*, 22(5), pp. 611–628.

Fortunati, L., 2001. The mobile phone, an identity on the move. *Personal and Ubiquitous Computing* 5, pp. 98–85.

Grodzins Gold, S., 2009. Tasteless profits and vexed moralities: assessments of the present in rural Rajasthan. *Journal of the Royal Anthropological Institute*, 15(2), pp. 365–385.

Höflich, J. R. and Hartman, M., eds., 2006. *Mobile communication in everyday life: ethnographic views, observations and reflections*. Berlin: Frank and Timme.

Horst, H. and Miller, D., 2006. *The cell phone: an anthropology of communication*. Oxford, UK: Berg.

Ito, M., Daisuke, O. and Matsuda, M., eds., 2006. *Personal, portable, pedestrian: mobile phones in Japanese life*. Cambridge, MA: MIT Press.

Jain, V. and Pant, S., 2015. Positioning generation Y for effective mobile communication: the case of three cities in India. *Transnational Marketing Journal*, 3(1), pp. 1–25.

Jouhki, J., 2013. A phone of one's own? Social value, cultural meaning and gendered use of the mobile phone in South India. *Journal of the Finnish Anthropological Society*, 38(1), pp. 37–58.

Kärki, J., 2013. 'If my daughter runs away, I will drink poison': an anthropological study of child marriage in North Indian villages. Unpublished Master's Thesis manuscript. Helsinki, Finland: University of Helsinki.

Kasesniemi, E.-L. and Rautiainen, P., 2002. Mobile communication of children and teenagers in Finland. In: J. Katz and M. Aakhus, eds. *Perpetual contact: mobile communication, private talk and public performance*. Cambridge, MA: Cambridge University Press, pp. 170–193.

Kertzer, D. L., 1983. Generation as a sociological problem. *Annual Review Sociology*, 9, pp. 125–149.

Kumar, S., 2016. Agrarian transformation and the new rurality in western Uttar Pradesh. *Economic and Political Weekly*, 37(19), pp. 61–71.

Kundu, T., 2000. Personal interview with Tapati Kundu.

Lim, S. S., ed., 2016. *Mobile communication and the family: Asian experiences in technology domestication*. Dordrecht, The Netherlands: Springer.

Lipset, D., 2013. Mobail: moral ambivalence and the domestication of mobile telephones in peri-urban Papua New Guinea. *Culture, Theory and Critique*, 54(3), pp. 335–354.

Mannheim, K., 1952 [1927]. The problem of generations. In: P. Kecskemeti, ed. *Essays on the sociology of knowledge*. London: Routledge and Kegan Paul.

Oreglia, E., 2014. ICT and (personal) development in rural China. *Information Technologies and International Development*, 10(3), pp. 19–30.

Otten, T. and Simpson, E., 2016. F G Bailey's Bisipara revisited. *Economic and Political Weekly*, 37(19), pp. 25–32.

Rustagi, P., ed., 2009. *Concerns, conflicts, and cohesions: universalization of elementary education in India*. New Delhi: Oxford University Press.

Selwyn, N., Johnson, N., Nemorin, S. and Knight, E., 2016. *Going online on behalf of others: an investigation of 'proxy' internet consumers*. Sydney: Australian Communications Consumer Action Network.

Stern, R. W., 1993. *Changing India*. New Delhi: Foundation Books.

Tenhunen, S., 2003. Culture and political agency, gender, kinship and village politics in West Bengal. *Contributions to Indian Sociology*, 37(3), pp. 495–518.

Tenhunen, S., 2008. Mobile technology in the village, ICTs, culture, and social logistics in India. *Journal of the Royal Anthropological Institute*, 14(3), pp. 515–534.

Tenhunen, S., 2011. Culture, conflict and translocal communication, mobile technology and politics in rural West Bengal, India. *Ethnos*, 76(3), pp. 398–420.

Tenhunen, S., 2014. Mobile technology, mediation and gender in rural India. *Contemporary South Asia*, 22(2), pp. 157–170.

The UNFPA report, 2014. The state of world population: the power of 1.8 billion, adolescents, youth and the transformation of the future. www.unfpa.org/sites/default/files/pub-pdf/EN-SWOP14-Report_FINAL-web.pdf.

Varshney, A., 2000. Is India becoming more democratic? *Journal of Asian Studies*, 59(1), pp. 3–25.

Wilska, T.-A., 2003. Mobile phone use as part of young people's consumption styles. *Journal of Consumer Policy*, 26, pp. 441–463.

Woodman, D. and Wyn, J., 2015. Class, gender and generation matter: using the concept of social generation to study inequality and social change. *Journal of Youth Studies*, 18(10), pp. 1402–1410.

Yoon, K., 2006a. The making of neo-Confucian cyberkids: representations of young mobile phone users in South Korea. *New Media and Society*, 8(5), pp. 771–753.

Yoon, K., 2006b. Local sociality in young people's mobile communications: a Korean case study. *Childhood*, 13(2), pp.174–155.

Part III

Consumption, lifestyles and markets

11 Necessities to all?

The role of ICTs in the everyday life of the middle-aged and elderly between 1999 and 2014

Terhi-Anna Wilska and Sanna-Mari Kuoppamäki

Introduction

The devices of the new information and communication technology (ICT) have become essential parts of everyday life. ICTs are incorporated in people's lives through forms of social networking and knowledge formation that promote new kinds of interactions and collaborations between people in different social and demographic groups. Nearly everyone owns a mobile phone, while the ownership of personal computers (PCs), smartphones and tablet computers has increased significantly in all age groups (Statistics Finland, 2015). However, there is little quantitative research on the significance of ICTs, as to how necessary they are considered in everyday life, especially among older users of these goods and services. Particularly, longitudinal studies in the older population are rare.

Much research has been conducted on the topic of digital divides, pointing out both socio-economic and socio-demographic differences in use and access. In terms of age related differences, younger generations are frequently regarded as 'born digital'. They have been called 'digital natives' whereas older generations seem doomed to be forever 'digital immigrants' (e.g. Prensky, 2001; Herold, 2012; Lugano and Peltonen, 2012). This view of a generational divide has been contested by many researchers, however, and the importance of time, period, life course stage and lifestyle-related matters offer a more nuanced understanding when explaining access, ownership and ICT use in different age groups (Helsper and Eynon, 2010; White and Le Cornu, 2011; Bolin, 2014; Gilleard *et al.*, 2015; Taipale, 2016). Research suggests that the use of and need for digital technologies varies over time and across the life course, as well as with changes in family composition, in patterns of work and leisure, and in people's social life (Spero and Stone, 2004; Livingstone *et al.*, 2005).

The aim of this chapter is to study how the perceived necessity of PCs, the internet and mobile phone for middle-aged and elderly people (aged 45–74) has developed during the period 1999–2014 in Finland. Drawing upon four waves of cross-sectional data, we explore both cohort/generation- and period-based approaches. The 15-year period that is covered by this research makes it possible to investigate if generational patterns (as distinct from patterns based upon period or age) can be found in the perceived significance of ICTs in people's lives.

We also look at the perceived necessity of mobile internet and tablet computers among all age groups (18–74) in 2014, in order to examine the significance of age, cohort and life course stage in the current diffusion of these more recent technological innovations.

ICT, generations and life course

The use of technology has been frequently explained by attributes related to generations, emphasising the importance of youth in the adoption of new technologies. The typologies and divisions of the age cohorts born in the Western world in the 20th century vary somewhat between countries (Smola and Sutton, 2002; Karisto, 2007; Hyde *et al.*, 2009; Parment, 2013). However, in most countries, the post World War II birth cohorts are regarded as being in a particularly pivotal position in terms of the development of modern lifestyles. The division that has been employed in the analysis of this study are the early 1900s Generation (born ca. 1900–29), the pre-Baby Boomers or War Generation (born ca. 1929–1944), the Baby Boomers (born ca. 1945–59),[1] Generation Xs (born ca. 1960–1974), Generation Ys (born ca. 1975–1989) and Generation Zs or the Millennials (those born ca. 1990–2005). The alphabetisation of the generations (as X, Y and Z generations), which is typical of American social and economic research,[2] is nowadays also commonly used in Europe.

In the 1980s and 1990s, most of the research looked at the use of ICTs from a generational viewpoint, calling the younger age cohorts (Y, Z) as the Net Generation, or the e-Generation. Researchers argued that exposure to ICT in youth leads to better knowledge and more ready inclusion in digital environments. For these young age cohorts, their generational identity was typically seen as being bound up with the new technology, particularly to mobile phones that penetrated the market during the 1990s (Tapscott, 1998; Turkle, 1996). In general, the use of ICTs was frequently seen as an important marker separating younger and older generations. Especially in the early 2000s, studies of the use of ICTs showed clear differences between age cohorts, which led to the assumption that technological skills are shaped in youth, and that this engagement with technology was shaping the core values of these generations, which in turn determines the interest in and competence of using new technology later in life. This pattern of differential adoption eventually results in a digital divide between the generations (Haddon, 2005; Green, 2010). Particularly in the 1990s, many researchers were fascinated by the ways young people used and appropriated ICTs, and the position of young users of ICTs became almost mythical by the 2000s. The generations of 'digital natives' were thought to mature earlier and to have become more knowledgeable than any previous generation (Rushkoff, 1996; Turkle, 1996; Tapscott, 1998; Gobé, 2001; Wilska, 2003; Wilska and Pedrozo, 2007). It was even argued that digital technologies had created a wider social and cultural gap between Generation X and the 'digital natives' generations Y and Z than the gap between Generation X and the Baby Boomers (Jones *et al.*, 2009; Parment, 2013).

Each generation is, however, tied to certain time periods that are characterised by their own distinct social, economic and cultural conditions. This wider cultural context is likely to affect ICT usage and the perceived necessity of ICTs for all age groups. In Finland, the ownership rate of mobile phone or internet does not now differ much between age groups (Statistics Finland, 2015). This suggests that the use and consumption of digital technologies are connected to certain time periods when technologies become available to the majority of consumers, regardless of their age. Changes in the life course also matter, and generationally determined engagement with technology is likely to change along with people's position in the life course. For instance, household structure and family context influence the use of digital technologies significantly (Livingstone *et al.*, 2005). The presence of young people in the household increases the use of ICTs for adults, for example, as young people and children are often the reason for acquiring the technology in the first place. There is also a bi-directional pattern of influence as young people also may help their parents in the use of the new technologies (Haddon, 2005; Eynon and Helsper, 2015).

As children grow up and move away from home when their parents typically approach late midlife, ICTs become the necessary means for keeping up the connection between the generations. Moreover, in late midlife and older adulthood, new demands for technologies emerge as the importance of social networks increases in terms of sustaining well-being. (Charles and Carstensen, 2010; Hutteman *et al.*, 2014). After retirement, older adults have an increased amount of leisure time (Helson *et al.*, 2006; Kokko, 2010), which facilitates engagement in leisure-based online services such as entertainment and social networking. Age differences in ICT use might also be blurring as lifestyles of different generations have been assimilated, particularly after the generational schism of the long 1960s, and middle-aged and older people want to become users of ICTs and participants in online activities in much the same way as younger people do (Räsänen and Koiranen, 2016).

Life course transitions and changes in social roles and personal relationships differ between men and women. These differences in turn may contribute to somewhat gendered practices in the use and consumption of ICTs in late midlife and old adulthood. Parenthood typically changes gender divisions, and the domestic division of labour often becomes more traditional within the household, which in turn affects the use of technologies in people's daily lives (Fortunati, 2011). Then, as children move away from home and the demands of daily housework decreases, the gendered division of household labour changes once more, which in turn may further affect the role of ICTs in daily life.

ICTs and consumption norms

Apart from being means of communication and ways of using technological skills, ICT goods and services are also consumable objects and provide access to other new consumable services. Thus, ICTs can be examined as the acquisition of material possessions, as sources of distinction and as essential parts of modern consumer lifestyles. As a result of the rapid development of technology, in Finland and other affluent countries, technological commodities such as mobile phones and computers, are increasingly regarded as part of life's necessities (Lehtinen *et al.*, 2011; Aro and Wilska, 2014). In consumer societies, the consensually accepted necessities create consumption norms; those items which households should own, and activities they should be able to participate in. Issues such as the capability to achieve an adequate standard of living and a lifestyle which is in accordance with prevailing norms, are relevant when conceptualising the necessities in people's everyday lives. (Halleröd *et al.*, 2006; Bradshaw *et al.*, 2008; Aro and Wilska, 2014). The notion of a 'good' or 'adequate' consumer in modern consumer society possesses both the material resources and the cognitive competences to know how to consume (Bauman, 1998; Wilska, 2001).

Consumer societies are dynamic and driven by change. The shifting perceptions of what constitute the necessities of life and lifestyle mean that commodities that may at one time have been regarded as specialities or luxuries may in a short time span become necessities and essential elements in contemporary lifestyles (Dwyer, 2009, p. 334). In some cases, a peak and a fall may occur, as some items rise in importance only to quickly become obsolete and are then replaced by the next wave of new technology. In terms of telephony, for example, the landline phone was first replaced with 'ordinary' mobile phones, which were subsequently quickly replaced by smartphones. DVDs are rapidly being replaced by digital TV platforms, and non-professional digital cameras with mobile phone cameras. Technological products are often expensive when first introduced to the market, and they also require technical competence which some may be able to afford and some may possess, thus enabling such technology to serve as sources of distinction and symbols of status (cf. Bourdieu, 1984). The prices and status value of the new technologies have led to discussions about digital divides between different socio-economic groups, linking ICTs to questions of what is necessary for a decent standard of living in a consumer society. Previous research has confirmed that both income and education have effects on both the use of ICTs and their perceived necessity (Räsänen, 2006; Bauerlein, 2011; Tondeur *et al.*, 2011; Aro and Wilska, 2014). In older age groups, in particular, people with high education and income are more likely to possess and use PCs and the internet than less educated and/or poorer older people (Zickuhr and Madden, 2012; Van Deursen and Helsper, 2015; Piper *et al.*, 2016; Räsänen and Koiranen, 2016). ICT goods cannot be seen solely in terms of their role as status commodities, though. They also serve as organisers of multiple functions in daily life and are increasingly needed for several errands in today's societies such as accessing public services, shopping, entertainment and participating in various forms of social networking. The more ICT goods are regarded as necessities, the more they become intrinsic elements of everyday life (Lehtonen, 2003; Røpke, 2003; Shove, 2003; Warde, 2005).

Generational differences in the perception of life's necessities, in the diffusion of the ICTs and in the ways that technology is incorporated into the lifestyles of people at different life course stages are undoubtedly intertwined (Hyde *et al.*, 2009; Carr *et al.*, 2012). Therefore, it is likely that the ways of using ICTs and the meanings they represent vary for different age cohorts, each growing up in different environments and time periods. Furthermore, broader social and economic macro circumstances also have an effect, as well as cultural variations between societies. From the viewpoint of Finnish generations, those cohorts born before World War II encountered digital technology only in their old age, after retirement. The Baby Boomers learned to use ICTs in their middle-age in the late 1990s and 2000s while at work and with their children at school. The members of Generation X were exposed to digital technology in their young adulthood, as the consumption of ICTs grew remarkably in Finland in the 1990s (Wilska, 2001, 2003). Even younger generations, the members of the Ys and the Zs, have in their turn grown up amidst digital technology and constant online communication, making their relation to ICTs unique compared with most other generations (Barbagallo, 2003; Valentine and Powers, 2013).

Differences between age cohorts might thus be considered likely to fade, particularly for items that have existed long enough and are thus incorporated as necessary elements sustaining the practices of everyday life. For instance, Hyde *et al.* (2009) found out that in the early 2000s, 'older' technical goods such as (landline) telephones and TVs were possessed almost equally often by both older and younger age cohorts, whereas the ownership of 1980s' innovations like VCRs, microwave ovens and PCs remained low in old age cohorts even in the 2000s (Hyde *et al.*, 2009, pp. 110–115). What is likely is that nowadays, since the diffusion of today's technological innovations is so much faster than before, it has become much more difficult to predict how today's middle-aged and elderly age cohorts will adopt the new technologies as part of the necessary architecture of modern lifestyles.

Research questions

Informed by the discussion above, we turn to our empirical research programme examining the perceived necessity of ICTs to those age cohorts frequently described as 'digital immigrants', those age cohorts that were 45–74 years old in 1999, 2004, 2009 and 2014. On the basis of previous research, it is obvious that over a 15-year period, many ICTs will have become part of everyday life and thereby the initial differences between age cohorts should be evened out over time. As people also tend to judge items that they already possess as necessities (e.g. Halleröd *et al.*, 2006; Aro and Wilska, 2014), it might be expected that as the perceived necessity of ICTs has grown with time, ownership rates will also increase across all age groups. Given these considerations, we examine potential determinants of the perceived necessity of more recent ICT innovations as well as mobile internet and tablet computer use among all age groups (18–74) in 2014, since new technologies have previously been detected as being adopted first by younger age groups. We also examined the effects of socio-demographic variables on the perceived necessity of these goods, as previous studies in Finland have suggested that people with high income and education are more likely than poorer people to regard technological devices as necessities. Previous studies have also detected differences within the middle-aged and older adults in terms of house-hold structure (life course stage) and gender (Räsänen, 2006; Aro and Wilska, 2014; Piper *et al.*, 2016; Räsänen and Koiranen, 2016; Taipale, 2016), so these factors were also taken into consideration in delineating possible digital divides.

The specific research questions are as follows:

1   What is the perceived necessity of ICT products (mobile phone, PC and inter-net connection) among different age/birth cohorts among 45- to 74-year-olds in 1999, 2004, 2009 and 2014?
2   Can cohort- or generation-based differences be detected throughout the period 1999–2014 in the perceived necessity of ICTs?
3   Can socio-demographic differences be detected across the various 45- to 74-year-olds' age cohorts regarding the perceived necessities of ICTs?
4   Can socio-demographic differences be detected in the perceived necessity of more recent technology (mobile internet and tablet computers) in 2014 across all age cohorts?

Data and methods

The data used in this study are derived from a postal survey 'Finland – Consumption and Lifestyle' that was repeated 4 times within 15 years. The surveys covered a wide range of questions regarding attitudes and practices related to consumption, work, income, lifestyles and perceived problems in society. The first survey was carried out in 1999 (N=2,417), the next in 2004 (N=3,574), five years later, in 2009 (N=1,202) and finally in 2014 (N=1,350). The size of the total sample of interviewees was N=8,543 (Koivula *et al.*, 2015). The overall design was a repeated cross-sectional survey. Each year question-naires were sent out to 18- to 74-year-old Finnish-speakers, randomly selected from the Finnish Population Register Database. In 1999, the response rate was 61 per cent, in 2004, 60 per cent, in 2009, 49 per cent, and in 2014, 46 per cent (Erola *et al.*, 2005; Sarpila *et al.*, 2010; Koivula *et al.*, 2015). In 2009 and 2014, the questionnaire could also be completed online (Koivula *et al.*, 2015). In the final data sampling, older age groups and females were overrepresented, which was corrected by weighting the data by age and gender.

In this study, we analysed the question: Which of the following do you regard as necessities in your daily life? This was asked in respect of mobile phones, PCs and the internet for all years under examination. In 2014, the tablet computer and mobile internet were included as new items in the questionnaire. Responses were rated as: 1 = necessity; 2 = useful, but not a necessity, and 3 = not necessary at all. To simplify interpretation of the analyses, the responses were reverse-scored; a larger value representing a higher level of perceived necessity.

Two-way ANOVA models were used as analytical tools. The perceived necessities of the internet, PCs and mobile phones were used as the dependent variables in the analysis. First, the differences between age cohorts in years 1999, 2004, 2009 and 2014 were measured by comparing the means of the perceived necessity of PC, internet connection and mobile phone in different age groups. The significance of the differences was tested with a two-way ANOVA model that included: (a) the interaction of the year of examination and age, (b) gender, (c) income quintile, (d) socio-economic status, (e) education and (f) absence/ presence of children (of any age) in the household as independent variables. The year and age interactions were significant in the overall models of all ICTs (sig. of F <0.05). The significance of age in each year were tested with unstandardised parameter estimates (B) that describe how much the means of the different categories of the independent variables deviate from the reference category. For the PC and internet connection, the differences between age groups were significant in 1999 and 2004 (sig. of B <0.05), but in 2009, only the differences between the two oldest age groups (aged 65–74) and the youngest age group were significant. For the mobile phone, the differences between age groups were all significant in 1999 and 2004, but in 2009 and 2014, the differences were not significant in any age groups (Figures 11.1–11.3). Subsequently, the socio-demographic predictors of the necessity values were analysed in terms of mobile phone, PC and internet among the six age cohorts in all years under examination. Another ANOVA model was built to examine the predictors for the perceived necessity for tablet and mobile internet in all age groups in 2014.

The age groups were divided into six categories, those aged 45–49 years, 50–54 years, 55–59 years, 60–64 years, 65–69 years and 70–74 years. In the analyses, these age groups were turned into birth cohorts. The 5-year birth cohorts in our analyses are shorter than the generations that are typically regarded as 15–20 years long, since we assumed that if the cohorts covered longer periods, it would be more difficult to detect differences in the perceived necessities of the products of the ICTs which typically spread rapidly, as new products flow constantly into the market (e.g. Dwyer 2009). Because the longitudinal data 1999–2014 were constructed from four cross-sectional datasets, it was not possible to do a proper cohort analysis. However, as the samples were large and nationally representative, it was possible to create pseudo cohorts of the individuals in the years under examination (see also Hyde *et al.*, 2009). In 1999, the oldest age cohort of 45- to 74-year-olds was born in 1925, and in 2014, the youngest cohort was born in 1969. Thus, if interpreted as generations, the samples of individuals ranged from those belonging to the early 1900s generations to members of Generation X.

Results

The perceived necessity of PC, internet and mobile phones, 1999–2014

Figure 11.1 shows that in 1999, although 40 per cent of all households already owned a PC (Kangassalo, 2002), most did not regard it as very necessary. However, there were clear differences between the age cohorts. The oldest cohorts, those born before WW2, regarded the PC as almost totally unnecessary, whereas the post-war Baby Boomer cohorts were clearly more interested in PCs. The perceived necessity of PCs increased rapidly for members of all six birth

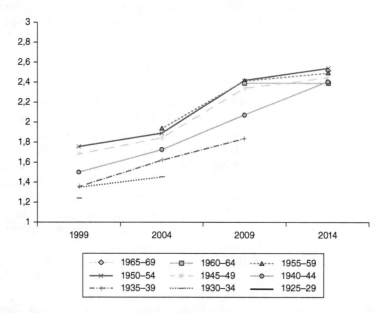

Figure 11.1 The mean perceived necessity of PCs among five-year pseudo cohorts aged from 45 to 74 between 1999–2014.

Note: Means in 1–3 scale, (1 = not a necessity at all, 2 = useful, but not a necessity, 3 = a necessity).

cohorts during the 2000s, but the differences between the cohorts remained until 2009, which suggests a slight cohort effect for most of the earlier period. But by 2014, the perceived necessity had reached a high level for all the samples, and these age cohort differences had evened out as members of all age cohorts now regarded the PC as more or less a necessity. The differences between cohorts born after WW2 were small during the whole period, and by 2014, the oldest surviving cohort (those born in 1940–44, who were now aged 70–74 years old) rated the necessity of these goods and services at almost the same level as the younger cohorts.

The perceived necessity of the internet followed a similar pattern as that for the PC, as shown in Figure 11.2. It too started as a non-necessity, rated even less necessary than the PC in 1999, probably because only about 20 per cent of all households had an internet connection at home at the time (Kangassalo, 2002). However, its perceived necessity increased rapidly during the 15-year period. The differences between birth cohorts were slightly larger for the internet than for the PC, as its perceived necessity developed more slowly for the older cohorts who were born before WW2 than for the Baby Boomers and subsequent younger cohorts. The age cohorts born after 1955 differed clearly from older cohorts and in 2014, the youngest cohort – those born between 1965 and 1969, who were aged 45–49 years old in 2014, – stands out from all other older cohorts reporting a clearly higher perceived necessity for the internet. However, for all age cohorts, the internet was regarded as more or less a necessity by 2014.

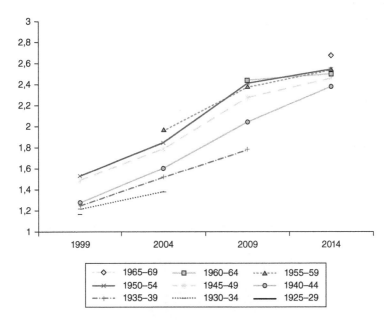

Figure 11.2 The mean perceived necessity of having internet connection at home among 5-year pseudo cohorts aged 45 to 74 between 1999–2014.

Note: Means in 1–3 scale, (1 = not a necessity at all, 2 = useful, but not a necessity, 3 = a necessity).

Changes in the perceived necessity of mobile phones developed rather differently (see Figure 11.3). In 1999, 80 per cent of all Finnish households already owned at least one mobile phone (Kangassalo, 2002), and in most families with children, there were as many mobile phones as there were members of the household (Wilska, 2003). Thus, the mean perceived necessity of a mobile phone was quite high in 1999 for all age cohorts (almost 1.9 on a 1–3 scale), even among the oldest age cohort (i.e. those born in 1925–29). Thus, at the start, even elderly people in Finland regarded the mobile phone as at least 'useful'. During the whole period from 1999 to 2014, the differences between age cohorts remained small, although interestingly, the perceived necessity of mobile phones seemed to reach a saturation point around the year 2009. From then until 2014, the perceived necessity did not grow any more. This might have been because during this latter five-year period, alternative means of communication had developed, via the internet, such as video calling. In 2015, for example, almost 20 per cent of people across the age range 45 to 74 years old were reported to have used online or video call applications in Finland (Statistics Finland, 2015).

Socio-economic and demographic predictors of the perceived necessity of ICTs

Next, we report analyses on the effects of other socio-demographic variables on the perceived necessity of ICTs among age cohorts 45–74 years old. Differences

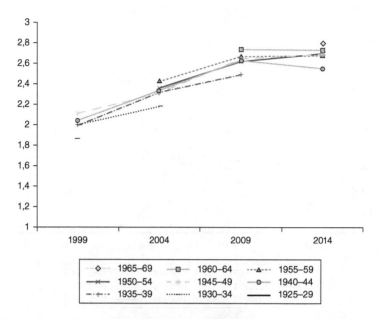

Figure 11.3 The mean perceived necessity of mobile phone among 5-year pseudo cohorts
      aged 45 to 74 between 1999–2014.

Note: Means in 1–3 scale, (1 = not a necessity at all, 2 = useful, but not a necessity, 3 = a necessity).

in the perceived necessity of the ICTs (using the range of 1–3) were explored
in relation to: (a) year of examination, (b) age, (c) gender, (d) income quintile,
(e) socio-economic status, (f) education and (g) absence/presence of children
(of any age) in the household. Table 11.1 displays the results from the main-
effect tests in two-way ANOVA (F- and *B*-values). The (adjusted) coefficients of
determination (R^2) show the proportions of variance explained by all independent
variables in the models.

As expected, Table 11.1 shows that the year of examination affected all
perceived necessities of the ICTs. For the perceived necessity of both the PC
and internet, the presence of children in the household was the most significant
other determinant; even more significant than age. High levels of education
and high income were significantly associated with higher ratings of the perceived necessity of these ICTs. Gender and socio-economic status also showed
some effects. Males, people in managerial or professional positions, and people
with high income, rated the PC a necessity slightly more often than females,
other socio-economic groups and people in lower income quintiles. However,
the effects of gender and socio-economic position were clearly smaller than the
effects of other predictors. For the perceived necessity of mobile phones, the
year under examination was significant only in 1999 and 2004 while determinants other than age and year had little significance. Males were slightly more
likely to regard the mobile phone as a necessity as were people in the three highest income quintiles. The presence of children in the household had no effect.

Table 11.1 Determinants of the perceived necessity of PC, internet and mobile phone between 1999–2014 among 45- to 74-year-olds (two-way ANOVA).

	Personal computer (PC) (B)	Internet (B)	Mobile phone (B)
Age (ref. 70–74)	F=8.738***	F=11.262***	F=5.241***
45–49	.280***	.318***	.247***
50–54	.267***	.287***	.181***
55–59	.275***	.271***	.133**
60–64	.231***	.205***	.154**
65–69	.133**	.124***	.138**
Year of the study (ref. 2014)	F=260.807***	F=423.451***	F=141.820***
1999	−.994***	−1.233***	−.687
2004	−.726***	−.835***	−.371
2009	−.235***	−.289***	n.s.
Children (ref. no children living at home)	F=93.404***	F=130.190***	F=.006
Children living at home	.317***	.356***	n.s.
Gender (ref. male)	F=7.323**	F=4.660*	F=6.400**
Female	−.068**	−.051*	−.060**
Education (ref. no education)	F=36.553***	F=23.193***	F=1.923
Vocational training	.140***	.101**	n.s.
College degree or post-secondary education	.294***	.206***	n.s.
University degree	.465***	.361***	n.s.
Socio-economic position (ref. worker, building, industry)	F=2.783*	F=2.819*	F=1.478
Manager	.148**	.099*	n.s.
Professional	.118**	.129***	n.s.
Worker, office, service or sale	n.s.	n.s.	n.s.
Farmer	n.s.	n.s.	n.s.
Net income/consumption unit (ref. quintile I)	F=17.518***	F=25.795***	F=4.096**
Quintile II	n.s.	n.s.	n.s.
Quintile III	n.s.	.109**	.095*
Quintile IV	.172***	.212***	.105*
Quintile V	.292***	.358***	.153***
R Squared (adjusted R²)	.314 (.310)	.382 (.378)	.137 (.131)

*** p <0.001; **p < 0.01; *p < 0.05

The perceived necessity of mobile internet and tablet computers in 2014

Questions on the perceived necessity of the new ICTs, mobile internet and tablet computer were asked only in 2014. Figure 11.4 illustrates the mean perceived necessity of these goods across all age cohorts. In 2014, the oldest cohort was born between 1940 and 1944 and the youngest between 1990 and 1996. The perceived necessity of mobile internet was highest in the two youngest cohorts and rated lower with increasing age, which is not surprising. Interestingly, however,

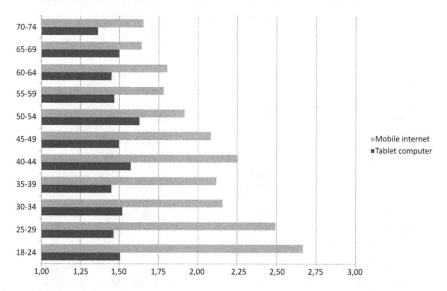

Figure 11.4 The mean perceived necessity of mobile internet and tablet computers across
all age cohorts in 2014.

Note: Means in 1–3 scale, (1 = not a necessity at all; 2 = useful, but not a necessity; 3 = a necessity).

the perceived necessity of tablet computers was not any higher among younger
cohorts than among the middle-aged and the elderly. This indicates that while
tablets and smartphones both have mobile internet, young people prefer the
smartphone over the tablet for those purposes.

Socio-demographic factors seemed to have little influence on the perceived
necessity of mobile internet and tablet computers in the age cohorts 45–74
years old in 2014, as shown in Table 11.2. Age, gender and socio-economic
position were not significant predictors for either tablet computers or mobile
internet and thus they were omitted from the models. The strongest determinant
for both technologies was the presence of children in the household, but also,
education and income had some effect. College or university level education
predicted higher perceived necessity ratings for both tablet computers and the
mobile internet, and people in the highest income quintile also regarded both
tablet computers and mobile internet as more necessary than those in the lowest income quintile. This suggests that people in those professions that require
higher education may be more likely to need tablets for their work than others.
The influence of income was not very high though, as there were differences
only between the highest and lowest income quintiles. Finally, the influence of
young people in the household on these goods' perceived necessity may mean
that these devices are bought for them or that the youngsters influenced their
parents' needs.

Table 11.2 Determinants of perceived necessity of tablet computer and mobile internet, 2014, 45- to 74-year-olds.

	Tablet computer	*Mobile internet*
Children (ref. no children living at home) *(B)*	F=11.979**	F=13.144***
Children living at home	.180**	.235***
Education (ref. no education) *(B)*	F=2.379*	F=5.490**
Vocational training	n.s.	n.s.
College degree or post-secondary education	.147*	.259**
University degree	.129*	.353**'
Income / per consumption unit (ref. quintile I) *(B)*	F=3.159*	F=3.961**
Quintile II	n.s.	n.s.
Quintile III	n.s.	n.s.
Quintile IV	n.s.	n.s.
Quintile V	.213**	.213*
R Squared (Adjusted R^2)	.036 (.027)	.057 (.048)

*** $p < 0.001$; ** $p < 0.01$; * $p < 0.05$

Discussion and conclusions

In this chapter, we have analysed the perceived necessity of ICT for middle-aged, young-old and elderly people during the period 1999 to 2014 in terms of PCs, access to the internet and mobile phones – ICT resources that were available throughout the period of the surveys. The differences that existed at the beginning of the surveys between the different age cohorts had mostly evened out by the end. On the other hand, the differences between the pre and post WW2 age cohorts widened between 1999 and 2009. Since the pre-war cohorts were no longer in the age sampling frame by the end of the survey period in 2014, it is hard to say whether these differences might also have narrowed. This seems unlikely since the trend up to 2009 had been for a widening, not a narrowing of this particular 'generational gap'.

Differences between the age cohorts in the perceived necessity of mobile phones were smaller when compared with those for PCs and the internet throughout the whole period, which probably reflected the early and relatively more rapid diffusion of mobile phones in Finland compared with most other countries. With regard to more recent ICTs, such as tablet computers and mobile internet, age cohort differences in 2014 were small, and for the tablet computer, there were no significant differences between the younger and older age cohorts. ICTs were rated as increasingly more necessary over time and this was the case for all age cohorts. However, between 1999 and 2009, differences between the very oldest pre-war birth cohorts and the younger, post-war birth cohorts remained clear and even grew wider (with the exception of the mobile phone). For all post-war generations, however, the differences in the perceived necessities of ICTs clearly evened out.

What should be noted is the significance of household composition, namely the presence of children in the household. This is consistent with the earlier discussion that pointed out the significance of *life course stage* in the engagement in ICTs. Our results suggest that younger generations exercise influence on their parents' attitudes toward ICTs, which supports previous findings about the important role young people play in the acquisition and use of ICTs within families (Haddon, 2005; Eynon and Helsper, 2015). Our findings strongly suggest that the use of and need for ICTs more often binds the generations together than creates gaps between them at least as it applies to successive post-war generations (see also Taipale, 2016). Gender differences were small in our study, although males regarded PC, internet access and mobile phone slightly more necessary than women. This is consistent with previous studies, which have suggested that women and girls have always been less interested in technical devices, although more in the social communication made possible with the ICTs (Gill and Grint, 1995; Cooper and Weaver, 2003; Wilska, 2003; Taipale, 2016).

We also analysed socio-economic variables affecting the perceived necessity of ICTs, on the grounds that social status influences the perceptions of what constitutes 'decent' living standards and *consumption norms* (Bauman, 1998; Halleröd *et al.*, 2006). Since acquiring and using new technology require both economic resources and technical competence, ICTs are likely to become viewed as necessities more rapidly among those in higher socio-economic groups (Räsänen, 2006; Aro and Wilska, 2014; Räsänen and Koiranen, 2016). Higher levels of education, income and socio-economic status were all associated with a higher perceived necessity for ICTs. For tablet computer and mobile internet, the effect of income was smaller. Some studies suggest that low socio-economic groups use only mobile devices to connect to the internet more than others, because they cannot afford both fixed and mobile broadband. Moreover, the different affordance of fixed use is not so much utilised by low-class and low-income people (Brown *et al.*, 2013; Pearce and Rice, 2013; Taipale, 2014). Socio-demographic divisions became less important as the devices were increasingly adopted as essential components of everyday life. The more our everyday life is shaped and constructed by technology, the more the perceived necessity of ICTs becomes part of people's everyday practices, regardless of their age (again within the limits of the ages and age cohorts we have studied). Our results revealed, for instance, that older people prefer tablet computers to smartphones to access the internet. This may have practical reasons as it is easier to operate larger screens and touchpads than with smartphones, which are preferred by younger people. Moreover, the requirements of ICTs at work may affect the perceptions of ICTs in leisure time too, as employees get used to certain practices, such as using tablet computers in meetings, while tablets are also used within families to entertain small children.

The obvious limitation of this study is that perceptions of the necessity of ICTs do not tell us much about the actual use of technology. Although ICTs are nowadays regarded as almost equally important to all age groups, the way technology is used varies between age groups. Different needs arise at different life course stages, which in turn affect the use of ICTs (see Oksman, 2006; Loos *et al.*, 2012).

Moreover, changes in consumer cultures over time need to be taken into account when interpreting generational differences. In this study, the youngest cohorts (born 1950–69) grew up in an expanding consumer society. This has undoubtedly had an effect on the adaptation of ICTs as consumer goods. The generational experience of material scarcity may be stronger for older cohorts (Hyde *et al.*, 2009), and for pre-war cohorts, ICTs were probably regarded throughout much of the period as unnecessary luxuries.

Although generational differences among post-war cohorts are undoubtedly narrowing in terms of ICT use, it is difficult to predict future developments. What makes research on any social aspects of ICTs difficult is the speed of new developments in ICTs. Technological innovations diffuse so rapidly that questions about the necessity of the internet, for instance, may soon become irrelevant. In the future, for both young and old, ICTs will be omnipresent along with other unforeseen innovations in the internet of things. We must recognise that the role of chronological age will only become ever more contingent as age too becomes an integral part of these cultural changes. New and more sensitive methods are thus needed for understanding the ways ICTs are perceived and appropriated in different age groups.

Notes

1 In Finland, the Baby Boomer's cohort is narrower in years than in many other countries such as in the UK (e.g. Karisto, 2007), The cohort born 1945-49 is disproportionately large in size compared to five-year cohorts born before or after that. However, the birth rate remained rather high in Finland during the whole 1950s, but started to decline rapidly in the 1960s.
2 The name 'Generation X' was first used in Douglas Coupland's (1991) novel *Generation X: tales from an accelerated culture* (New York: St. Martin's Press).

References

Aro, R. and Wilska, T.-A., 2014. Standard of living, consumption norms, and perceived necessities. *International Journal of Sociology and Social Policy*, 34(9), pp. 710–728.

Barbagallo, P., 2003. Teens. *Target Marketing*, 26(4), pp. 65–68.

Bauerlein, M., 2011. *The digital divide: arguments for and against Facebook, Google, texting, and the age of social networking*. New York: Jeremy P. Tarcher/Penguin.

Bauman, Z., 1998. *Work, consumerism and the new poor*. Milton Keynes, UK: Open University Press.

Bolin, G., 2014. Media generation: objective and subjective media landscapes and nostalgia among generations of media users. *Journal of Audience & Reception Studies*, 11(2), pp. 108–131.

Bourdieu, P., 1984. *Distinction: a social critique of the judgement of taste*. London: Routledge.

Bradshaw, J., Middleton, S., Davis, A., Oldfield, N., Smith, N., Cusworth, L. and Williams, J., 2008. *A minimum income standard for Britain: what people think*. Loughborough, UK: Loughborough University/Joseph Rowntree Foundation.

Brown, K., Campbell, S. W. and Ling, R., 2013. Mobile phones bridging the digital divide for teens in the US? *Future Internet*, 3(2), pp. 144–158.

Carr, D. J., Gotlieb, M. R., Lee, N. J. and Shah, D. V., 2012. Examining overconsumption, competitive consumption and conscious consumption from 1994 to 2004: disentangling cohort and period effects. *The Annals of the American Academy of Political and Social Science*, 664(1), pp. 220–233.

Charles, S. T. and Carstensen, L. L., 2010. Social and emotional aging. *Annual Review of Psychology*, 61, pp. 383–409.

Cooper, J. and Weaver, K. D., 2003. *Gender and computers: understanding the digital divide*. London: Routledge.

Coupland, D., 1991. *Generation X: tales for an accelerated culture*. New York: St. Martin's Press.

Dwyer, R. E., 2009. Making a habit of it: positional consumption, conventional action and the standard of living. *Journal of Consumer Culture*, 9(2), pp. 328–347.

Erola, J., Räsänen, P., Halenius, L., Vasunta, V. and Haapanen, T., 2005. *Suomi 2004: aineistonkeruu ja tutkimusseloste sekä yhteiskunnan ja kulutuksen muutos 1999–2004*. Keskustelua ja raportteja 5: 2005. Turku, Finland: Turun kauppakorkeakoulu.

Eynon, R. and Helsper, E., 2015. Family dynamics and internet use in Britain: what role do children play in adults' engagement with the internet? *Information, Communication and Society*, 18(2), pp. 156–171.

Fortunati, L., 2011. ICTs and immaterial labour from a feminist perspective. *Journal of Communication Inquiry*, 35(4), pp. 426–432.

Gill, R. and Grint, K., 1995. *The gender-technology relation: contemporary theory and research*. London: Taylor & Francis.

Gilleard, C., Jones, I. and Higgs, P., 2015. Connectivity in later life: the declining age divide in mobile cell phone ownership. *Sociological Research Online*, 20(2), 3. www.socresonline.org.uk/20/2/3.html

Gobé, M., 2001. *Emotional branding: the new paradigm for connecting brands to people*. New York: Allworth Press.

Green, L., 2010. *Understanding the life course: sociological and psychological perspectives*. Cambridge, UK: Polity Press.

Haddon, L., 2005. Personal information culture: the contribution of research on ICTs in everyday life. In: *UNESCO between two phases of the World Summit on the Information Society*. St. Petersburg, Russia: UNESCO.

Halleröd, B., Larsson, D., Gordon, D. and Ritakallio, V.-M., 2006. Relative deprivation: a comparative analysis of Britain, Finland and Sweden. *Journal of European Social Policy*, 16(4), pp. 328–345.

Helson, R., Soto, C. J. and Cate, R. A., 2006. From young adulthood through the middle ages. In: D. K. Mroczek and T. D. Little, eds. *Handbook of personality development*. Mahwah, NJ: Psychology Press, pp. 337–352.

Helsper, E. J. and Eynon, R., 2010. Digital natives: where is the evidence? *British Educational Research Journal*, 36(3), pp. 503–520.

Herold, D., 2012. Digital natives: discourses of exclusion in and inclusive society. In: E. Loos, L. Haddon and E. Mante-Meijer, eds. *Generational use of new media*. Farnham, UK: Ashgate, pp. 71–86.

Hutteman, R., Hennecke, M., Orth, U., Reitz, A. K. and Specht, J., 2014. Developmental tasks as a framework to study personality development in adulthood and old age. *European Journal of Personality*, 28(3), pp. 267–278.

Hyde, M., Higgs, P., Gilleard, C., Victor, C., Wiggins, D. and Rees Jones, I., 2009. Ageing, cohorts, and consumption: the British experience 1968–2005. In: I. R. Jones, P. Higgs and D. J. Ekerdt, eds. *Consumption and generational change: the rise of consumer lifestyles*. New Brunswick, NJ: Transaction Publishers, pp. 93–128.

Kangassalo, P., 2002. Matkapuhelin lähes kaikilla talouksilla. Uusin elektroniikka kuitenkin vielä harvinaista. *Tietoaika* 4/2002. Statistics Finland. www.stat.fi/tup/tietoaika/tilaajat/ta_04_02_matkapuhelin.html.

Karisto, A., 2007. Finnish baby boomers and the emergence of the third age. *International Journal of Ageing and Later Life*, 2(2), pp. 91–108.

Koivula, A., Räsänen, P. and Sarpila, O., 2015. *Suomi 2014 – kulutus ja elämäntapa. Tutkimusseloste ja ainestojen 2009 ja 2014 vertailua.* Working Papers in Economic Sociology. Turku, Finland: University of Turku.

Kokko, K., 2010. Keski-iän määrittelyä ja kuvailua. In: L. Pulkkinen and K. Kokko, eds., *Keski-ikä elämänvaiheena*. Publications of the Department of Psychology, University of Jyväskylä. Jyväskylä: University of Jyväskylä.

Lehtinen, A.-R., Varjonen, J., Raijas, A. and Aalto, K., 2011. *What is the cost of living? Reference budgets for a decent minimum standard of living in Finland.* Working Papers 132/2011. National Consumer Research Center, Helsinki. www.referencebudgets.eu/budgets/images/finnland_refbud.pdf.

Lehtonen, T.-K., 2003. The domestication of new technologies as a set of trials. *Journal of Consumer Culture*, 3(3), pp. 363–385.

Livingstone, S., Van Couvering, E. and Thumin, N., 2005. *Adult media literacy. A review of the research literature.* https://core.ac.uk/download/files/161/4155054.pdf.

Loos, E., Haddon, l. and Mante-Meijer,E., eds., 2012. *Generational use of new media.* Farnham, UK: Ashgate.

Lugano, G. and Peltonen, P., 2012. Building intergenerational bridges between digital natives and digital immigrants: attitudes, motivations and appreciation or old and new media. In: E. Loos, L. Haddon and E. Mante-Meijer, eds. *Generational use of new media*. Farnham, UK: Ashgate, pp. 151–170.

Oksman, V., 2006. Young people and seniors in Finnish 'mobile information society'. *Journal of Interactive Media in Education*, 2. http://dx.doi.org/10.5334/2006-3.

Parment, A., 2013. Generation Y vs. baby boomers: shopping behavior, buyer involvement and implications for retailing. *Journal of Retailing and Consumer Services*, 20(2), pp. 189–199.

Pearce, K. E. and Rice, R. E., 2013. Digital divides from access to activities: comparing mobile and personal computer internet users. *Journal of Communication*, 63(4), pp. 721–744.

Piper, A. M., Cornejo Garcia, R. and Brewer, R. N., 2016. Understanding the challenges and opportunities of smart mobile devices among the oldest old. *International Journal of Mobile Human Computer Interaction*, (8)2, pp. 83–98.

Prensky, M., 2001. Digital natives, digital immigrants. *On the Horizon*, 9(5), pp. 1–6.

Räsänen, P., 2006. Consumption disparities in information society: comparing the traditional and digital divides in Finland. *International Journal of Sociology and Social Policy*, 26(1–2), pp. 48–62.

Räsänen, P. and Koiranen, I., 2016. Changing patterns of ICT use in Finland: the senior citizens' perspective. In: J. Zhou and G. Salvendy, eds. *ITAP 2016*, Part I, LNCS 9754, pp. 226–237. http://link.springer.com/chapter/10.1007/978-3-319-39943-0_22

Røpke, I., 2003. Consumption dynamics and technological change: exemplified by the mobile phone and related technologies. *Ecological Economics*, 45(2), pp. 171–188.

Rushkoff, D., 1996. *Playing the future: how kids' culture can teach us to thrive in an age of chaos.* New York: HarperCollins.

Sarpila, O., Räsänen, P., Erola, J., Kekki, J. and Pitkänen, K., 2010. Suomi 2009. Tutkimusseloste ja aineistojen 1999–2009 vertailua. Turku, Finland: Turun yliopisto.

Shove, E., 2003. *Comfort, cleanliness and convenience. The social organization of normality.* Oxford, UK: Berg.

Smola, K. V. and Sutton, C. D., 2002. Generational differences: revising generational work values for the new millennium. *Journal of Organizational Behavior,* 23(4), pp. 363–382.

Spero, I. and Stone, M. 2004. Agents of change: how young consumers are changing the world of marketing. *Qualitative Market Research: An International Journal,* 7(2), pp. 153–159.

Statistics Finland, 2015. *Väestön tieto- ja viestintäteknologian käyttö.* Helsinki: Statistics Finland. http://tilastokeskus.fi/til/sutivi/2015/sutivi_2015_2015–11–26_fi.pdf.

Taipale, S., 2014. Do the mobile-rich get richer? Internet use, travelling and social differentiations in Finland. *New Media & Society,* 18(1), pp. 44–61.

Taipale, S., 2016. Synchronicity matters: defining the characteristics of digital generations. *Information, Communication and Society,* 19(1), pp. 80–89.

Tapscott, D., 1998. *Growing up digital: the rise of the net generation.* New York: McGraw-Hill.

Tondeur, J., Sinnaeve, I., Van Houtte, M. and Van Braak, J., 2011. The ICT as cultural capital: the relation between socioeconomic status and the computer-use profile among young people. *New Media & Society,* 13(1), pp. 151–168.

Turkle, S., 1996. *Life on the screen: Identity in the age of the internet.* New York: Touchstone.

Valentine, D. B. and Powers, T. L., 2013. Generation Y values and lifestyle segments. *Journal of Consumer Marketing,* 30(7), pp. 597–606.

Van Deursen, A. and Helsper, E., 2015. A nuanced understanding of internet use and non-use amongst older adults. *European Journal of Communication,* 30(2), pp. 171–187.

Warde, A., 2005. Consumption and theories of practice. *Journal of Consumer Culture,* 5(2), pp. 131–153.

White, D. S. and Le Cornu, A., 2011. Visitors and residents: a new typology for online engagement. *First Monday,* 16(9). http://firstmonday.org/ojs/index.php/fm/article/view/3171/3049.

Wilska, T.-A., 2001. The role of states in the creation of consumption norms. In: A. Warde and J. Gronow, eds. *Ordinary consumption.* Routledge, London, pp. 179–198.

Wilska, T.-A., 2003. Mobile phone use as part of young people's consumption styles. *Journal of Consumer Policy,* 26(3), pp. 441–463.

Wilska, T.-A. and Pedrozo, S., 2007. New technology and young people's consumer identities: a comparative study between Finland and Brazil. *Young,* 15(4), pp. 557–576.

Zickuhr, K. and Madden, M., 2012. *Older adults and internet use.* www.sainetz.at/dokumente/Older_adults_and_internet_use_2012.pdf.

12 A risk to privacy or a need for security?

Digital domestic technologies in the lives of young adults and late middle-agers

Sanna-Mari Kuoppamäki, Outi Uusitalo and Tiina Kemppainen

Introduction

In studies of consumption, it has been argued that different generations possess unique values and attitudes that significantly affect their daily consumption choices, preferences and behaviours (Carr *et al.*, 2012; Chhetri *et al.*, 2014; Eastman and Liu, 2012; Parment, 2011, 2013; Valentine and Powers, 2013). As a consequence of the development of digital devices, consumption is digitalising and new digital solutions are being provided for consumers regardless of age (Dholakia, 2012). This chapter investigates how digital technologies are perceived by young adults and late middle-agers in the daily contexts of housing and living in Finland. More specifically, we investigate what kinds of socially shared meanings young adults and late middle-agers, understood as members from different generations, have towards consumption of digital technologies in domestic environments.

Digitalisation of domestic environments refers to processes where new technologies, such as smart home solutions and other digital devices from smart phones to robot lawn mowers, are intertwined with the daily practices of home, housing and living (Balta-Ozkan *et al.*, 2013; De Silva *et al.*, 2012; Dholakia, 2012). First, we discuss concepts of life course, generations and the digitalisation of domestic environments in terms of attitudes towards digital technologies. Second, we analyse qualitative data from 8 focus group interviews with 68 participants. Third, we discuss the empirical results with respect to new approaches to generations and the marketing of digital devices, arguing that values and attitudes towards technologies are affected by both shared generational aspects and individual life-course events. By utilising data collected in the Finnish Housing Fair environment, the chapter combines aspects of sociology and marketing with qualitative, interview-based research.

Life-course stages and new technologies

In life-course literature, the stages of life course are usually classified into young adulthood (years 18 to 30), middle age (years 31 to 45), late middle age (years 46 to 65) and old adulthood (years 65 and over) (Hutteman *et al.*, 2014). Each life stage involves particular transitions, such as changes in roles and statuses, and readjustments to new social roles and expectations (Hutchison, 2011). Young adulthood is characterised by identity formation, formation of romantic relationships and the significance of peers. In late mid-life, transitions occur in work-life balance, in relationships towards ageing parents and children leaving home (Hutteman *et al.*, 2014). In late mid-life, leisure time typically increases (Helson *et al.*, 2006; Kokko, 2010). Consumer decisions, based on economic resources, social capital, health and wellbeing, lifestyle values and aspirations (Beer and Faulkner, 2011) are therefore necessarily affected by the life-course stage.

Use of new technologies is typically influenced by life experiences. Although late middle-aged adults are familiar with technologies such as the telephone, television and radio, most of them have learnt to use computers, mobile phones and the internet as adults, and are less familiar with them than young adults who have grown up with these technologies (Green, 2010, p. 137; Haddon, 2005). In previous research, older adults are often represented as lacking skills in using new technologies (e.g. Barnard *et al.*, 2013), and for expressing less comfort and ease in using technology, and less confidence in their abilities to use new technology (Chen and Chan, 2011; Smith, 2010). For older adults, communication with family and loved ones, as well as access to social support have been the most common motivations for computer and internet use (Thayer and Ray, 2006). Other motivations include a safety link to others (Ling, 2004) and a way to support independent living (Mikkonen *et al.*, 2002).

Today, the boundaries and lengths of each life stage are flexible and life-course transitions, such as transformations in roles and expectations in working life, do not necessarily appear as linear. People have ever more possibilities to transform and adjust their own biographies in non-conventional ways (Beck and Beck-Gernsheim, 2002; Izuhara, 2015; Kohli, 2007). For young adults, for instance, accessing home ownership is often considered a rite of passage to full adulthood, backed by a stable income, career prospects and the need for space for a growing family (Izuhara, 2015). Today, many life-course transitions, including leaving the parental home, family formation and purchasing a home, which used to occur in the twenties, now often occur in the thirties. In old adulthood, as general living standards and life expectancies have risen, people have more possibilities to pursue a lifestyle that addresses quality of life and self-expression (Koivula *et al.*, 2015). New technologies and social media applications focused on self-expression, for instance, provide opportunities for creating a life course of one's own with individualised and customised choices.

Generational archetypes

Studies of generations argue that consumption practices and use of new technologies are influenced by shared generational experiences. The concept of 'generation' refers to a group of individuals who have experienced similar historical events in their early adulthood that later constitute shared experiences or consciousness (Karisto, 2007; Mannheim, 1952; Purhonen, 2007). Generational experiences are said to remain unchangeable throughout the life course, although typically generational experiences are influenced by life-course transitions as well (Carr *et al.*, 2012; Meredith and Schewe, 1994; Ryder, 1985). 'Generation' is also applied in marketing studies to understand consumer practices such as buyer involvement, brand loyalty and lifestyle segments of generations, arguing that generations are distinguishable in orientations towards adopting technologies, sustainable consumption practices and early adoption of new products (Chhetri *et al.*, 2014; Eastman and Liu, 2012; Parment, 2011, 2013; Syrett and Lamminman, 2004; Valentine and Powers, 2013).

Studies of generations typically argue that each generation shares distinctive features, such as values and attitudes that would be somewhat typical for members of each generation. Members of Generation Y, born approximately between the years 1979 and 1994, aged 21 to 36 in 2015, have spent their early adulthood in a period of economic growth and emergence of new media, and consequently appear as individualistic but well-educated and technologically skilled with positive orientations towards consumer culture and new technological innovations (Paul, 2001). Generation Ys are often illustrated as 'digital natives' who possess positive attitudes towards new technologies and carry well-developed technological skills. Also called the 'Millennials', Generation Ys have grown up in a global mindset with unrestricted communication where mobile devices are instantly used for social networking (Parment, 2011).

Members of Generation X, born approximately between the years 1964 and 1978, aged 37 to 51 in 2015, are rarely identified as a discrete group of individuals in the Finnish context and have not been empirically investigated to the same extent as other generations. Generation Xs lived their youth during the 1980s and became adults in the 1990s and consequently encountered the financial recession in adulthood; hence the lives of Generation Xs have been influenced by economic uncertainties (Smola and Sutton, 2002).

Prior to Generation Xs, Baby Boomers, born in the Finnish context between the years 1945 and 1950, represent the first post-war generation in Western societies. Growing up during a period of revolutionary societal changes, Boomers are often associated with untraditional and idealistic values (Karisto, 2007; Purhonen, 2007); marketers interpret Boomers as an extravagant and brand loyal generation. Unlike younger generations, Boomers were not influenced by technological innovations until the age of 35 to 40, indicating that they were not similarly engaged with emerging digital technologies as younger generations.

In Finland, those born in the 1960s and currently aged approximately 50 to 55 are not usually acknowledged as members of any particular or well-defined generation based on international classifications. According to Finnish longitudinal studies, the birth cohort born in the 1960s, aged approximately 50 and over in 2015, most value benevolence in the form of the promotion of the wellbeing of close relatives, and universalism in the form of taking care of other people and nature (Pulkkinen and Polet, 2010, pp. 82–83). People aged 50 and over also value safety, implying the security of society, personal relationships and life in general. As the values of different generations are examined, it becomes clear that orientations towards and shared meanings regarding digitalisation are diverse, indicating the possibility of identifying generational values towards digitalisation of domestic environments.

Digitalisation of domestic environments

Digitalisation of domestic environments refers to processes where daily contexts of housing and living are influenced by digital devices. Technology available to consumers has expanded, and consumer markets offer constantly changing products related to the digitalisation of households: new smart home solutions, for instance, are presented to consumers (Balta-Ozkan *et al.*, 2013; De Silva *et al.*, 2012; Ehrenhard *et al.*, 2014). Content creation is not limited only to certain service providers; consumers have become the creators of technology via communication platforms which also aid consumers in organising their lives (Dholakia, 2012, p. 17). Consumption of technologies occurs in households where socio-cultural resources, as well as family dynamics, significantly influence the use and adoption of technologies (Livingstone and Lunt, 1991). In households, technologies are generally consumed for multiple purposes, including entertainment, online shopping, communication and household tasks. At the moment, these technologies are becoming digital, indicating that digital devices such as smartphones and tablet computers are used for the management of everyday living.

Often, digital technologies have different meanings for different social groups, and these meanings typically differ by age (Oksman, 2006). These meanings, such as values and attitudes regarding technologies, are typically negotiated, reflected and maintained in social relationships (Bijker and Law, 1992; Kline and Pinch, 1999; Pinch and Bijker, 1984; Selwyn, 2012). In the remainder of this chapter, we investigate socially shared meanings concerning consumption of digital technologies in domestic environments. We also present empirical findings from group discussions to highlight the shared meanings among consumers at different life-course stages. More specifically, we investigate:

1   What kinds of socially shared meanings do young adults and late middle-agers express towards digitalisation of domestic environments, and consumption of new technologies in general, during group discussions?
2   Can values and attitudes regarding digital technologies shared by members of each generation be interpreted as reflecting a generational experience or do they rather emerge from individual life-course events?

Data and methods

Data

This study analyses qualitative interview data from eight focus group discussions that were conducted in the context of the Finnish Housing Fair[1] in 2015. Four of the groups consisted of people aged 50–65 and three groups of people aged 18–35.

One group had both older and younger participants. A total of 68 participants attended the discussions. Each discussion, conducted as a semi-structured group interview, included 7 to 12 participants and lasted approximately 60 to 75 minutes.

Participants

About half of the participants belonged to the age group of 18- to 35-year-olds (N=31) and the other half to the age group of 50- to 65-year-olds (N=37). Over half of the participants were women (N=44). The majority lived in an urban area in an apartment building, and the participants were mainly employed and held a master's or college degree. In terms of family relations, one-third were married or in co-habitation and did not have children living at home; another third were married or in co-habitation with children living at home. The participants were randomly selected for the focus groups so that each group contained both women and men. About half of the participants attended the interviews as couples or families. Concerning their socio-demographic background, the participants were a rather homogenous group, which indicates that the findings are limited to urban and educated people with a middle-class background.

Procedure

The data were collected in the following way. First, participants were recruited through an advertisement in a decoration magazine, on the Housing Fair's website and on the website and Facebook site of the research project. In the advertisement, two focus groups based on age definitions were recruited: 18- to 35-year-olds (young adults) and 50- to 65-year-olds (late middle-agers). Out of approximately 200 contacts, 70 participants were selected for the interviews. Selection of the participants was based on the order of registration, and participants were awarded free entrance to the Housing Fair area.

Group discussions were organised in the Housing Fair area. Participants were met at the entrance of the Housing Fair and informed of the basic principles of the study. Participants were given two hours to walk around the area, after which group discussions were conducted in a separate room. There were two researchers moderating the discussions, and two researchers made notes about the situation and the participants. After the discussions, participants were asked to fill in a background information form that included questions on socio-demographic variables (birth year, gender, residential area, form of dwelling, occupation, education and family relationships). The discussions were taped and transcribed, resulting in 146 pages of transcribed text.

Methods

The analysis of focus group discussions in which participants represent a specific group of people, such as young adults or late middle-agers, aims to understand and explain shared meanings that participants produce during discussions

(Halkier, 2010; Rabiee, 2004; Thomas *et al.*, 1995). These shared meanings are considered to represent and describe the life stage of each participant and, within these shared meanings, it is possible to understand and explain orientations towards digital technologies among different consumer groups. The group discussions conducted during this research were semi-structured, covering three research areas derived from the literature (Carù and Cova, 2015; Coolen and Hoekstra, 2001; Dholakia, 2012): 1) customer experience related to the Housing Fair, 2) consumption behaviour related to housing, and 3) use of digital technologies in everyday life. The sub-questions varied according to situational factors, such as participants' interests, group dynamics and the conversation process. The transcribed text was analysed with a qualitative content analysis method, which aimed to understand and explain meanings in the context of the text (see Hsieh and Shannon, 2005; Rabiee, 2004).

In the first phase of analysis, all data expressions related to use of technologies were separated from the main text. These data expressions comprised sentences and statements that the interviewees articulated during the group discussions. This analysis produced 121 statements related to use and adoption of new technologies. In the second phase, the raw data expressions were interpreted into upper categories that reflected shared meanings towards digital technologies in domestic environments. In this phase, the sentences and statements were interpreted in terms of barriers and difficulties related to the adoption of technologies. This produced 24 upper categories of shared attitudes towards technologies. In the final phase, the upper categories were combined further into main categories in order to reduce the number of upper categories. A total of 15 main categories was formulated. In all phases, the analysis was grounded in empirical data expressions and the analysis unit was a sentence or statement articulated by one interviewee.

Results

Among all participants, the digitalisation of housing and living aroused shared values and attitudes that varied from rejection to careful optimism towards technologies. Participants reflected on their relationship to technologies in an environment that represented housing and living in terms of the latest innovations where new technologies of housing were characterised as expensive commodities. Many participants interpreted digital domestic technologies as non-necessities in daily life and, generally, they aroused more sceptical resistance than positive orientations.

Shared meanings among young adults

During the interviews, it was generally easier for younger participants to reflect on the role of technology in their everyday lives than for participants representing older generations. Many young adults interpreted new technologies, already involved in many aspects of their lives, as inseparable from daily life. Despite this, many younger people saw obstacles to the use of new technologies in domestic surroundings, relating mostly to adopting and becoming familiar with them. Younger female respondents in particular saw the use of technology as requiring too much time to become familiar with and hence referred to the use of technologies in general as *time-consuming*:

> I don't want the whole house to be digital . . . It would take so much time to become familiar with it . . . My stress level would get higher if I had to know how to use all these.
>
> (Female, 33)

> If I got used to technology, it would be handy, but of course it takes time to adapt to it first.
>
> (Female, 35)

Younger participants also perceived the digitalisation of housing as something they should have control over. The idea that "technology takes control over people" came up among female participants who perceived the domestic environment as something that humans and not machines should have control over. Younger participants understood technology as smart and self-imposed: something that is inherently part of daily life and hence has to be controlled. Controlling the use of technologies was related to time spent with the devices and many shared the viewpoint that technology already occupies too much of their daily lives. Some participants described time spent without digital devices as 'liberating' and, especially, many young participants wanted to 'shut down' the technology that is already constantly close to them. For participants in their thirties, it was responsibilities towards work, and for participants in their twenties, responsibilities towards social networks that created the need to control the time spent using technologies.

Many of the younger participants reflected on digital technologies with respect to social relationships; for younger people social aspects of digital technologies were not necessarily perceived as positive. Due to the intertwining of new technologies in domestic environments, maintaining boundaries between personal and social life was perceived as important, especially by younger females. The idea that *new technologies risk privacy* included negative evaluations of social media in domestic surroundings; from this framework, technologies were not perceived as something that could easily be adapted to private life. Rather, many wanted to make clear distinctions between private and social life with the use of technologies.

Male participants regarded digital technologies above all as consumer goods. New technologies were identified as *incomplete* when they lacked the qualities that would make them worth purchasing. In particular, younger male respondents in their thirties identified new technologies as inadequate in terms of functionality and technical characteristics, and they wanted "to see how they develop" and not be "the first one to buy them". They were conscious of the marketing and production processes of digital technologies and represented themselves as careful consumers of the latest innovations. This reflects a critical attitude of young males towards purchasing digital technologies in general.

Shared meanings among late middle-agers

Many late middle-agers identified new technologies in domestic surroundings as something they often lack skills in using. Male and female respondents shared experiences of new technologies as difficult and something they need help with. Whereas young adults understood difficulties in adopting new technologies in terms of time management, late middle-agers perceived the difficulties as originating from their own inner qualities:

> When my computer breaks, I don't know what to do. My kids will help me.
>
> (Male, 59)

> If I have problems with technology, I need help. It's difficult to solve the problems by myself.
>
> (Female, 52)

> I am a technically unskilled person. I have my own support person; he is my son.
>
> (Female, 51)

Late middle-agers relied on family members, and especially their children, for help in using technologies. Many older respondents share the perception of their children as 'digital natives' who will help them in the adoption and use of technologies. Digital technologies in domestic environments were thus perceived as 'common' to the whole family and something the whole family shares together through experiences, meanings and practices between generations (Piper *et al.*, 2016; Selwyn, 2004; Zickuhr and Madden, 2012). The obstacles and also the motivations were related to how they are used in interactions between family members and how the whole family is engaged in their use.

In addition to lack of skills, many late middle-agers recognised characteristics of technologies as not fitting with their lifestyle. In general, older generations, and female respondents in particular, understood technologies to be too complicated and dysfunctional and recognised that "technologies have to be simple" in order to fit their own values. From this viewpoint, technologies were not seen as valuable in themselves but only by virtue of their functions:

> But I don't want to get it [digital device] for myself, if it's complicated. It has to be good and functional, so that I can utilise it. Making things simple, that's a good thing nowadays.
>
> (Female, 53)

In many cases, late middle-agers did not want to see themselves as too dependent on technologies. For older generations, functionality was perceived as a core value for digital devices: digital devices are used for banking, purchasing and shopping, information and communication with others (Dholakia, 2012). Dysfunctionality, on the other hand, was conceptualised as a key feature for most devices: "Now when it's all digital, the system does not work in our house" (Male, 52). Also, power cuts were mentioned as a risk factor in digital technologies. Whereas younger respondents understood technologies as developing devices that are constantly under construction, among older generations it was scepticism towards the qualities of the devices in general that caused the critical attitudes towards them.

Late middle-agers significantly differed from young adults in their viewpoints on *safety*. For older generations, digitalisation was connected to values of safety, such as safety of domestic appliances or safety of housing and living in general. Late middle-agers reflected on safety in terms of their relationships with their own parents, and the connection between digitalisation and safety was associated with old adulthood rather than middle age. Safety, besides referring to the safety of digital technologies, was defined through personal relationships:

> In the future, older people can live a longer life with digitalisation . . . nowadays, it is known that some floors can identify whether a person has fallen or is standing, this kind of increases safety to the living of old people.
>
> (Male, 51)

> I was thinking of my mom, she lives alone. It would be a good thing to have digital devices that create safety in living.
>
> (Male, 51)

For late middle-agers, digital technologies represented something that constituted generational experiences and differences between younger and older generations. Although young adults did not recognise themselves as digital natives, for late middle-agers younger adults were represented as the digital generation that utilises new technologies in a different way compared to their own generation. Late middle-agers identified that generational experiences during early adulthood, for instance growing up with a technology in one's twenties, have a significant influence on the ways people use technologies in later life. In their discussion, late middle-agers composed generational experiences and boundaries and their identities through technologies:

> We belong to that age group that it [technology] didn't belong to our lives when we were in our 30s. When I'm thinking about my own kids, who are 25 to 30, they take a shower with their cell phones. Let alone the kids in school. They live in a totally different world.
>
> (Female, 57)

> Last year our son announced that he would like to have a television for a Christmas present, he told me all the models and all. Together we went to see it, and he used the television through a tablet . . . his generation utilises the possibilities in a completely different way.
>
> (Female, 63)

Shared meanings among all participants

Despite the fact that participants shared some values, ideals or attitudes that were age or generation specific, attitudes towards digital domestic technologies also connected participants across generation, age and life-course boundaries. Notably, female participants – regardless of age – shared the experience that they are "not interested in technology", and that technologies in general are not a part of their lifestyle. The use of technologies was interpreted as something that people should naturally have an interest in, and in these respondents' lives, technologies did not have a significant role. These opinions varied from "I'm not at all a digi-person" (Female, 32) to "I'm not at all interested in technology, I use it as little as possible" (Female, 52).

Fears and anxieties related to digital technologies were common among participants regardless of age, generation, life course and gender. Use of new technologies was perceived as a *risk* not only in terms of power cuts but also in terms of health, wellbeing and general safety. In addition, unfamiliarity about the health risks that use of technology involves, such as risk of radiation, was mentioned. The use of digital technologies, and especially smart phones, was also conceptualised as *addictive*; digital devices have already become necessities in most people's lives and therefore "you are anxious when it is not in your pocket" (Male, 65). Digital devices break boundaries in everyday life practices, and in online shopping, for instance, a fear of losing control appeared in some respondents' discussions:

> It is very scary. Many of my friends buy clothes every week on the internet. They just click and it's very scary, how easy the shopping has become.
>
> (Female, 32)

Moreover, respondents in the different age groups identified the *information flow* of digital technologies as *exhausting*. This was especially connected to the use of smartphones associated with the working environment: "My phone rings, I am on the phone all day. After that I want to be in a quiet place" (Male, 57). In today's lifestyles, people perceived not having technologies at home as necessary for their wellbeing, and especially in the domestic environments, living without technologies was perceived as ideal:

> I think the information flow is very exhausting. Now when I have the smartphone, I'm stuck to it all the time. It would be better for me to claim a place in my house which doesn't involve technology.
>
> (Female, 30)

For all participants, not having technologies at home was justified by the idea that "people can do it by themselves". For late middle-agers, managing daily lives without technologies was almost a matter of a pride: "I can manage to turn off the light by myself" (Female, 55) and "I can manage to switch the lighting on and off and push the vacuum cleaner by myself" (Male, 61). Late middle-agers understood technologies in domestic environments as assisting, meaning that technologies will assist the lives of elderly people, with whom they don't identify. In the lives of young adults, managing their lives without technologies was associated with the future: "We will plant such a small lawn that we can cut it by ourselves" (Female, 27). In both young adults and late middle-agers, a preference for living without technologies was associated and justified with a desire for physical activity.

In the context of housing and living, new technologies are still perceived as a *vanity*. When technologies are presented in domestic surroundings, people do not acknowledge them as necessities but rather as outcomes of the markets. In participants' speech, a need for technologies is negotiated between concepts of 'vanity', 'necessity', 'need' and 'desire'. Consumption of technologies is conceptualised in terms of a moral framework (Silverstone and Hirsch, 1992) where the use of new technologies is comprehended as "splurging on non-necessities" which, in terms of housing and living, have negative connotations. Simultaneously, this symbolises the profound distinction between consumer desires and normative restrictions, where consuming technologies for hedonistic purposes is conceptualised as morally suspicious (Lehtonen, 1998, pp. 224, 229–231; Sarantola-Weiss, 2003, pp. 37–39). Therefore, throughout the group discussions, interviewees reassured us and each other of their ability to manage their home without technologies, although they identified the addictive features of them.

Conclusions and discussion

In many previous studies, Finnish people are typically represented as technologically skilled consumers who adopt and orient themselves positively towards new technologies (Desai *et al.*, 2002). When consumption of digital technologies is discussed in groups, digital technologies arouse more negative resistance than positive attitudes. Well-educated, urban and middle-class consumers are very conscious of the markets and the life cycles of products and services, which may result in critical attitudes towards marketing of new technologies. In Finland, consumer attitudes in general, and those of ageing consumers in particular, highlight values and attitudes of ecological and ethical consumption over the values of self-indulgent and hedonistic consumption (Nyrhinen and Wilska, 2012; Wilska, 2002). This, due to an understanding of digital technologies as expensive commodity goods, might lead to perceiving them as 'non-necessities' and 'vanity' in daily lives. Additionally, cultural interpretations of technology reflect the binary codes and symbolic good versus bad, and, therefore, this can connote the profound tendency of consumers to label technologies as something suspicious (Mick and Fournier, 1998; Pantzar, 2000, p. 242). The study asked whether these values and attitudes reflect generational experiences or if they emerge from individual life events. The perception of digital technologies as a vanity connected consumers regardless of generational boundaries, which might imply that these attitudes are not greatly affected by generational experiences.

Although digital domestic technologies are predicted to expand in the future (Ehrenhard *et al.*, 2014), participants in our study understood the digitalisation of domestic environments as a risk to privacy and general wellbeing. Moreover, the participants perceived technology as a risk in different ways, depending on their age and life-course stage. Young adults highlight the risk to privacy and independence whereas late middle-agers perceive technology as a risk to security. These perceived risks can reflect the life course and generation membership of each consumer: members of Generation Ys are said to value independence (Parment, 2011, 2013; Paul, 2001), which may lead to their need to emphasise privacy in the use of technologies. Millennials, being affected by technologies starting in early childhood (Green, 2010), have experienced the all-encompassing effects of technologies in their social relationships and therefore might highlight privacy as a core value and similarly a risk of technologies.

Moreover, the lives of young adults, involving transitions in social relationships from student to employee or from single to married couples and later on to parents (Green, 2010; Hutteman *et al.*, 2014) are characterised by rapid changes and juggling different social roles and responsibilities; thus technologies can also be perceived as a risk in terms of time management, pointing to the need to have control over them. Hence, the commonly known stereotype of those born in the 1980s and early 1990s as 'digital natives' (Dulin, 2008) is not supported in this study; rather, many participants aged 25 to 35 speak about technologies in a belittling way. In young adults' speech, generational experiences or consciousness in the use of digital appliances seemed nevertheless stronger than among late middle-agers, indicating that young adults might have a stronger generational identity in terms of digital technologies than late middle-agers.

Older adults – those aged 50 and over – generally value safety (Pulkkinen and Polet, 2010), and new technologies represent functions related to safety (Ling, 2004; Mikkonen *et al.*, 2002). In our discussions, late middle-agers connected digital technologies to ideals of security, and in the case of smart home solutions, 'digital security' is connected to old adulthood in late middle-agers' speech. Moreover, late middle-agers were much more insecure about their ability to manage technology which resulted in a careful orientation towards it. Late middle-agers became engaged with technologies in their thirties so they might not have had the opportunity to integrate technologies into their already established daily routines (Haddon, 2005). From this perspective, the use of digital technologies seems to be a matter of generation or cohort experience (Ling, 2008).

In our group discussions, however, insecurities towards technologies were interpreted by participants as stemming from inadequate skills. Rather than generational or cohort experience, attitudes towards digital technologies reflect the life-course stage of late middle-agers: with ageing, maintaining satisfactory social relationships becomes important (Charles and Carstensen, 2010; Hutteman *et al.*, 2014), and for ageing consumers, digital technologies represent means of maintaining relationships and communication with family members (Thayer and Ray, 2006). In this study, late middle-agers recognised generational differences in terms of technological skills, but in themselves the differences did not represent a generational consciousness as much as the individual life events related to changes in personal relationships and the need to 'stay in touch' with their family members.

The findings of this study highlight the importance of understanding the particularities of different generations as market segments. Although young adults and middle-agers seem to adhere to similar values and meanings concerning the digitalisation of domestic environments, the subtle differences in perceived risks and benefits of technology provide a basis for cohort-based differentiation of marketing practices. Product design, branding and communication could create personal appeal and a sense of familiarity (Parment, 2013) among middle-agers by demonstrating that digitalised products result in benefits such as safety and the wellbeing of others. Conversely, privacy and independence are focal concerns for young adults, and thus brand, product design and communication personalised to this cohort could be designed accordingly.

Note

1 The Housing Fair is an annual event in Finland that showcases ongoing trends in the housing industry, such as building, architecture and interior design. The Housing Fair is a set area where the houses are built and decorated for the audience to visit (www. asuntomessut.fi).

References

Balta-Ozkan, N., Davidson, R., Bicket, M. and Whitmarsh, L., 2013. Social barriers to the adoption of smart homes. *Energy Policy*, 63, pp. 363–374.

Barnard, Y., Bradkey, M. D., Hodgson, F. and Lloyd, A. D., 2013. Learning to use new technologies by older adults: perceived difficulties, experimentation behaviour and usability. *Computers in Human Behaviour*, 29, pp. 1715–1724.

Beck, U. and Beck-Gernsheim, E., 2002. *Individualization*. London: SAGE.

Beer, A. and Faulkner, D., 2011. *Housing transitions through the life course: aspirations, needs and policy*. Bristol, UK: The Policy Press.

Bijker, W. and Law, J., 1992. *Shaping technology/building society: studies in sociotechnical change*. Cambridge, MA: MIT Press.

Carr, D. J., Gotlieb, M. R., Lee, N. J. and Shah, D. V., 2012. Examining overconsumption, competitive consumption and conscious consumption from 1994 to 2004: disentangling cohort and period effects. *The Annals of the American Academy of Political and Social Science*, 664(1), pp. 220–233.

Carù, A. and Cova, B., 2015. Co-creating the collective service experience. *Journal of Service Management*, 26 (2), pp. 276–294.

Charles, S. T. and Carstensen, L. L., 2010. Social and emotional aging. *Annual Review of Psychology*, 61, pp. 383–409.

Chen, K. and Chan, A. H. S., 2011. A review of technology acceptance by older adults. *Gerontechnology*, 10(1), pp. 1–12.

Chhetri, P., Hossain, M. I. and Broom, A., 2014. Examining the generational differences in consumption patterns in South East Queensland. *City, Culture & Society*, 5(4), pp. 1–9.

Coolen, H. and Hoekstra, J., 2001. Values as determinants of preferences for housing attributes. *Journal of Housing and Built Environment*, 16(3–4), pp. 285–306.

Desai, M., Fukuda-Parr, S., Johansson, C. and Sagasti, F., 2002. Measuring the technology achievement of nations and the capacity to participate in the network age. *Journal of Human Development*, 3(1), pp. 95–122.

De Silva, L. C., Morikawab, C. and Petra, I. M., 2012. State of the art of smart homes, Engineering Applications of Artificial Intelligence, 25(7), pp. 1313–1321.

Dholakia, R. R., 2012. *Technology and consumption: understanding consumer choices and behaviors*. New York: Springer.

Dulin, L., 2008. Leadership preferences of a Generation Y cohort: a mixed-method investigation. *Journal of Leadership Studies*, 2(1), 43–59.

Eastman, J. K. and Liu, J., 2012. The impact of generational cohorts on status consumption: an exploratory look at generational cohort and demographics on status consumption. *Journal of Consumer Marketing*, 29(2), pp. 93–102.

Ehrenhard, M., Kijl, B. and Nieuwenhuis, L., 2014. Market adoption barriers of multi-stakeholder technology: smart homes for the aging population. *Technological forecasting and social change*, 89, pp. 306–315.

Green, L., 2010. *Understanding the life course: sociological and psychological perspectives*. Cambridge, UK: Polity Press.

Haddon, L., 2005. Personal information culture: the contribution of research on ICTs in everyday life. In: *UNESCO between two phases of the World Summit on the Information Society*. St. Petersburg, Russia: UNESCO.

Halkier, B., 2010. Focus groups as social enactments: integrating interaction and content in the analysis of focus group data. *Qualitative Research*, 10(1), pp. 71–89.

Helson, R., Soto, C. J. and Cate, R. A., 2006. From young adulthood through the middle ages. In: D. K. Mroczek and T. D. Little, eds. *Handbook of personality development*. Mahwah, NJ: Psychology Press, pp. 337–352.

Hsieh, H. F. and Shannon, S. E., 2005. Three approaches to qualitative content analysis. *Qualitative Health Research*, 15(9), pp. 1277–1288.

Hutchison, E. D., 2011. *Dimensions of human behaviour: the changing life course*, 4th ed. Los Angeles, CA and London: SAGE.

Hutteman, R., Hennecke, M., Orth, U., Reitz, A. K. and Specht, J., 2014. Developmental tasks as a framework to study personality development in adulthood and old age. *European Journal of Personality*, 28(3), pp. 267–278.

Izuhara, M., 2015. Life-course diversity, housing choices and constraints for women of the 'lost' generation in Japan. *Housing Studies*, 30(1), pp. 60–77.

Karisto, A., 2007. Finnish Baby Boomers and the emergence of the third age. *International Journal of Ageing and Later Life*, 2(2), pp. 91–108.

Kline, R. and Pinch, T., 1999. The social construction of technology. In: D. MacKenzie and J. Wajcman, eds. *The social shaping of technology*. 2nd ed. Milton Keynes, UK: Open University Press, pp. 113–115.

Kohli, M., 2007. The institutionalization of the life course: looking back to look ahead. *Research in Human Development*, 4(3–4), pp. 253–271.

Koivula, A., Räsänen, P. and Sarpila, O., 2015. *Suomi 2014 –kulutus ja elämäntapa. Tutkimusseloste ja aineistojen 2009 ja 2014 vertailua. Working Papers in Economic Sociology*. Turku, Finland: Turun yliopisto.

Kokko, K., 2010. Keski-iän määrittelyä ja kuvailua. In: L. Pulkkinen and K. Kokko, eds. *Keski-ikä elämänvaiheena*. Jyväskylän yliopiston psykologian laitoksen julkaisuja 352. Jyväskylä, Finland: Jyväskylän yliopisto.

Lehtonen, T. K., 1998. Rajallista ostamista: itsekuri, omatunto ja mielihyvä. In: J. P. Roos and T. Hoikkala, eds. *Elämänpolitiikka*. Tampere, Finland: Gaudeamus.

Ling, R., 2004. *The mobile connection: the cell phone's impact on society.* San Francisco, CA: Morgan Kaufman.

Ling, R., 2008. Should we be concerned that the elderly don't text? *The Information Society,* 24, pp. 334–341.

Livingstone, S. M. and Lunt, P. K., 1991. Generational and life cycle differences in experiences of ownership. *Journal of Social Behaviour and Personality,* 6(6), pp. 229–242.

Mannheim, K., 1952. Essay on the problem of generations. In: P. Kecskemeti, ed. *Essays on the sociology of knowledge by Karl Mannheim.* New York: Routledge & Kegan Paul.

Meredith, G. and Schewe, C. D., 1994. The power of cohorts. *American Demographics,* 16(12), pp. 22–31.

Mick, D. G. and Fournier, S., 1998. Paradoxes of technology: consumer cognizance, emotions, and coping strategies. *Journal of Consumer Research,* 25(2), pp. 123–143.

Mikkonen, M., Väyrynen, S., Ikonen, V. and Heikkilä, M. O., 2002. User and concept studies as tools in developing mobile communication services for the elderly. *Personal and Ubiquitous Computing,* 6, pp. 113–124.

Nyrhinen, J. and Wilska, T.-A., 2012. Kohti vastuullista ylellisyyttä? Eettiset ja ekologiset trendit sekä luksuskulutus Suomessa. *Kulutustutkimus.Nyt,* 6(1), pp. 20–41.

Oksman, V., 2006. Young people and seniors in Finnish mobile information society. *Journal of Interactive Media in Education,* 2, pp. 1–21.

Pantzar, M., 2000. *Tulevaisuuden koti: arjen tarpeita keksimässä.* Helsinki, Finland: Otava.

Parment, A., 2011. *Generation Y in consumer and labor markets.* New York: Routledge.

Parment, A., 2013. Generation Y vs. Baby Boomers: shopping behavior, buyer involvement and implications for retailing. *Journal of Retailing and Consumer Services,* 20(2), pp. 189–199.

Paul, P., 2001. Getting inside Generation Y. *American Demographics,* 23(9), pp. 42–49.

Pinch, T. and Bijker, W., 1984. The social construction of facts and artefacts: or how the sociology of science and sociology of technology might benefit each other. *Social Studies of Science,* 14, pp. 399–441.

Piper, A. M., Cornejo Garcia, R. and Brewer, R. N., 2016. understanding the challenges and opportunities of smart mobile devices among the oldest old. *International Journal of Mobile Human Computer Interaction,* 8(2), pp. 83–98.

Pulkkinen, L. and Polet, J., 2010. Tyydytystä ja huolta aiheuttavat asiat elämässä. In: L. Pulkkinen and K. Kokko, eds. *Keski-ikä elämänvaiheena.* Jyväskylän yliopiston psykologian laitoksen julkaisuja 352. Jyväskylä, Finland: Jyväskylän yliopisto.

Purhonen, S., 2007. Sukupolvien ongelma: tutkielma sukupolven käsitteestä, sukupolvitietoisuudesta ja suurista ikäluokista. PhD. Research Reports No. 251. Helsinki, Finland: University of Helsinki.

Rabiee, F., 2004. Focus-group interview and data analysis. *Proceedings of the Nutrition Society,* 63, pp. 655–660.

Ryder, N. B., 1985. The cohort as a concept in the study of social change. In: W. M. Mason and S. E. Fienberg, eds. *Cohort analysis in social research.* New York: Springer.

Sarantola-Weiss, M., 2003. *Sohvaryhmän läpimurto: kulutuskulttuurin tulo suomalaisiin olohuoneisiin 1960- ja 1970-lukujen vaihteessa.* Helsinki, Finland: Suomalaisen Kirjallisuuden Seura.

Selwyn, N., 2004. The information aged: a qualitative study of older adults' use of information and communications technology. *Journal of Aging Studies,* 18(4), pp. 369–384.

Selwyn, N., 2012. Making sense of young people, education and digital technology: the role of sociological theory. *Oxford Review of Education,* 38(1), pp. 81–96.

Silverstone, R. and Hirsch, E., 1992. *Consuming technologies: media and information in domestic spaces*. London: Routledge.

Smith, A., 2010. *Home Broadband 2010*. Washington, DC: Pew Internet and American Life Project.

Smola, K. V. and Sutton, C.D., 2002. Generational differences: revising generational work values for the new millennium. *Journal of Organizational Behavior*, 23(4), pp. 363–382.

Syrett, M. and Lamminman, J., 2004. Advertising and millennials. *Young Consumers*, 5(4), pp. 62–73.

Thayer, S. E. and Ray, S., 2006. Online communication preferences across age, gender and duration of internet use. *CyberPsychology & Behaviour*, 9(4), pp. 432–440.

Thomas, L., MacMillan, J., McColl, E., Hale, C. and Bond, S., 1995. Comparison of focus group and individual interview methodology in examining patient satisfaction with nursing care. *Social Sciences in Health*, 1, pp. 206–219.

Valentine, D. B. and Powers, T. L., 2013. Generation Y values and lifestyle segments. *Journal of Consumer Marketing*, 30(7), pp. 597–606.

Wilska, T.-A., 2002. Me – a consumer? Consumption, identities and lifestyles in today's Finland. *Acta Sosiologica*, 45(3), pp. 195–210.

Zickuhr, K. and Madden, M., 2012. Older adults and internet use. www.sainetz.at/dokumente/Older_adults_and_internet_use_2012.pdf.

13 Personality traits and computer use in midlife

Leisure activities and work characteristics as mediators

Tiia Kekäläinen and Katja Kokko

Background

Nowadays, computers and the internet are part of everyday life. According to a survey conducted by Eurostat (2015) in 2014, 78 per cent of adults in European Union countries had used the internet during the previous three months. The survey found that the younger the age group, the greater the proportion of internet users. The reasons for using the internet appear similar across age, and the most common reasons are: information searches, email and other communications, and internet banking (Keenan, 2009; Statistics Finland, 2015). The most noteworthy difference between age groups is in the use of social networking sites (SNS); in Finland, 87 per cent of people aged 25–34, 51 per cent of people aged 45–54 and 19 per cent of people aged 65–74 used the internet for social networking (Statistics Finland, 2015).

In addition to age, gender has some link to computer and internet use such that although the frequency of internet use is similar between men and women, they use the internet for somewhat different purposes (Keenan, 2009; Statistics Finland, 2015). For example, men use internet for reading news and seeking information about goods and services more than women, whereas women use it for reading blogs and seeking information about health issues more than men (Statistics of Finland, 2015). It is noteworthy that the reasons for computer use in general extend beyond the use of the internet, but then, internet use is no longer linked solely to computers. In this chapter, we present research in both domains: computer use and internet use. Research has increasingly focused on the use of SNS, Facebook in particular, which is the most popular social networking site in the world, with over one billion users in December 2015 (Facebook Company Info, 2016).

Computer, internet and SNS use have been widely studied, and many individual factors predict their use, for example age, life satisfaction and social resources (education, income) are linked to computer use in different age groups (Hills and Argyle, 2003; Kim and Jeong, 2015; Livingstone and Haddon, 2009; Papacharissi and Rubin, 2000; Wagner *et al.*, 2010). In addition to age, generation and age cohort contribute to computer and internet use such that younger generations, X (born 1965–1979) and Y (born 1976–1994) use computers and the internet much more than older generations, such as baby boomers (born 1946–1964) (Anderson *et al.*, 2010). Generations differ in when they started using modern digital technology: generation Y since they were kids, generation X before entering the working life and baby boomers in their midlife. Hence, according to Shah *et al.* (2001), the most important media for generation X is the internet, whereas for baby boomers it is television, which reflect their perceptions.

The biggest difference between generations is in the use of SNS, but studies have mainly been conducted among children, youth and young adults (Amichai-Hamburger and Vinitzky, 2010; Guadagno *et al.*, 2008; Kuo and Tang, 2014; Özgüven and Mucan, 2013; Tuukkanen *et al.*, 2013; Wilson *et al.*, 2010). Relatively little attention has been paid to middle-aged adults' use of computers and SNS, particularly from the viewpoint of personality. Therefore, this chapter focuses on middle-aged adults and their individual characteristics as predictors of computer use. The chapter also investigates whether leisure activities or work characteristics mediate the associations between personality and computer use among middle-agers.

Personality traits

Besides socio-demographic factors such as age and education, computer use is associated with other characteristics of an individual. In this chapter, we analyse personality, which describes the ways individuals think, feel and behave (McCrae and Costa, 2003), as a potential antecedent of computer use. We conceptualise personality here using the Big Five taxonomy (also known as the five-factor model), where the five personality traits are extraversion, neuroticism, agreeableness, conscientiousness and openness to new experiences (Goldberg, 1993; John and Srivastava, 1999; McCrae and Costa, 2003).

Every personality trait can be seen as a continuum. For example, McCrae and Costa (2003) and John and Srivastava (1999) describe typical characteristics of individuals who are in extremes of a continuum, in other words high or low in the traits. According to them, *extraversion* is a personality trait reflecting activity, optimism and the desire to be with other people, while individuals with low extraversion are reserved and quiet. Individuals who score high in *neuroticism* typically have negative feelings, whereas individuals with low scores in neuroticism have high emotional stability and can handle difficult and stressful situations well. Furthermore, McCrae and Costa note that *openness to new experiences* is related to a desire to seek new experiences and broaden a way of thinking, whereas individuals with low scores are down-to-earth and prefer routine. People with high scores in *conscientiousness* are well-organised, hardworking and dutiful, and those with low scores are aimless and negligent. *Agreeableness*, on the other hand, is a trait related to good-natured, unselfish and altruistic behaviour, whereas individuals with low agreeableness are critical, antagonistic and hardheaded.

An individual's personality is considered to be quite stable across situations and the life course (Caspi *et al.*, 2005; McAdams and Olson, 2010). With respect to the relative stability in the rank-ordering of the Big Five, the same longitudinal data used in the present study show a high level of continuity in adulthood (Kokko *et al.*, 2013). There is also significant continuity from childhood temperamental characteristics to adult personality traits; for example, behavioural activity in childhood contributes to extraversion-related characteristics in adulthood, particularly in males (Pulkkinen *et al.*, 2012). As regards absolute stability, some general changes in the levels of the personality traits take place over time in adulthood, as conscientiousness and agreeableness tend to increase in midlife, whereas neuroticism tends to decrease (Kokko *et al.*, 2013; Roberts and Mroczek, 2008).

Personality traits and computer use

The links between the Big Five personality traits and computer or internet use have been analysed in several studies. Recently, the role of personality traits in social media use has also been studied, although mostly among younger adults. In the majority of previous studies, extraversion has not been linked to internet use in general (Berner *et al.*, 2012; Chen and Persson, 2002; Hills and Argyle, 2003; Kim and Jeong, 2015; Swickert *et al.*, 2002). However, extraversion has specifically been linked with more frequent use of social media (Correa *et al.*, 2010; Ryan and Xenos, 2011; Wilson *et al.*, 2010), especially for communication (Ryan and Xenos, 2011). Moreover, this association was similar among both young (aged 18–29) and older adults (aged 30+) (Correa *et al.*, 2010). The studies also suggest that individuals with high and low scores in extraversion use social media for different purposes (Orchard and Fullwood, 2010); individuals high in extraversion may use social media to communicate with friends and to broaden their social network, while individuals low in extraversion may also use social media because they prefer online communication to real-life communication (Orchard and Fullwood, 2010).

Like extraversion, neuroticism was not correlated with computer or internet use in general (Berner *et al.*, 2012; Chen and Persson, 2002; Hills and Argyle, 2003; Landers and Lounsbury, 2006), but it has been linked to social media use. Several studies found that individuals who are high in neuroticism use social media more than individuals low in neuroticism (Correa *et al.*, 2010; Kuo and Tang, 2014; Ryan and Xenos, 2011). However, according to Correa *et al.* (2010), this association has been found only in adults aged 30 and over, and only in men. Individuals who have high or low scores in neuroticism may, like individuals with high or low scores in extraversion, have different motives for using Facebook: individuals high in neuroticism may use it to boost their self-assurance, while individuals low in neuroticism share information for self-actualisation (Amichai-Hamburger and Vinitzky, 2010). It has also been reported that individuals high in neuroticism perceive Facebook as a part of their everyday lives and feel lost if they have not used it for a while (Kuo and Tang, 2014). It may be that the resemblance between individuals who have high scores in neuroticism and low scores in extraversion is explained by a preference for both types for online communication to real-life communication.

Openness to new experiences has been positively associated with internet use (Chen and Persson, 2002; Kim and Jeong, 2015) and especially with social media use (Correa *et al.*, 2010; Guadagno *et al.*, 2008; Kuo and Tang, 2014). Correa *et al.* (2010), observed that high openness predicts social media use in individuals aged 30 and older, but not in younger adults, and only in women. These results may not come as a surprise since it can be assumed that the adoption of new technologies interests individuals with intellectual curiosity and willingness to engage in new activities, but why the association is found only among older adults remains unclear.

For conscientiousness, again, the results are somewhat inconsistent. Some studies show that individuals with high scores in conscientiousness use computers for academic purposes (Landers and Lounsbury, 2006; Orchard and Fullwood, 2010), but less frequently for leisure purposes (Landers and Lounsbury, 2006), and less for social media (Hughes *et al.*, 2012; Ryan and Xenos, 2011; Wilson *et al.*, 2010). In other studies, no associations were found between conscientiousness and internet use (Berner *et al.*, 2012; Chen and Persson, 2002; Swickert *et al.*, 2002). These results on computer use are reasonable considering individuals who are characterised by high conscientiousness may want to do their jobs well and carefully, and use the computer more for those purposes than for recreation.

Moreover, in previous research, agreeableness has shown no associations with computer or internet use in general (Berner *et al.*, 2012; Kim and Jeong, 2015; Swickert *et al.*, 2002) or with social media use (Guadagno *et al.*, 2008; Özgüven and Mucan, 2013; Ross *et al.*, 2009; Ryan and Xenos, 2011; Wilson *et al.*, 2010). In studies where some significant associations have been found, high agreeableness has been linked to infrequent use of computers (Landers and Lounsbury, 2006) and Facebook (Kuo and Tang, 2014).

Leisure activities as possible mediators between personality traits and computer use

Although different personality traits seem to have associations with different types of leisure activities, to the best of our knowledge no previous research has been published on the factors mediating personality traits and computer and internet use. We hypothesise that leisure might be one such mediator since it is linked to both personality and computer use (Figure 13.1). In order to function as mediator, certain criteria need to be met, as suggested by Baron and Kenny (1986). First, the personality traits in question and computer use have to correlate with each other. Second, the personality traits have to correlate with the mediator variables, and finally, the mediators have to correlate with computer use. As described above, personality traits show some significant, though inconsistent, associations with computer, internet and social media use, but they are also associated with other types of leisure activities. Extraversion and openness to new experiences, in particular, are positively associated with different kinds of leisure activities, such as sports activities and outdoor leisure (Jopp and Hertzog, 2010; Kuo and Tang, 2014). Conversely, high neuroticism is associated with less frequent participation in outdoor leisure and fitness (Kuo and Tang, 2014) and in experiential activities (e.g. gardening, reading) (Jopp and Hertzog, 2010). Furthermore, both agreeableness and conscientiousness have been positively associated with religious activities and experiential activities (Jopp and Hertzog, 2010).

A few studies investigated the associations between computer use and other leisure activities. One key suggestion is that a high level of internet use is associated, although not linearly, with more active leisure (Näsi *et al.*, 2011; Zhou *et al.*, 2014). Janković *et al.* (2016) found an association between Facebook use and higher participation in other leisure activities among students, but only to a certain extent; if Facebook takes too much time, then that time is taken away from other activities. According to Näsi *et al.* (2011), having a higher number of other leisure activities predicted more frequent internet use among a sample of elderly persons (aged 60–79). In general, older adults use computers less than younger people, which may reveal what an active life means at different ages. Associations may also depend on the types of activities engaged in: according to Zhou *et al.* (2014), internet users go to movies and amusement parks more often than others, but are less active in the domain of physical exercise. One reason for the inconsistencies in the results may be the method of measurement. For example, Robinson (2011) compared three national samples and found that according to self-assessment data, internet users were also more active in other leisure activities, whereas diary-based data showed no differences between internet users and non-users in the amount of leisure activities.

We found that with the exception of Kuo and Tang (2014), no studies have investigated personality traits, leisure activities and Facebook simultaneously. In addition, to the best of our knowledge, the same applies to computer and internet use in general. Kuo and Tang (2014) found an association between high extraversion and higher frequency of Facebook use and a higher number of friends on Facebook, which in turn was positively associated with participation in team sports. It follows that openness to new experiences, number of Facebook friends and participation in team sports are all positively correlated with each other. On the other hand, neuroticism correlates positively and agreeableness negatively with the frequency of Facebook use, which in turn correlated negatively with fitness activities. Hence, diverse paths may exist between personality, leisure activities and the use of Facebook. However, Kuo and Tang (2014) did not analyse them in the same model, and they recommended the use of structural equation modelling in future studies.

Work characteristics as possible mediators between personality traits and computer use

While computer and social media use are obviously a way of spending leisure time, for middle-aged adults computer use does not mean leisure entertainment alone, as it is also used for work-related activities. Accomplishing work-related tasks is one of the most common reasons for computer use among middle-agers (Mann *et al.*, 2005), and for this group, with the diffusion of technical devices and the internet, the boundary between work and leisure has become blurred, as personal computers have made it possible to work during leisure time and at home.

According to Berkowsky (2013), 86 per cent of adults check work-related emails at least sometimes at home. Therefore, we analyse computer use for business matters outside of working hours along with computer use for leisure purposes and social media use.

Studies show that personality contributes to many aspects of the working career, such as occupational status and income (Judge *et al.*, 1999; Viinikainen *et al.*, 2010). Openness to new experiences, extraversion and conscientiousness have been associated with higher occupational status and better job performance (Barrick and Mount, 1991; Judge *et al.*, 1999), and extraversion is also associated with higher income (Judge *et al.*, 1999; Viinikainen *et al.*, 2010). Both the studies by Viinikainen *et al.* 2010, which is based on the same data as the present article, and by Judge *et al.* (1999) found that even childhood personality correlated with adulthood career success. Thus, because business-related computer use could be hypothesised to depend on work characteristics, we also consider them as possible mediating factors between personality traits and computer and internet use (Figure 13.1).

The purpose of this study

Previous studies have analysed the associations between personality traits, leisure activities, work characteristics and different types of computer use as single links. Those studies were based mainly on cross-sectional data, yet the present study analyses these different variables simultaneously, using longitudinal data. Figure 13.1 shows our study design, where we hypothesise that personality traits, measured at age 42, are linked to computer and social media use, assessed at age 50. We further assume that work characteristics and leisure activities, measured at age 42, mediate this direct link; that is, personality traits are associated with these mediating factors, which for their part, relate to computer and social media use. The moderating role

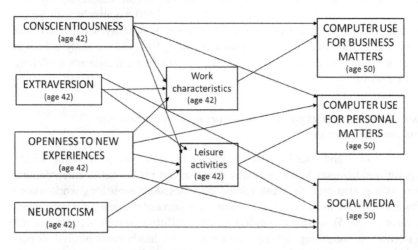

Figure 13.1 Hypothesised path model.

of gender in the associations between personality and computer use has remained unclear, as some studies found no differences between men and women (Kim and Jeong, 2015; Özgüven and Mucan, 2013) while others did (Amichai-Hamburger and Vinitzky, 2010; Correa *et al.*, 2010; Guadagno *et al.*, 2008). Therefore, we also studied the gender differences in the associations.

Our research questions were as follows:

1   Which personality traits contribute to different kinds of computer use in midlife?
2   Do work characteristics and leisure activities mediate the associations between personality traits and computer use?

Methods

Participants

This study is based on the Jyväskylä Longitudinal Study of Personality and Social Development (JYLS). The JYLS was started in 1968 by Professor Lea Pulkkinen and the same participants have thus far been followed from age 8 to 50 (initial N=369) (Pulkkinen, 2009; 2017). Most participants were born in 1959 and are representative of their respective Finnish age cohort (Pulkkinen and Kokko, 2010), belonging to the tail of baby boomers, also called the younger baby boomers (Reisenwitz and Iyer, 2007). In these analyses for this study, we use information gathered in 2001 when the participants were 42 years old (N=285) and in 2009 when they were 50 (N=271). The number of participants varied as a function of missing information on different variables in a range from 213 to 279. Data were collected using life situation questionnaires (LSQ), semi-structured psychological interviews (in the context of which several self-report inventories were filled in) and a medical examination.

Measures and variables

The main outcome variables in this study are different types of computer use at age 50. First, the participants answered in the LSQ whether they used or had used a computer (1) or not (0). They were also asked how many hours a week they used a computer for business matters outside of working hours and how many hours a week they used a computer for personal matters or enjoyment. Based on the distribution of responses, computer use for business matters was categorised into 0 (1), 1–2 (2) and ≥3 (3) hours per week, and computer use for personal matters into ≤1 (1), 2–4 (2) and ≥5 (3) hours per week. The use of social media (Facebook, chat, blogs) was elicited as part of a more extensive leisure time and activity self-report inventory and utilised a response scale from 1 (not at all or very seldom) to 4 (twice a week or more frequently). Response categories were dichotomised into non-users and users. Non-users represented category 1, who answered not at all or very seldom (0), and users categories 2 to 4 (1).

Antecedents of computer use were measured at age 42 and personality was measured with the NEO-FFI[1] (Costa and McCrae, 1989; Kokko *et al.*, 2013), a shortened 60-item version of the NEO-PI[2] questionnaire (Costa and McCrae, 1985; Pulver *et al.*, 1995). Each personality trait was measured by 12 statements with a response scale from 1 = strongly disagree to 5 = strongly agree, and mean scores calculated. Cronbach's alphas for the traits were .87 for neuroticism, .75 for extraversion, .78 for openness to new experiences, .78 for conscientiousness and .79 for agreeableness (Kokko *et al.*, 2013).

Occupational status and weekly working hours were used as work-related characteristics, and we used three categories of occupational status: 1 = blue-collar, 2 = lower white-collar and 3 = higher white-collar (Pulkkinen *et al.*, 1999). Acquired using the LSQ, weekly working hours ranged from 0 to 100 and leisure activities were elicited as frequency of participation in 22 different activities using a self-report inventory with a response scale from 1 (daily) to 5 (never) and the participants' responses were reverse-scored (Pulkkinen, forthcoming). New mean scores were formed: 'watching TV' (watching informative or topical TV series, entertainment programmes, crime or action programmes, videos), 'reading' (reading books, visiting a library) and 'attending events' (going to see a film, attending cultural events). The variable 'creative activities' includes writing, visual activities, playing a musical instrument and singing, and was dichtomised into 0 (never doing any of these) and 1 (doing at least one of them) with the remaining leisure activity variables based on single questions. Based on their distribution, 'religious activity' and 'organisational activities' were dichotomised into 0 (never) and 1 (all other options) and 'socialising', 'handicrafts', 'outdoor activities' and 'exercise' were used with the original categorisation. Exercise was measured with a 7-category scale from 0 (never) to 6 (practically every day).

Data analyses

We carried out the analyses using IBM SPSS Statistics 22.0 (IBM Corp., 2013) with the exception of the path analyses, for which we used Mplus 7-software (Muthén and Muthén, 1998–2015). First, for descriptive statistics, differences between men and women were estimated by independent samples t-test and chi-square test, then Pearson's rank-order correlations separately for men and women for all the personality traits, work characteristics, leisure activities, and computer use variables. Furthermore, gender differences were tested using Fisher's r-to-z transformation (McNemar, 1969).

Based on the previously mentioned mediator criteria (Baron and Kenny, 1986), we chose variables for the path analyses according to their correlations. Here, personality traits that did not correlate with any computer use variable were excluded, and only work characteristics and leisure activities that correlated with at least one personality trait and one computer use variable were included. In the path analysis, we used weighted least squares (WLSMV) as the estimator method, which is a robust method when a model includes categorical dependent variables (Muthén and Muthén, 1998–2015). Lastly, the parametrisation used was theta.

Results

Descriptive statistics

The frequency of computer use for different purposes and the number of overall users are reported in Table 13.1. Men and women differed significantly only in computer use for business matters, which men did more. With respect to personality traits, as previously reported by Kokko *et al.* (2013), women had significantly higher openness to new experiences and agreeableness, but there were also some gender differences in work characteristics and leisure activities.

Table 13.1 Frequencies and means with gender differences.

	All (n=213–279)	Women (n=109–132)	Men (n=104–147)	x^2-test/ t-test p
Have used a computer %				.581
No	5.8	5.0	6.6	
Yes	94.2	95.0	93.4	
Social media %				.294
No	80.8	78.0	83.7	
Yes	19.2	22.0	16.3	
Computer use for business matters %				.011
0 h/w	58.0	57.1	58.8	
1–2 h/w	24.2	31.4	17.6	
3≤ h/w	17.9	11.4	23.5	
Computer use for personal matters %				.281
1≥ h/w	29.1	33.0	25.8	
2–4 h/w	34.5	35.9	33.3	
5≤ h/w	36.3	31.1	40.8	
Neuroticism	2.37	2.40	2.33	.475
Extraversion	3.30	3.33	3.24	.469
Openness	3.32	3.45	3.17	<.001
Conscientiousness	3.69	3.75	3.60	.063
Agreeableness	3.63	3.72	3.48	.005
Occupational status %				.001
blue-collar	34.6	12.8	54.0	
lower white-collar	38.9	62.4	24.5	
higher white collar	26.5	24.8	28.0	
Weekly working hours	38.80	36.46	40.90	.032
Watching TV	4.08	3.93	4.22	.001
Reading	2.69	2.95	2.46	.001
Attending events	1.91	1.99	1.84	.009
Socialising	3.55	3.45	3.64	.041
Handicrafts	2.94	2.80	3.07	.026

(continued)

Table 13.1 (continued)

	All (n=213–279)	Women (n=109–132)	Men (n=104–147)	x^2-test/ t-test p
Outdoor activities	3.27	3.44	3.12	.007
Exercise	3.07	3.18	2.97	.332
Creative activities %				.057
No	68.5	62.9	73.5	
Yes	37.1	26.5	31.5	
Religious activity %				.014
No	68.9	62.6	76.2	
Yes	30.2	37.4	23.8	
Organisational activity %				
No	65.1	67.2	63.3	.495
Yes	34.9	32.8	36.7	

Note: Computer use was measured at age 50, and personality traits, work characteristics and leisure activities at age 42.

In studying whether the small group of computer non-users (n=15) differed from users (n=243) in personality traits (Table 13.2), we found three significant differences: the non-users have higher scores in neuroticism, lower scores in extraversion and openness to new experiences than the computer users. Because the non-user group was so small, further analyses were not considered reasonable.

Correlations between computer use, personality traits, work characteristics and leisure activities for men and women are presented in Table 13.3. As already mentioned, to meet the criteria for mediators (Baron and Kenny, 1986), first, personality has to correlate with computer use, and, second, both personality and computer use have to relate to potential mediators, that is, work characteristics and leisure activities. In women, we discovered that the only association between personality traits and computer use was between extraversion and computer use for business matters. In men, however, extraversion and openness correlated positively with computer use for business matters, agreeableness negatively with computer use for personal matters, and openness positively with social media use. Work characteristics and leisure activities had several correlations with personality traits and

Table 13.2 Differences in personality traits between computer users and non-users, independent samples t-test.

	Have used a computer		
	No (n=15)	Yes (n=243)	p
Neuroticism	2.95	2.34	**.004**
Extraversion	2.80	3.31	**.006**
Openness to new experiences	2.87	3.36	**.010**
Agreeableness	3.42	3.64	.200
Conscientiousness	3.52	3.69	.320

Note: Statistically significant (p<.05) coefficients are in bold.

Table 13.3 Correlations between personality, computer use, work characteristics and leisure activities for women/men.

	N	E	O	A	C	CB	CP	SM
CB	-.12/-18	.24*/.37*	.15/.27*	-.16/.01	-.03/.15	—	—	—
CP	.08/-.07	-.05/-.03	.06/.10	-.12/-.17*	.00/.00	-.02/.24*[a]	—	—
SM	-.02/.06	-.04/-.03	.16/.32*	-.03/-.04	-.01/-.18	.16/.98	-.34*/.33*	—
W1	-.42*/-.32*	.28*/.26*	.31*/.24*	.04/.11	.03/.21	.24*/.31*	.08/.23*[a]	.02/.15*[a]
W2	-.08/-.04	.18/.27*	-.04/-.08	-.04/-.13	.06/.03	.36*/.29*	-.09/-.01	.18/.07
A1	.01/-.06	.16/.06	.17/.17	.11/-.04	.11/.01	.08/.06	-.08/-.20*	-.08/-.02
A2	-.03/-.18	.15/.24*	-.09/.18	-.03/.17*[a]	-.07/-.05	.20*/.14	.26*/.09	.32*/.23*
A3	-.08/-.15	.05/.09	.05/.12	.01/-.02	-.17/.18[a]	-.05/.07	-.00/.05	.15/.02
A4	-.07/-.01	.08/.21*	.05/.16	.25*/.20*	.01/-.22*[a]	-.04/.01	-.17/-.04	-.04/.03
A5	-.08/-.01	.08/-.10	.09/-.06	.21*/.20*	.14/.09	.04/-.08	-.20*/-.01	-.03/-.05
A6	-.08/-.02	.10/.07	-.12/-.05	.00/.11	-.00/-.13	-.10/.04	.01/.06	-.04/-.07
A7	.17/.13	.04/-.06	.00/.13	-.21*/.00[a]	-.07/-.10	-.01/.13	-.10/.00	-.17/.20*[a]
A8	.03/.11	-.04/-.07	-.25*/-.14	-.00/-.08	-.03/-.06	-.10/-.18	.14/-.03	.06/.08
A9	.09/-.07	.10/.17	.35*/.25*	-.07/.18*[a]	-.09/.02	.21*/.19	.04/.22*	.16/-.07[a]
A10	.00/-.06	-.12/.06	.38*/.25*	-.04/.23*[a]	-.13/.01	.01/-.05	-.02/.01	-.07/.00

Notes: N=neuroticism, E=extraversion, O=openness, A=agreeableness, C=conscientiousness, CB=computer use for business matters, CP=computer use for personal matters, SM=social media, W1=occupational status, W2=weekly working hours, A1=religious activity, A2=organisational activity, A3=handicrafts, A4=socialising, A5=outdoor activities, A6=going out, A7=exercise, A8=watching TV, A9=creative activities, A10=reading; *p<.05; [a] significant difference between men and women (Fisher's z-test).

computer use. However, only work characteristics and leisure activities that met the criteria for the mediator according to their correlations were included in the path analysis. Occupational status correlated positively with extraversion, openness to new experiences, computer use for business matters and social media use for men. In addition, weekly working hours correlated positively with extraversion and computer use for business matters. Regarding leisure activities, organisational activities correlated positively with extraversion and computer use for business matters, and outdoor activities correlated positively with agreeableness and negatively with computer use for personal matters.

In summary, we included variables in the path analyses according to their significance, as shown by their correlations; independent variables included were extraversion, agreeableness and openness to new experiences. As possible mediator variables, we included occupational status, weekly working hours, participating in organisational activities and outdoor activities, and dependent variables incorporated in the analyses were computer use for business matters, computer use for personal matters and social media use.

Path analysis

To see whether the differences in structural paths across gender were statistically significant, we conducted multiple group path analysis.[3] We first estimated a model with no constraints on gender, but according to the indices,[4] the model fit was not satisfactory. Because of their high modification indices, the variable measuring participation in organisational activities was allowed to correlate with computer use for personal matters and social media, while the measure for occupational status was allowed to correlate with computer use for personal matters only. With these changes, the free baseline model showed a good fit to the observed data,[5] so next, we compared the fit of this baseline model with no constraints to a model where all paths were constrained to be equal for men and women. Using these results,[6] the

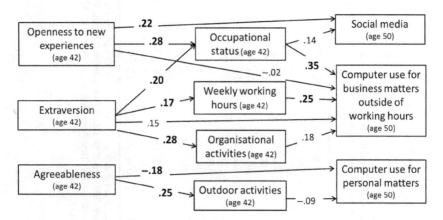

Figure 13.2 The mediator path model between personality traits and computer use.

final model was then estimated with the whole sample. Given the high modification index, weekly working hours and outdoor activities were also allowed to correlate with each other. The fit of the final model was good,[7] and the results of the mediator model are presented in Figure 13.2 with standardised coefficients.

In the path model, openness to new experiences was directly linked to social media use (p=.041) and agreeableness to computer use for personal matters (p=.033), as already shown by the correlations. Conversely, extraversion showed insignificant associations with business-related computer use (p=.135). It was linked to higher occupational status and weekly working hours which, in turn, were related to computer use for business matters. Hence, the association between extraversion and computer use for business matters was mediated by work characteristics.

Discussion

The purpose of this study was to investigate which personality traits predict computer use in midlife, and whether work characteristics and leisure activities mediate these associations. The chapter also discussed the moderating role of gender. Some significant results are presented here. First, a small group of computer non-users differ from computer users in their personality, and the study found that high neuroticism, low extraversion and low openness to new experiences predicted non-use of a computer at age 50. These results indicate that personality relates to whether or not technology is adopted. Second, the hypothesis that gender would moderate the associations is not supported in this study because it is possible that gender differences are more significant among other age groups than middle-agers.

Third, we found that computer use for business matters outside of working hours is predicted by extraversion mediated by work characteristics, thereby supporting our hypothesis. Extraversion appears to contribute to having the kind of job where computer use for business matters is also necessary during leisure time. On the other hand, contrary to our expectations, conscientiousness is not associated with computer use for business matters.

Fourth, computer use for personal matters was predicted by agreeableness: individuals with high scores in agreeableness used computers for personal matters less than individuals with low scores in agreeableness. The results are in line with those of Landers and Lounsbury (2006), who suggest that agreeableness correlates negatively with internet use among students. They assume that students low in agreeableness are less popular and therefore have more time to spend on the internet. Agreeable people are, for example, altruistic and compliant (McCrae and Costa, 2003), hence it is possible that in midlife, agreeable individuals prefer other types of activities, such as those focused on the needs of others through personal interaction. Therefore, the only possible mediator between agreeableness and computer use is outdoor activities, but it does not mediate the association. It seems that the association between agreeableness and leisurely computer use is either direct or is mediated by other factors that remain unidentified in this study.

Furthermore, our hypotheses that computer use for personal matters would show a negative association with conscientiousness and a positive association with openness to new experiences, did not receive support. In addition, our further, unreported, ANOVA comparison shows that computer use for personal matters was average among individuals with high scores in extraversion, whereas for low-scoring individuals, it was either on a low or high level. Hence, the association between extraversion and personal computer use may not be linear. This may be one reason why previous studies found hardly any associations between extraversion and computer or internet use (Berner *et al.*, 2012; Chen and Persson, 2002; Swickert *et al.*, 2002), and why in this study no significant correlation was found between extraversion and personal computer use. Because extraverts are sociable and active persons, they may spend some of their leisure time using a computer, but their interest also extends to other leisure activities.

Fifth, the only personality trait that predicted social media use was openness to new experiences. This is consistent with previous results, where openness was associated with Facebook and other social media use (Kuo and Tang, 2014; Özgüven and Mucan, 2013). Contrary to our expectations, extraversion and neuroticism showed no associations with social media use. One explanation for this may be that at the time of data collection (2009) social media was a recent phenomenon, especially for middle-agers and older adults. This would also explain the finding that only one-fifth of our sample reported using social media at least sometimes. Therefore, openness to new experiences, in particular, may have been a significant predictor of adoption of this phenomenon, new in 2009. The only possible mediator between openness and social media use in this study was occupational status, and it did not mediate the association. Hence our hypothesis that leisure activities would mediate personality and leisure computer or social media use was not supported.

When interpreting the results of this study, it is important to bear in mind that the data were collected in 2009, hence the results are not directly applicable to the 50-year-olds of today. The development of technology is so rapid that its use will have characteristics specific to every age cohort. For example, in the recent past, using the internet was clearly connected to the use of a stationary computer; this is no longer the case. Nevertheless, this study offers interesting information on the seldom-studied longitudinal associations between personality and computer use using representative data, and deepens our knowledge on the individual characteristics underlying adoption and use of technology.

In addition, even though these results may not be completely applicable to the 50-year-olds of today, they may be interpreted within the present generation. The present participants represent their respective Finnish age cohort group born in 1959. Those born in 1959 belong to young baby boomers, and most of them used the internet for the first time in their thirties (Reisenwitz and Iyer, 2007). As the results showed, personality clearly has some effect on how that generation responds to new technology and how they use it. In future research, it would be important to analyse whether similar individual characteristics link to the adoption of other types of recent technology (e.g. intelligent domestic appliances) than computer and internet use, and whether the current middle-aged adults use computers for similar reasons as the present participants. Furthermore, it would be important to replicate the results with different age cohorts and a larger sample size.

In light of these findings, personality should be seen as a meaningful topic of research in connection with the adoption of new technologies and/or the motives driving their uses. It would also be interesting to investigate personality profiles instead of single personality traits. Combinations of personality traits may reveal even more about the associations between personality and behaviour than personality traits separately. Kinnunen *et al.* (2012) found five longitudinally stable personality profiles in the same sample that was used in this study: for example, resilient individuals low in neuroticism and high in all the other traits and under-controlled individuals high in extraversion and openness and low in conscientiousness. It is noteworthy that even though personality is quite stable over the life course (Caspi *et al.*, 2005; McAdams and Olson, 2010), there are some general changes in personality traits during adulthood. Agreeableness, which was linked to lower personal computer use in this study, tends to increase during adulthood, and openness, which was linked to higher social media use, tends to decrease (Kokko *et al.*, 2013; Roberts and Mroczek, 2008). These personality differences between age groups may also play a role in computer use differences between age groups. Moreover, in future research, it should be borne in mind that personality traits may also have non-linear associations with the use of technologies, as individuals with different personalities may have different reasons for using the same technology. It will also be interesting to see how personality directs technology use among baby boomers and generations X and Y, as they age and technology changes.

Acknowledgments

The Jyväskylä Longitudinal Study of Personality and Social Development (JYLS) has been funded by the Academy of Finland, most recently in 2009 through grants #127125 and #118316. We appreciate Professor Lea Pulkkinen's contribution to the JYLS over the years. The use of the NEO Personality Inventory in Finnish in the JYLS is based on the permission granted to Professor Pulkkinen.

Notes

1 Neuroticism-Extraversion-Openness Five-Factor Inventory
2 Neuroticism-Extraversion-Openness Personality Inventory
3 Model fit was evaluated by the chi-square test of model fit and other indices: RMSEA (Root mean square error of approximation), CFI (Comparative Fit Index), TLI (Tucker and Lewis Index), and WRMR (Weighted root mean square residual). The values indicating good fit are $\geq.95$ for the CFI and TLI, $\leq.06$ for the RMSEA (Hu and Bentler, 1999), and ≤ 1 for the WRMR (Yu, 2002).
4 $x^2(50)=95.816$, p<.001, RMSEA=.08, CFI=.78; TLI=0.61, WRMR=1.20.
5 $x^2(44)=43.67$, p=.486, RMSEA=.00, CFI=1.00; TLI=1.00, WRMR=.76.

6 According to the difference test, the constrained model did not differ from the uncon-
strained model: $x^2(30)=38.43$, p=.144, suggesting that there were no significant gender
differences in the paths.
7 $x^2(21)=21.38$, p=.436, RMSEA=.01, CFI=1.00; TLI=1.00, WRMR=.53.

References

Amichai-Hamburger, Y. and Vinitzky, G., 2010. Social network use and personality.
Computers in Human Behavior, 26(6), pp. 1289–1295.

Anderson, J., Reitsma, R., Sorensen, E. and Munsell, M., 2010. *The state of consumers and
technology: benchmark 2010, US*. Cambridge, MA: Forrester Research.

Baron, R. M. and Kenny, D. A., 1986. The moderator–mediator variable distinction in
social psychological research: conceptual, strategic, and statistical considerations.
Journal of Personality and Social Psychology, 51(6), pp. 1173–1182.

Barrick, M. R. and Mount, M. K., 1991. The Big Five personality dimensions and job
performance: a meta-analysis. *Personnel Psychology*, 44(1), pp. 1–26.

Berkowsky, R. W., 2013. When you just cannot get away. *Information, Communication &
Society*, 16(4), pp. 519–541.

Berner, J., Rennemark, M., Jogreus, C. and Berglund, J., 2012. Distribution of personality,
individual characteristics and internet usage in Swedish older adults. *Aging & Mental
Health*, 16(1), pp. 119–126.

Caspi, A., Roberts, B. W. and Shiner, R. L., 2005. Personality development: stability and
change. *Annual Review of Psychology*, 56, pp. 453–484.

Chen, Y. and Persson, A. 2002. Internet use among young and older adults: relation to
psychological well-being, *Educational Gerontology*, 28(9), pp. 731–744.

Correa, T., Hinsley, A. W. and De Zúñiga, H. G., 2010. Who interacts on the Web?: The
intersection of users' personality and social media use. *Computers in Human Behavior*,
26(2) pp. 247–253.

Costa, P. T. J. and McCrae, R. R., 1985. *The NEO Personality Inventory manual*. Odessa,
FL: Psychological Assessment Resources.

Costa, P. T. J. and McCrae, R. R., 1989. *The NEO/NEO-FFI manual supplement*. Odessa,
FL: Psychological Assessment Resources.

Eurostat, 2015. *Information society statistics: households and individuals*. http://ec.europa.
eu/eurostat/statistics-explained/index.php/Information_society_statistics_-_house
holds_and_individuals#Internet_usage.

Facebook Company Info, 2016. http://newsroom.fb.com/company-info/.

Goldberg, L. R., 1993. The structure of phenotypic personality traits. *The American
Psychologist*, 48(1), pp. 26–34.

Guadagno, R. E., Okdie, B. M. and Eno, C. A., 2008. Who blogs? Personality predictors of
blogging. *Computers in Human Behavior*, 24(5), pp. 1993–2004.

Hills, P. and Argyle, M., 2003. Uses of the internet and their relationships with individual
differences in personality. *Computers in Human Behavior*, 19(1), pp. 59–70.

Hu, L. and Bentler, P. M., 1999. Cutoff criteria for fit indexes in covariance structure
analysis: conventional criteria versus new alternatives. *Structural Equation Modeling:
A Multidisciplinary Journal*, 6(1), pp. 1–55.

Hughes, D. J., Rowe, M., Batey, M. and Lee, A., 2012. A tale of two sites: Twitter vs.
Facebook and the personality predictors of social media usage. *Computers in Human
Behavior*, 28(2), pp. 561–569.

IBM Corp., 2013. *IBM SPSS Statistics for Windows, Version 22.0*. Armonk, NY: IBM Corp.

Janković, B., Nikolić, M., Vukonjanski, J. and Terek, E., 2016. The impact of Facebook and smart phone usage on the leisure activities and college adjustment of students in Serbia. *Computers in Human Behavior*, 55, pp. 354–363.

John, O. P. and Srivastava, S., 1999. The Big-Five trait taxonomy: history, measurement, and theoretical perspectives. In: L. Pervin and O. P. John, eds. *Handbook of personality: theory and research*. 2nd ed. New York: Guilford, pp. 102–138.

Jopp, D. S. and Hertzog, C., 2010. Assessing adult leisure activities: an extension of a self-report activity questionnaire. *Psychological assessment*, 22(1), pp. 108–120.

Judge, T. A., Higgins, C. A., Thoresen, C. J. and Barrick, M. R., 1999. The Big Five personality traits, general mental ability, and career success across the lifespan. *Personnel Psychology*, 52(3), pp. 621–652.

Keenan, T. A., 2009. *Internet use among midlife and older adults. AARP Bulletin Poll.* Washington, DC: AARP.

Kim, Y. and Jeong, J. S., 2015. Personality predictors for the use of multiple internet functions. *Internet Research*, 25(3), pp. 399–415.

Kinnunen, M., Metsäpelto, R., Feldt, T., Kokko, K., Tolvanen, A., Kinnunen, U., Leppänen, E. and Pulkkinen, L., 2012. Personality profiles and health: longitudinal evidence among Finnish adults. *Scandinavian Journal of Psychology*, 53(6), pp. 512–522.

Kokko, K., Tolvanen, A. and Pulkkinen, L., 2013. Associations between personality traits and psychological well-being across time in middle adulthood. *Journal of Research in Personality*, 47(6), pp. 748–756.

Kuo, T. and Tang, H., 2014. Relationships among personality traits, Facebook usages, and leisure activities: a case of Taiwanese college students. *Computers in Human Behavior*, 31, pp. 13–19.

Landers, R. N. and Lounsbury, J. W., 2006. An investigation of Big Five and narrow personality traits in relation to internet usage. *Computers in Human Behavior*, 22(2), pp. 283–293.

Livingstone, S. and Haddon, L., 2009. *EU kids online: final report*. London: LSE, EU Kids Online.

Mann, W. C., Belchior, P., Tomita, M. R. and Kemp, B. J., 2005. Computer use by middle-aged and older adults with disabilities. *Technology and Disability*, 17(1), pp. 1–9.

McAdams, D. P. and Olson, B. D., 2010. Personality development: continuity and change over the life course. *Annual Review of Psychology*, 61, pp. 517–542.

McCrae, R. R. and Costa, P. T. J., 2003. *Personality in adulthood: a five-factor theory perspective*. 2nd ed., New York: The Guilford Press.

McNemar, Q., 1969. *Psychological statistics*. 4th ed. New York: Wiley.

Muthén, L. K. and Muthén, B. O., 1998–2015. *Mplus user's guide*. 7th ed. Los Angeles, CA: Muthén & Muthén.

Näsi, M., Räsänen, P. and Sarpila, O., 2011. ICT activity in later life: internet use and leisure activities amongst senior citizens in Finland. *European Journal of Ageing*, 9(2), pp. 169–176.

Orchard, L. J. and Fullwood, C., 2010. Current perspectives on personality and internet use. *Social Science Computer Review*, 28(2), pp. 155–169.

Özgüven, N. and Mucan, B., 2013. The relationship between personality traits and social media use. *Society for Personality Research*, 41(3), pp. 517–528.

Papacharissi, Z. and Rubin, A. M., 2000. Predictors of internet use. *Journal of Broadcasting & Electronic Media*, 44(2), pp. 175–196.

Pulkkinen, L., 2009. Personality: a resource or risk for successful development. *Scandinavian Journal of Psychology*, 50(6), pp. 602–610.

Pulkkinen, L., 2017. *Growing up to the middle-aged: a longitudinal study on human development (in collaboration with Katja Kokko)*. London: Routledge.

Pulkkinen, L. and Kokko, K., eds., 2010. *Keski-ikä elämänvaiheena*. Reports from the Department of Psychology 352. Jyväskylä, Finland: University of Jyväskylä.

Pulkkinen, L., Kokko, K. and Rantanen, J., 2012. Paths from socioemotional behavior in middle childhood to personality in middle adulthood. *Developmental Psychology*, 48(5), pp. 1283–1291.

Pulkkinen, L., Ohranen, M. and Tolvanen, A., 1999. Personality antecedents of career orientation and stability among women compared to men. *Journal of Vocational Behavior*, 54(1), pp. 37–58.

Pulver, A., Allik, J., Pulkkinen, L. and Hämäläinen, M., 1995. A Big Five personality inventory in two non-Indo-European languages. *European Journal of Personality*, 9(2), pp. 109–124.

Reisenwitz, T. and Iyer, R., 2007. A comparison of younger and older baby boomers: investigating the viability of cohort segmentation. *Journal of Consumer Marketing*, 24(4), pp. 202–213.

Roberts, B. W. and Mroczek, D., 2008. Personality trait change in adulthood. *Current Directions in Psychological Science*, 17(1), pp. 31–35.

Robinson, J. P., 2011. IT use and leisure time displacement. *Information, Communication & Society*, 14(4), pp. 495–509.

Ross, C., Orr, E. S., Sisic, M., Arseneault, J. M., Simmering, M. G. and Orr, R. R., 2009. Personality and motivations associated with Facebook use. *Computers in Human Behavior*, 25(2), pp. 578–586.

Ryan, T. and Xenos, S., 2011. Who uses Facebook? An investigation into the relationship between the Big Five, shyness, narcissism, loneliness, and Facebook usage. *Computers in Human Behavior*, 27(5), pp. 1658–1664.

Shah, D. V., Kwak, N. and Holbert, R. L., 2001. 'Connecting' and 'disconnecting' with civic life: patterns of internet use and the production of social capital. *Political Communication*, 18(2), pp. 141–162.

Statistics Finland, 2015. Use of information and communications technology by individuals. www.stat.fi/til/sutivi/tau_en.html.

Swickert, R. J., Hittner, J. B., Harris, J. L. and Herring, J. A., 2002. Relationships among internet use, personality, and social support. *Computers in Human Behavior*, 18(4), pp. 437–451.

Tuukkanen, T., Wilska, T. A., Iqbal, A. and Kankaanranta, M., 2013. Children's social participation in virtual worlds. *International Journal of Virtual Communities and Social Networking (IJVCSN)*, 5(4), pp. 59–73.

Viinikainen, J., Kokko, K., Pulkkinen, L. and Pehkonen, J., 2010. Personality and labour market income: evidence from longitudinal data. *Labour*, 24(2), pp. 201–220.

Wagner, N., Hassanein, K. and Head, M., 2010. Computer use by older adults: a multidisciplinary review. *Computers in Human Behavior*, 26(5), pp. 870–882.

Wilson, K., Fornasier, S. and White, K. M., 2010. Psychological predictors of young adults' use of social networking sites. *Cyberpsychology, behavior and social networking*, 13(2), pp. 173–177.

Yu, C., 2002. Evaluating cutoff criteria of model fit indices for latent variable models with binary and continuous outcomes. Ph.D. University of California.

Zhou, R., Fong, P. S. and Tan, P., 2014. Internet use and its impact on engagement in leisure activities in China. *PloS one*, 9(2). http://dx.doi.org/10.1371/journal.pone.0089598.

14 Electronic emotions, age and the life course

Jane Vincent

Introduction

In the late 1990s, the World Wide Web (WWW) and digital mobile phones were in their infancy; email and text messaging were the new mass market opportunity. The United Kingdom's BT Cellnet, a mobile phone network operator and service provider had launched an innovative lifestyle service 'Genie' (BT Group, 1998) which, for the first time, combined mobile phone use with internet access and text messaging. Targeted at a new audience of younger people, Genie was designed to attract a new generation of customers, typically male students, who were seen as the trail blazers for technology-rich products that converged mobile phones with the WWW and data services. The marketing team were thus puzzled, and some a little dismayed, to find that early adopters of their services also included women in their late forties – why would they want a product tailored to a much younger generation of male users? Recalling this anecdote is a reminder that regardless of marketing expectations, people of all ages will buy products if they meet their emotional and practical needs, whether they are within the target audience or identify with the advertising image.

The telecommunications industry is not alone in targeting age and generation cohorts as the focus of marketing activity but, as I will show in this chapter, age specific advertising is not the only criteria people use when choosing information and communication technology (ICT) products and services. It was the conundrum of the role of emotion in the mismatch between targeted customers and actual customers that prompted the research, which since 2002 and together with colleagues from across the globe, has explored people's social practices with regard to ICTs and in particular mobile phone use. Early on in the research into the social shaping of technology, it became apparent that emotion played a significant role in the adoption and use of mobile phones (Vincent, 2003; Vincent and Harper, 2003) and, working with Leopoldina Fortunati, these studies led to the development of the concept of 'electronic emotions' (Vincent and Fortunati, 2009) – emotions that occur as a result of human interaction with ICTs.

Electronic emotions are felt and expressed directly as a result of interaction with a machine – often this is the presence of the mobile phone at a particular moment – either physically handled, or felt, or just being thought about. Expressed emotionally, this melding of awareness of what the device contains and how it is used combines with the role of the mobile phone in the presentation of self, and the inner thoughts and feelings of each individual mobile phone user.

Electronic emotions are not different emotions from those we experience in everyday life (sadness, joy, anger, frustration and so on) but they occur directly as a consequence of an interaction uniquely enabled or elicited when using ICTs. People turn to their mobile phones in moments of anxiety; they use apps on smartphones or tablets to relive happy memories of loved ones, and social media and emails to express emotions about all kinds of things. They feel emotions when they think about their mobile phone or other ICT device, when it enables them to do their job better, to solve a problem, or reduce stress, but the emotions can also be negative, such as if unwanted calls and communications are received or anticipated.

One of the findings from studying older age mobile phone users (Vincent, 2011a, p. 145) is that the emotions associated with their mobile phone use were influenced by activities related to their life stage and were irrespective of age, for example parenting or grandparenting young children, juggling home and work life, and death of loved ones. Subsequent studies of children aged 9–16 and their ICT use also highlight emotions in relation to their life course and life stages that influenced how they used ICTs, e.g. change of school year, moving schools and friendship groups (Vincent, 2004, 2010, 2015; Vincent and Haddon, 2004; Mascheroni and Cuman, 2014; Haddon and Vincent, 2015; Mascheroni and Vincent, 2016). What appears to be emerging from my research findings, and what I will expand upon in this chapter, are similarities with regard to electronic emotions in the social practices of ICT users, and mobile phone users in particular, that relate to life events regardless of age. Furthermore, as research about ICT use is frequently conducted using age as the main typology, there appears to be less known about these generational and life course aspects, especially with regard to emotion. The launch of mobile phones in its various generations over the years has meant that people have had to grapple with unfamiliar devices, technologies and interfaces on a regular basis. That they do so willingly is a consideration for this present analysis, which highlights that the life course of the mobile phone in particular and the length of time ICT devices have been used might also be factors in the electronic emotions experienced (Vincent, 2011a).

In this chapter I thus draw upon 12 years of primary qualitative research data gathered in Europe, mostly in the UK, to explore these findings further. The key studies from this research portfolio used to explicate this chapter are listed in Table 14.1.

I aim to use these data to understand more about the links between the electronic emotions elicited by ICTs, especially mobile phones, in relation to age and the life course by exploring two research questions. First: How do electronic emotions relate to the life course and life stages of ICT and especially mobile and smartphone users? Second: Are there similarities and differences in the electronic emotions experienced by respondents from different generations of ICT users?

Table 14.1 Summary of primary research sources on mobile phone and ICT users cited in this chapter.

Research topic and date	Methodology and number of respondents	References and comment
Social shaping of 3G mobile communications technology (2002/03)	Questionnaires, focus groups, interviews. 120 adults	(Vincent and Harper, 2003; Vincent, 2003) Study for UMTS Forum and EITO 2003 (included respondents from Germany)
Social shaping of mobile communications (2003/04)	Focus groups, diaries, interviews 41 adults 3×3 generations of one family	(Vincent and Haddon, 2004) Study for UMTS Forum
11 to 16 year olds' use of mobile phones (2004)	Diaries, focus groups, interviews 105 children	(Vincent, 2004; Haddon and Vincent, 2007) Children from the same
11 to 16 year olds' use of mobile phones and ICT (2006/07)	Diaries, focus groups, interviews 80 children	schools were used for both studies conducted for Vodafone
Emotions and mobile phones (2007/08)	Open ended interviews 40 adults	(Vincent, 2010, 2011; Vincent and Fortunati, 2009) Respondents older than 40 (average age 50). Doctoral thesis
'Net Children Go Mobile' Children aged 9–16 safe use of mobile internet (2012–2015)	(3,500 questionnaires) Interviews, focus groups 327 children and adults (EU Kids Online)	(Haddon and Vincent, 2015; Vincent 2015; Livingstone *et al.*, 2014a; Mascheroni and Cuman, 2014) Comparative data from EU Kids Online also used in reports

Following this introduction and overview of contextual literature and research, this chapter first outlines the methodological approach used in the data sources for this present analysis; it then explores the theoretical perspectives that frame the studies regarding both the data sources cited in this chapter and in the broader context of this volume. The two research questions are then explored by drawing on illustrative examples from the aforementioned research projects and this discussion leads to final conclusions in response to these questions.

Methodology

This chapter uses a content analysis approach (Altheide, 1996) to examine and analyse published reports, articles and data content from primary research studies which the author has led or participated in since 2002. The chapter is informed by these studies, outlined in Table 14.1, and in particular, by two studies conducted for the industry body The UMTS Forum (Vincent and Harper, 2003; Vincent and Haddon, 2004); by the author's Doctoral research (Vincent, 2011a), and by the Net Children Go Mobile project (Mascheroni and Ólaffson, 2014; Vincent, 2015; Vincent and Haddon, 2015). Each of these studies involved qualitative research gathered variously in questionnaires, interviews, diaries, focus groups and observational studies. The first UMTS study was conducted in the UK and Germany and involved focus groups and interviews with adults, including students. The second study conducted in the UK included a diary record made by three generations of three families who were also interviewed about their ICT use, as well as interviews with industry and academic experts. Published as reports for The UMTS Forum membership and in the European Information Technology Observatory 2003, these studies were used by industry to contribute to the planning for the launch of 4G mobile communications services. The Doctoral research explored emotion in the social practices of mobile phones users, and was based on 40 open-ended interviews with people aged 45–80 living in the UK. The findings from this study inspired this present chapter. Funded by the European Commission's Better Internet for Kids Programme, the 'Net Children Go Mobile' project examined children's use of mobile internet and followed a larger study, EU Kids Online that explored children's use of the internet on personal computers. Both studies commenced with quantitative research in European countries, followed by qualitative research including interviews and focus groups with children, parents, teachers and youth workers (Livingstone *et al.*, 2014b). In conjunction with these studies, I concurrently explored and developed the notion of electronic emotion and the emotional attachment people have to their mobile phones. These additional studies also inform this present chapter (cf. Vincent, 2003, 2009, 2013; Vincent and Sugiyama, 2013). The studies of social shaping and electronic emotion followed a sociological and social psychological approach, and the studies of children, media and communication studies, and social psychology.

Theoretical perspectives: balancing generation and emotion studies among ICT users

The exploration of people's use of mobile phones and ICTs touches on many aspects of individual and societal identities. The foundational theoretical literature for the analysis of many mobile phone and ICT research projects is found in interactionist theory, and my own studies have similarly focused on the dramaturgical approach of Goffman, and also on the understanding of the inner self expounded by Mead (1967 [1943]) and later by Hochschild (2003 [1983]). Indeed, much of the research cited in this chapter was framed by interactionist theory: Goffman's (1969 [1959]) presentation of self; the domestication approach of Silverstone and Hirsch (1992) and Silverstone and Haddon (1996); and Hochschild's (2003 [1983]) emotion management and feeling rules. This volume, in exploring generations and the life course, opens the door to contrasting these interactionist perspectives with Mannheim's sociological analysis of generations (Mannheim, 1927), and the work of others on age and life course (e.g. Hepworth, 1998; Burnett, 2010; Green, 2010; Bristow, 2015), as well as studies of digital technologies and generation (e.g. Colombo and Fortunati, 2011; Loos *et al.*, 2012; Garattini and Prendergast, 2015) and mobilities (Urry, 2000; Taipale, 2014). These mutually inclusive theoretical and conceptual perspectives highlight how communications technology use, such as the mobile phone, has cut through the sociological analysis of society according to generations and class, with those that explore the role of individual interactions and mobility.

Furthermore, following Urry's definition of 'scapes': "the networks of machines, technologies, organisations, texts and actors that constitute various interconnected nodes" (Urry, 2000, p. 36), one could argue that infrastructures of ICTs now provide for a constant 'always on' mobility that has an effect on all aspects of society and the self (see also Taipale, 2014 for his analysis of the dimensions of mobilities). Examining electronic emotions and ICT use is no longer a matter of exploring individual experiences such as absence and presence, time and space, presentation of self and emotion management. Now, one must add constant co-presence enabled via devices such as smartphones, laptops and wi-fi connectivity. All these combine to effectively eliminate the stark rawness of physical separation and the strong feelings that this elicits. Described by Bassett in the context of travel, she posits:

> For the mobile phone user, travel no longer presumes a broken connection. There is no dislocation between the world of the train and the world beyond: not even the temporary dislocation the journey used to produce. Each world is shot through with the other.
>
> (Bassett, 2005)

Framing many research studies is the notion that ICTs – especially mobile phones – bring together multitudes of individual temporal and spatial worlds into a carousel of connectivity, delivering social relationships whenever and wherever needed. Note, however, that much of this research, including my own, is based on gathering data about the individual's use of mobile phones and other ICTs and extrapolating a societal, or at least, cohort perspective using age, generation and/or gender typologies. This is where the theoretical perspectives of exploring the presentation of self and domestication begin to intersect with Mannheim's exposition on the role of generations in society. His argument does, indeed, hold sway when exploring ICT use from an age perspective, and especially when one introduces technology into the mix. Young Europeans below the age of 20 have lived their entire lives with mobile phones freely available, whereas their grandparents would have experienced adulthood without a mobile phone or other forms of digital communication devices such as laptops and smartphones. Their contextual influencing generational experiences are bound to be different as, indeed, it will for every individual within that generation.

The challenge to Mannheim's approach comes when one considers how people are responding to the electronic emotions associated with the communicative affordances of mobile phones. Defined as "an interaction between subjective perceptions of utility and objective qualities of the technology that alters communicative practices or habits" (Schrock, 2015, p. 1130), communicative affordances highlight the likelihood for similar responses to new technology irrespective of age. This is especially the situation when it is introduced simultaneously (as in the case of a new generation of mobile technology), or adopted by people experiencing the same life stage, regardless of age.

An interesting point of convergence between the domestication and generational approaches discussed herein is with regard to the speed of change within the respective human and technological generations. Mannheim argues that a new *generation entelechy*, in other words a new generation style, can occur when old traditions are overcome by new impulses. Just such a situation occurs when the mobile phone is simultaneously encountered for the first time by all generations and ages in relation to a life stage event such as a new baby, divorce, house move and so on.

Nevertheless, and notwithstanding Mannheim's emphasis only on men as his subjects, his arguments are set forth in *The sociological problem of generations* (1927), which assume throughout that older generations must compensate for the lack of experience of youth – an attitude being turned on its head now by some who believe that children have overtaken the technological experience of their forebears and are more advanced and competent with their ICT use. A 2016 advertising campaign by Bartle Bogle Hegarty for Virgin Media inferred that operating a television is so complicated that children are now needed to help older people change a channel.

> The ad . . . features six children, portrayed as being sinisterly powerful due to their innate understanding of technology. The last child to speak, a boy wearing a hoodie, approaches the camera saying: "We are the masters of entertainment because we are seven, and you are not. You need help".[1]

Our research of children (Livingstone *et al.*, 2014a; Mascheroni and Cuman, 2014; Haddon and Vincent, 2015) showed that although some people, particularly young children, do believe children are more competent when using smartphones and the internet, this is not necessarily the case as they may be more knowledgeable about a few aspects but not wholly competent.

> Two in three children say they know more than their parents about the internet, and 86% claim to know more than their parents about smartphones. However, 9- to 10-year-olds generally think their parents know more about using the internet than they do.
>
> (Livingstone *et al.*, 2014a, p. 4)

We do know that as each generation is located differently, they will inevitably experience the same events in different ways. I contend that whilst this is true for many aspects of everyday life, the first encounter of mobile phone and ICT services – as in the earlier example of Cellnet's Genie – is not necessarily differentiated by generation, age or gender but by other life events. Furthermore, if we consider the electronic emotions engendered by the constant presence of mobile phones and the always on connectivity it affords its users, the emotional attachment that quickly builds between the user and their ICT device is similar across all generations.

Electronic emotions and life stages of mobile phone users

As illustrated by the theoretical and conceptual perspectives that frame the discourse on generation, age and life course, emotions are present in all layers of technology adoption and appropriation. Furthermore, the 'communicative affordances' of the mobile phone present extraordinary opportunities to stimulate or trigger electronic emotions (Mascheroni and Vincent, 2016). This apparent omnipresence of emotion or emotional associations that occur when using ICTs is associated with uses of the device that are not necessarily particular to age cohorts or generations, but rather are in relation to similarity of use to which the device is put, such as keeping in contact with an absent loved one or keeping a child safe en route to school. In this regard, the question of the similarities and differences in the electronic emotions experienced by different generations of ICT users is now considered.

Smartphones, tablets, laptops and ICT devices are now integral to daily life in this second decade of the twenty-first century. As we walk through towns, cities and countryside, everywhere people are using their smartphones: talking, texting, messaging on social media, taking photos, using satnav (satellite navigation), playing games, or simply holding the phone in anticipation of use. Research of mobile phone users shows that many people hold their phone in their hand at all times, others keep it close to hand in a bag or their pocket, ready for quick access to deal with incoming communications or to make contact with someone themselves. Ensuring the mobile phone is close to hand is something respondents have commented upon:

> I always check in my handbag that it's there. It's very rare I haven't got it with me. If I go to the gym, because I literally take my keys and my phone and that's it, so I put the phone along with my keys, which I have to obviously have for the car and the house; the next thing is the mobile phone. I'd leave a purse quite happily but I wouldn't leave my phone behind, strangely enough.
>
> *June, 45* (Vincent, 2011a, p. 94)

> I've got to have my mobile phone; it's like you having your keys. You don't leave home without your keys and you don't leave home without your mobile phone.
>
> *John, 46* (Vincent, 2011a, p. 76)

In the case of this young girl she will have it with her in bed, and then cannot resist using it:

> Even when I have to go to bed and it's school, I'm not allowed to use the phone, only so it can wake me up in the morning, because I put an alarm on it, so it can wake me up. And when it's in the night, I'll go under the covers and start playing games or looking at my pictures to delete, things like that.
>
> *Angela, 9–10* (Vincent, 2015, p. 48)

In the research of UK mobile phone and ICT users, and in that of others (Lasen, 2004; Baron, 2008; Turkle, 2008) this 'always on' link between the user and their mobile phone has been a constant theme; some studies also explore the emotion associated with this attachment between user and device (Vincent, 2003; Cumiskey, 2005; Vincent and Fortunati, 2014). In this section I draw on my research to explore how emotions have been shown to be key triggers for mobile phone use throughout the life course and in so doing challenge the preponderance of age typologies in academic analysis of mobile phone use. Fewer and fewer people never use a mobile phone, or never contact someone who is using a mobile phone, and this technological and communicative turn in the everyday life of UK (and global) society is shaping a new understanding of why and for what people use mobile phones.

The bond between mobile phone and user is driven by emotions, and indeed I have argued that the combination of the personalised mobile phone and individual user creates a personalised social robot (Vincent, 2013). The ability to remain in constant contact with friends and family, as well as care workers and commercial and business users, elicits positive emotions, but there are also negative emotions experienced such as from ended relationships, bullying or bad deals. The emotional response to the mobile phone – and now smartphone or tablet computer – is immediate and constant from the moment it is acquired. Whether it is in constant use or kept for emergencies, the mobile phone is now an integral part of the everyday lives of most Europeans over 10 years old – although, perhaps, not yet among all those aged over 80. The respondents in the first of the UMTS Reports certainly considered that mobiles were so important for them that an emotional paradox of it being too important to lose had begun to emerge:

> But [I] might be getting too dependent on them . . . the importance is so great it makes the mobile too valuable: I don't take it to the club 'cause it would be terrible if I lost it.
>
> (Vincent and Harper, 2003, p. 18)

Other respondents have made the mobile phone an integral part of their everyday life, especially regarding child minding responsibilities:

> I've just adapted my life around the phone to some extent, and happily so because I think it's more me.
>
> *Christine, 45* (Vincent, 2011a, p. 134)

To ring friends to say, you know, to get you to just keep an eye on the girls, I may or may not be back in time, and that's when I tend to use a mobile phone.

Martha, 70 (Vincent, 2011a, p. 80)

Whilst personal computers, laptops and tablets are often used and shared by all ages from toddlers onwards, mobile phones are rarely shared and are acquired as a direct result of a planned or unexpected life event. Looking first at the children in the UK, acquisition typically occurs during the transition to secondary school such as in the final years of primary school; in some other European countries, a mobile phone is given as a gift on religious confirmation. Now that smartphones offer child friendly applications allowing safe access online, gaming and some social media, they are also being acquired at the start of school or sooner. Older people acquiring them for the first time do so as birthday gifts, as a result of family crisis, for work or due to family pressures to be contactable, as in the example of one respondent, Nina (80), who has a mobile phone for use in emergencies although she does not rely on it (Vincent, 2011a, p. 80). For both older and younger users, mobile phones may be donated or gifted from other family members, a practice that was re-affirmed by recent research (Piper *et al.*, 2016). These examples are life events that involved the transition from one life stage to another, and it appears that the first acquisition of a mobile phone has become a rite of passage; itself an emotionally charged event. Adult children with new responsibilities for ailing parents and parents who are letting go of being wholly in control of their children's lives use the mobile phone as a safety net or digital leash (Ling, 2004). Once at secondary school the children use their mobiles for social contact, and their parents use them to keep in touch and to know where they are at all times. This emotional attachment to their mobile phone was evident in the study I conducted in 2004 of 11–16 year olds and in the more recent European studies of children, as well as in the other studies involving adults. The only recent change is that the children are acquiring their phones at a younger age. Here we see that the mobile phone has a different function for parents and children, but the role it performs in placating their emotional need to stay connected is common and age is immaterial. One of the respondents found, to her cost, that relying on the mobile phone to keep connected with young sons who had gone off alone shopping failed when there was no coverage:

[s]o I had to start thinking about where they might be. And then I started panicking because I thought if I can't get them on his mobile, I don't quite know where we're going to meet in this massive, great big shopping centre.

Margaret (Vincent, 2011a, p. 93)

Another respondent, George, lost his smartphone whilst on a business trip and after a week without it he missed the intimacy of calls to his family at the end of a busy day, and the inability to communicate with business colleagues or access his contacts. He said: "And I went onto Facebook having been away a week at this time and I updated my profile to say: 'George is missing his wife and family but at this moment he is actually missing his mobile more'" *George 50* (Vincent, 2011a, p. 100).

Children's attachment to their mobile phones is highlighted in these comments from a teacher and, second, from a mother:

> We've got quite a few new teachers from Ireland and Australia, and one of the Australian teachers was saying to me that, in the end, their school was so big, it was [had] over 2,000 pupils, they said, we more or less have given up on it. We just couldn't fight the battle of phones in lessons anymore, it was just too difficult.
>
> *Alex, Teacher at secondary school, UK*
> (Haddon and Vincent, 2015, p. 30)

> All the time, if I say that you've had enough on the PlayStation, they will go and pick up an iPad. If I say, you've had enough on the iPad and the PlayStation, they'll go and find a laptop, and then I end up saying, no, it's just no screens whatsoever, no screen, nothing with a screen.
>
> *Sally, mother of boys aged 10 and 7, UK*
> (Haddon and Vincent, 2015, p. 29)

Current research by the European COST Action IS1402 on ageism highlights that among the older age population, ICTs, not just mobile phones, have become integral to everyday life. Keeping connected with family, friends and care workers becomes more challenging with the frailties of age and there are increasing interventions for healthcare and support. There is evidence that older people are appropriating smartphone technology such as in Spain where WhatsApp is used to socialise with peers and family members (Fernández-Ardèvol and Rosales, forthcoming). There is still work to be done to ensure ease of accessibility, but the use of ICTs for monitoring and safety are commonplace, and accompanying this are the electronic emotions associated with using devices such as personal alarms, or carrying a portable or mobile phone everywhere in case of a fall. That adaptive mobile phones and emergency buttons must become part of everyday life is a watershed for many, and this passive surveillance of the frail elderly highlights the tensions between people's willingness to accept assistive technologies such as a personal alarm and their denial of the impact of ageing on their mobility or cognitive skills (see Garattini and Prendergast, 2015). The additional stresses associated with wearing a surveillance device elicit further electronic emotions as the touch of the button on the skin provides reassurance at moments of anxiety as well as alarm if or when it has to be used.

These 'watershed' life stages are more often considered in the context of old age, but, as has been shown already, they are not exclusive to this older generation. In the small study of three generations of family users conducted in 2004, the mobile phone had acquired a key role in the household. It was significant in the communicative relationship between the generations who all used their mobiles, albeit for different purposes, as this extract from the Report findings explains:

The families had needs for mobile phones that differed a little between generations but in principle were based on the same needs of connectivity, reassurance and to avoid risk. They used them quite differently within their own social groups. For example the oldest generation tended not to use their mobile phone to call friends whilst the children's volume of use would have been greater had they not been influenced by their tariff, budgetary and parental control. The middle generation mothers were the most intensive users calling friends during the day and keeping their mobile phone with them because their friends used it to contact them.

(Vincent and Haddon, 2004, p. 33)

Nowadays children mostly use smartphones, and their attachment to their device develops very quickly, so much that they cannot imagine life without it. Mobile phone applications such as WhatsApp and Snapchat are constantly in use and present the children with challenges for keeping up to date to continue to be included in friendship groups – especially if their parents are unwilling to allow them free rein on when and where they can use their mobile. A quarter of the children admitted they missed "eating or sleeping because of their use of the internet, and nearly two-thirds say that the internet gets in the way of time they should spend with family, friends or schoolwork" (Mascheroni and Cuman, 2014, p. 5). A 16-year-old girl, Bea, said she could manage an hour without her mobile, but when her younger sister asked if she could manage a week she said "A week, oh gosh, I'd die, I couldn't live with that" (Haddon and Vincent, 2014, p. 30). Another 16-year-old described how she managed the high volume of social media on her smartphone:

I follow so many people on Twitter that I can't actually physically read everything that they say, so what I do . . . I probably go onto my mentions because my mentions are full of the people that I want to see their tweets and I . . . then I just go through that and look at the people's tweets I want to see, instead of reading everyone's, so I probably just go through my Twitter but it takes so long.

Eliza, 16 (Vincent, 2015, p. 5)

The adult respondents may not be as voracious users of mobile applications as the children but they are similarly attached to their mobile phones as a response to being in contact with whomever they want, anywhere and at any moment. Juggling the work-life balance is frequently managed via the mobile phone, which augments the emotional attachment to the device, but it can also be a means of checking up on one's partner or spouse, and for some the freedom it affords is tempered by this unwanted contact. Maria describes misunderstandings over mobile phone accessibility that occurred in the long-distance relationship with her boyfriend:

So he says "Why aren't you answering your phone?" – Because I didn't hear it and I was walking – "But you had it in your pocket!" – Yes but my trousers are loose what do you want me to do? Hold it in my hand all the time? – "YES

I want you to hold it in your hand! I know that the breakdown in communication frustrates him but I get frustrated when he gets frustrated. I get annoyed because when he gets frustrated he switches off his phone and doesn't speak to me and then I have the big space, no, a void, of not being able to communicate with him and then I get frustrated and so I'd rather hold my phone and check it every single moment all the time rather than go through that roller coaster of him being annoyed, switching his phone off, me trying to contact him, then ending up just having a fight for some stupid reason.

Maria, 42 (Vincent, 2011a, p. 128)

Another respondent uses his mobile phone to keep in touch with his mates whilst he is overseas, and he shares moments with them over the phone in the same way as if they were together, such as the excited celebration of a team win en route home from a rugby match he had attended with another friend:

We had to talk to somebody so we rang my rugby mate's son who'd obviously been watching it and we had rather a long and amusing conversation which helped the time pass.

Nigel, 62 (Vincent, 2011a, p. 134)

Emotions in relation to mobile phone use are not always acknowledged or realised by the users – rather, they are simply expressed in words or behaviours as they talk about their mobile phone use such as about holding the phone in a hand, having conversations on it, keeping it close to hand, or referring to the potential loss of the device with horror.

These quotes from the respondents of the various studies show how emotion words are used when they talk about their mobile phones and about other ICTs. They express their feelings spontaneously and mostly these are positive, but their reaction was often one of discomfort if asked to think about not having their mobile phone. It was unusual for a respondent to be immediately negative about their mobile phone, instead they would share how they used it and then occasionally they would give examples of problems they had to overcome to continue to make it work for them.

Conclusion

Based on this analysis, review of literature and the illustrative quotes, this section draws some conclusions regarding the challenges presented by the theoretical perspectives framing the discussion, as well as the outcome of this development of summative material from studies based on age and cohort typologies. This approach is pertinent to understanding how it can be that people of all generations are now comfortable using mobile phones, despite those who are older having to change their communicative practices from already domesticated modes of communications such as the telephone and paper mail.

One of the challenges is against the frame on which to analyse this ICT use when exploring the life course. In effect, we have two axes – on the one hand, the longitudinal Mannheimian view that places generations apart from each other, each influenced only by their life experience which collectively, is similar for each generation or member of a generation. On the other, is the more dynamic individual who encounters technological opportunities as they appear on the market. One such opportunity is the affordance of mobile phones and other ICT taken up at particular life stages irrespective of the generation, age or class. What began as a problem-solving device purchased irrespective of generation, albeit influenced by peer groups which include one's generation, goes on to penetrate the intimacy of everyday life in ways for which they were not originally designed or perhaps acquired. The electronic emotion, the utility, the communicative affordances of the device and the essential role it plays in an individual's emotion management of their everyday lives, cuts through familiar age and generational analysis that is so popular. The categorisations such as Millennials, Generation Y, Silver Surfers, Elders, Youth, Adolescents and Children are designed to monetise a product, or for cohort analysis are valid research structures, which are less effective when exploring electronic emotions. Each have their similarities and differences that create the cohort but when it comes to the electronic emotions elicited via their mobile phones, and their attachment to their mobile phone or other ICT, these are transparent of generation. People long for contact, touch the phone, take and store photos, phone or text a friend for advice, clutch the phone when anxious, use it to play games, use it for identity management, social media and for so many things that are not necessarily age or generation specific.

Whilst it is clear from Mannheim's articulation of the sociological problem of generations that each new generation has a different experience from that which comes after them, further honed by differences in education, life stage and so on, when it comes to examining electronic emotions there is another contributory factor – the technological input. Each generation of ICT and mobile phone especially (1G through to the forthcoming 5G, Android or iOS operating system and so on), will be delivered as a new experience at a point in time that is separated by fewer years than human generations. Following Bassett's articulation of mobile phone use on trains (2005) we can see that ICT use cuts through the everyday scapes of every generation and, furthermore, depending on the content and services used, each technology generation stimulates electronic emotions regardless of the age of the user. These emotions are the glue linking technology with users: the desirability, the usefulness, the importance of not losing a contact or missing an important communication or being able to limit accessibility, are all enabled by the ability to implement and use the new generation of technology. Notwithstanding the myth that a child of seven is always better informed about technology than adults, this is transparent to the traditional age and class generations described by Mannheim and is, instead, associated with the communicative affordance of the device (Schrock, 2015; Mascheroni and Vincent, 2016). Thus, it would appear the combination of electronic emotions, technological savviness and needs for particular communicative affordances are not necessarily related to human generations.

I wrote previously about the feral nature of mobile phones (Vincent, 2011b); following the domestication approach of Silverstone and Hirsch (1992) and

Silverstone and Haddon (1996), it is this capturing, 'taming' and tailoring of the communicative affordances of the mobile phone and other ICT to meet the needs of users that cuts through the generational divisions. A new mother, be she 16 or 46, or a bereaved friend, be he 10, 20 or 80, will use their mobile phone to express their feelings and to manage their emotions in these new life stage situations. George, for example, has not been able to remove the contact details from his mobile phone for his friend who has died: "Well it's just, well why is that? It's not logical; there's no logical reason why, it's almost like he's still here if he is in my address book . . . Weird". (Vincent, 2011a, p. 110). Electronic emotions such as those experienced by George, are not differentiated by the age or generation of the user, but rather by the life stage or life event that prompts the emotions.

The ICT machines and the technologies that enable electronic emotions are a perturbation that cuts orthogonally through the existing architecture of life course analysis. The emotional attachment to devices, especially mobile and smart-phones, and the electronic emotions they engender refute the experience of the heredity of generation and prevents it from dominating actions, linking it instead with new found knowledge and shared experience available simultaneously to all ages and without prior experience. How one responds to a new technology may well be influenced by generational life experience and one's position in the life course; but explored through the lens of electronic emotions it is neither one thing nor the other. Rather, it is a combination of individual and collective generational experience across the human life course.

Note

1 www.campaignlive.co.uk/article/virgin-media-brings-all-powerful-children-screen-new-campaign-tv/1408452#.

References

Altheide, D. L., 1996. *Qualitative media analysis.* Thousand Oaks, CA: SAGE.

Baron, N. H., 2008. *Always on: language in an on line and mobile world.* Oxford, UK: Oxford University Press

Bassett, C., 2005. How many movements? *Open, Cahier on Art and the Public Domain,* 9, pp 38–48.

Bristow, J., 2015. *Baby boomers and generational conflict.* Basingstoke, UK: Palgrave, Macmillan

BT Group, 1998. *Annual report and accounts.* www.btplc.com/report/1997-98/pdfs/full report.pdf.

Burnett, J., 2010. *Generations: the time machine in theory and practice.* Farnham, UK: Ashgate.

Colombo, F. and Fortunati, L., eds., 2011. *Broadband society and generational changes.* Berlin: Peter Lang.

Cumiskey, K., 2005. "Can you hear me now?" Paradoxes of techno-intimacy resulting from the public use of mobile communication technology. In: K. Nyiri, ed. *A sense of place: the global and local in mobile communication.* Vienna, Austria: Passagen Verlag, pp 151–158.

Fernández-Ardèvol, M. and Rosales, A., forthcoming. Older people, smartphones and WhatsApp. In: J. Vincent and L. Haddon L., eds. *Smartphone cultures*. Abingdon, UK: Routledge.

Garattini, C. and Prendergast, D., 2015. Introduction: critical reflections on ageing and technology in the twenty-first century. In: D. Prendergast and C. Garattini, eds. *Aging and the digital life course*. Oxford, UK: Berghahn.

Goffman, E., 1969 [1959]. *The presentation of self in everyday life*. Harmondsworth, UK: Penguin Books.

Green, L., 2010. *Understanding the life course: sociological and psychological perspectives*. Cambridge, UK: Polity.

Haddon, L. and Vincent, J., 2007. Growing up with a mobile phone: learning from the experiences of some children in the UK. DWRC Report for Vodafone UK. www.lse.ac.uk/media@lse/WhosWho/AcademicStaff/LeslieHaddon/Date.aspx.

Haddon, L. and Vincent, J., eds., 2014. *European children and their carers' understanding of use, risks and safety issues relating to convergent mobile media* Report D4.1. Milan, Italy: Unicatt.

Haddon, L. and Vincent, J., 2015. *UK children's experience of smartphones and tablets: perspectives from children, parents and teachers*. Net Children Go Mobile. London: The London School of Economics and Political Science. http://eprints.lse.ac.uk/62125/.

Hepworth, M., 1998. Ageing and emotions. In: G. Bendelow and S. J. Williams, eds. *Emotions in social life: critical themes and contemporary issues*. London: Routledge.

Hochschild, A. R., 2003 [1983]. *The managed heart commercialization of the human feeling*. 20th ed. Berkeley, CA: University of California Press.

Lasen, A., 2004. Affective technologies: emotions and mobile phones. *Receiver #11* Vodafone UK. www.academia.edu/472410/Affective_Technologies._Emotions_and_Mobile_Phones.

Ling, R., 2004. *The mobile connection*. San Francisco, CA: Morgan Kaufmann Publishers.

Livingstone, S., Haddon, L., Vincent, J., Mascheroni, G. and Ólafsson, K., 2014a. Net Children Go Mobile: the UK report. London: London School of Economics and Political Science.

Livingstone, S., Mascheroni, G., Ólafsson, K. and Haddon, L., with the networks of EU Kids Online and Net Children Go Mobile, 2014b. Children's online risks and opportunities: comparative findings from EU Kids Online and Net Children Go Mobile. http://eprints.lse.ac.uk/60513/.

Loos, E., Haddon, L. and Mante-Meijer, E., 2012. *Generational use of new media*. Farnham, UK: Ashgate.

Mannheim, K., 1927. The sociological problem of generations. http://mediaspace.new museum.org/ytjpressmaterials/PDFS/ARTICLES_ABOUT_THE_GENERATION/01_The_Sociological_Problem.pdf.

Mascheroni, G. and Cuman, A., 2014. *Net Children Go Mobile. Final report deliverables D6.4 & D5.2*. Milan, Italy: Educatt.

Mascheroni, G. and Ólafsson, K., 2014. *Net Children Go Mobile: risks and opportunities*. 2nd ed. Milan, Italy: Educat.

Mascheroni, G. and Vincent, J., 2016. Perpetual contact as a communicative affordance: opportunities, constraints, and emotions. *Mobile Media and Communication*, 4(3), pp. 310–326.

Mead, G. H., 1967 [1943]. *Mind, self and society*. Chicago, IL: Chicago University Press.

Piper, A. M., Cornejo Garcia, R. and Brewer, R. N., 2016. Understanding the challenges and opportunities of smart mobile devices among the oldest old. *International Journal of Mobile Human Computer Interaction*, (8)2, pp. 83–98.

Schrock, A., 2015. Communicative affordances of mobile media: portability, availability, locatability, and multimediality. *International Journal of Communication*, 9, pp. 1229–1246.

Silverstone, R. and Haddon, L., 1996. Design and the domestication of information and communication technologies: technical change and everyday life. In: R. Silverstone and R. Mansell, eds. *Communication by design. the politics of information and communication technologies*. Oxford, UK: Oxford University Press, pp. 44–74.

Silverstone, R. and Hirsch, E., eds. 1992. *Consuming technologies: media and information in domestic spaces*. London, Routledge.

Taipale, S., 2014. The dimension of mobilities: the spatial relationship between corporeal and digital mobilities. *Social Science Research* 43, pp. 157–167.

Turkle, S., 2008. Always-on/always-on-you: the tethered self. In J. E. Katz, ed. *Handbook of mobile communication studies*. Cambridge, MA: The MIT Press.

Urry, J., 2000. *Sociology beyond societies: mobilities for the twenty-first century*. London: Routledge.

Vincent, J., 2003. Emotion and mobile phones. In: K. Nyiri, ed. *Mobile democracy: essays on society, self and politics*. Vienna, Austria: Passagen Verlag, pp. 215–230.

Vincent, J., 2004. 11–16 mobile: examining mobile phone and ICT uses amongst children aged 11 to 16. DWRC Report funded by Vodafone UK. www.lse.ac.uk/media@lse/WhosWho/AcademicStaff/LeslieHaddon/Date.aspx.

Vincent, J., 2009. Emotion, my mobile, my identity. In: J. Vincent and L. Fortunati, eds. *Electronic emotions: the mediation of emotions via information and communications technologies*. Oxford, UK: Peter Lang, pp 187–206.

Vincent, J., 2010. Living with mobile phones. In: J. R. Höflich, G. F. Kircher, C. Linke and I. Schlote, eds. *Mobile media and the change of everyday life*. Berlin: Peter Lang, pp. 155–170.

Vincent, J., 2011a. *Emotion in the social practices of mobile phone users*. PhD. University of Surrey http://epubs.surrey.ac.uk/770244/.

Vincent, J., 2011b. The mediation of emotion: taming the mobile phone. In: ICA (International Communications Association), *61st Annual ICA Conference, Division of Communication and Technology, Structural Transformation of the Private Sphere*. Boston, MA, 26–30 May 2011. Washington, DC: ICA.

Vincent, J., 2013. Is the mobile phone a personalised social robot? *Intervalla*, 1, pp. 60–70.

Vincent, J., 2015. *Mobile opportunities: exploring positive mobile media opportunities for European children*. London: London School of Economics and Political Science.

Vincent, J. and Fortunati, L., eds. 2009. *Electronic emotions: the mediation of emotions via information and communications technologies*. Oxford, UK: Peter Lang.

Vincent, J. and Fortunati, L., 2014. The emotional identity of the mobile phone. In: G. Goggin and L. Hjorth, eds. *The Routledge companion to mobile media*. Abingdon, UK: Routledge, pp. 312–331.

Vincent, J. and Haddon, L., 2004. Informing suppliers about user behaviours to better prepare them for their 3G/UMTS. Customers Report 34 for UMTS Forum. www.umts-forum.org.

Vincent, J. and Harper, R., 2003. Social shaping of UMTS: preparing the 3G Customer Report 26 for UMTS Forum. www.umts-forum.org.

Vincent, J. and Sugiyama, S., 2013. Social robots and emotion: transcending the boundary between humans and ICTs. *Intervalla* 1, pp. 1–6.

15 Conclusions

*Chris Gilleard, Terhi-Anna Wilska
and Sakari Taipale*

This edited volume is concerned with the changing relationships that are emerging between the new digital technologies, generational identity and the life course. Both theoretical models and empirical research findings have been reported in the diverse contributions that illuminate particular aspects of these relationships. They have been examined through the lens of family and intergenerational relations as well as from what might be called a consumerist perspective and have drawn upon both quantitative and qualitative, cross-sectional, longitudinal and cross-sequential studies of age groups, life stages and birth cohorts. Its central concern has been to evaluate how these technologies are instrumental in effecting – or realising – social and cultural change.

If modernity can, as Ulrich Beck believed, be broadly periodised into a 'first' and a 'second' modernity, there is no doubt that these new technologies form part of the 'second' modernity (Beck *et al.*, 2003). They are penetrating the systems and the life world in equal measure, in ways that the technologies of the first modernity barely dreamed of. The concerns of the first generation of European sociologists were with the processes of industrialisation, urbanisation and the struggle for citizenship and solidarity within the nation state. Among the pantheon making up sociology's founding fathers, Karl Mannheim alone evinced an interest in generational location as a source of social change. Georg Simmel was perhaps the lone figure of that era who evinced a similar interest in culture, media and technology (Bouchet, 1998; Frisby, 1997). In the second modernity, sociological interests have expanded to give increasing prominence to questions of identity and lifestyle within what is now termed 'the network society' (Castells, 1996; Rainie and Wellman, 2012).

Both generation and technology are closely linked to topics of identity and lifestyle. If the generational schism of the long 1960s witnessed new demands in Western societies, not for universal or class-based rights, but for the rights to equal citizenship of previously under-recognised groups, this brought to prominence and gave power to what were effectively new generational demands. These included demands for equal recognition for women, for racial and ethnic minorities, for sexual minorities and for people with disabilities. Framed as either cultural politics or identity politics, this transformation in social political life was interwoven with socio-economic changes that saw increases in the stand-ard of living, the rise of mass consumerism and the marketing of 'lifestyle'. This combination of cultural, economic and political change made this not so much a generational *phenomenon* as a wider and more profound generational *schism*. In the process, there has been a steady breaking down of previously solid age and generational boundaries.

Since this break, the second modernity has witnessed further changes, not least in the penetration of new technologies into the home, changing the nature of families and of intergenerational relationships. While the earlier changes fos-tered a degree of generational separation such as the introduction of transistor radios and portable TVs, the new technologies seem to have first created and then collapsed new sites of distinction. A pervasive individualisation of society seems to be coinciding with new forms of connectivity. Time and space no longer serve as the coordinates of social division. Generation as a more or less fixed unit of social time seems to have been rendered a fluid imaginary. As a social location determined by age and chronology, it pre-occupies the media and the market and – perhaps not yet so prominently – the political classes, but Mannheim's question remains unanswered – namely 'what can and what cannot be attributed to the generation factor as one of the factors impinging upon the social process' (Mannheim, 1997, p. 61).

Several chapters in this volume have been exercised by this question. Some have considered how the term 'generation' should best be framed, particularly as a social identity and location within Europe's cosmopolitan networked societies; and assuming it functions as such a structuring influence, others have sought to explore how far the new digital technologies have penetrated the system world of the workplace and the market and the life world of home and family, and in the process, how far new generational identities have emerged based upon the consumption and engagement with this digital technology. As Göran Bolin has shown in his research, technologies and media play important roles in forming generational identities in developed countries, in what could be termed a 'gen-erationing' process (Bolin, 2016; Chapter 3 in this book). The increasing role played by the media and technology in such processes, however, compounds their structuring influence. Their very generationing power requires new definitions, new boundaries, new formations – recalling what Simmel described as modern culture's transformation of 'life' into 'more life' into 'more than life' (Oakes, 1984). Time and again, the empirical evidence confounds attempts at generational delineations; other contingencies arise, whether concerning the differential use and meanings of the technology according to age, gender or life stage; position within the workforce or 'generational role' within the family; or whether as a result of individual differences in personality, temperament and experience; or simply time itself.

Seeking to apply Marx's model of class consciousness to generational identity, Mannheim emphasised both the 'objective' location of generational identity based upon the confluence of birth cohorts and distinct historical events (generation-in-itself) and the collective consciousness of being of a generation

(generation-for-itself). Such understandings remain of value, but his underlying assumptions are too essentialist for these more liquid times. Generational identities are co-constructed through cultural narratives, and the new technologies – and their marketing – have stimulated an outpouring of such accounts. But as Mannheim recognised, attempts to establish generations through a sort of sociology of chronological tables [*Geschichtstabelensoziologies*] risks giving birth to an inexorably jumbled up set of categories (Mannheim, 1997, p. 53). Equal caution needs to be exercised in assuming that engagement with technology by one age group at one point in time also constitutes a generational identity (see Buckingham, 2013, p. 1). Their 'generationing' power both creates and undermines generational identities and formations.

What then of generational identities within the family? As several chapters have noted, and as has long been recognised (cf. Kertzer, 1983), there clearly exist generational identities within families based upon kinship. This appeared as particularly pronounced in the study on rural India. What several of the studies reported here have shown, however, is that the exchanges afforded by the new technologies (of buying them, using them, offering help and assistance) seem as likely to be forging new bonds between older and younger family members as they are to developing new divisions within the family. While such interchanges are not necessarily significant in fashioning a social generational identity, they do indicate the contingencies that operate in making, breaking and reshaping generational boundaries within families.

In the introduction to this book, we noted that our approach is 'post-Mannheimian', arguing that digital technologies have the potential to shape generational experiences in ways that are no longer confined to youth. Increasingly, these experiences are taking place at later stages of life, with very different consequences. This is happening at the same time as the staging of the life course is itself undergoing change. This theme was strongly present in all chapters of this book that described how the new technologies impact on different domains of life, in different ways among differing cultural and social groups. Indeed, the shared experiences related to technology among middle-aged and older people in communication with family members, peers and relatives, in their organisation of time and work, and in consumption and lifestyle were shown to be strongly related both to the life situation and also to the particular period under examination. What is becoming evident now is likely to become much more so in future as identities and lifestyles are continuously renegotiated in and through these evolving information and communication technologies.

One final point perhaps can be made and that concerns the changing nature of time that is afforded by the new technologies. Several authors reporting on longitudinal or pseudo cohort cross-sequential studies that track changes in attitudes towards or the use of these new technologies have observed how differences discerned between age groups or cohorts at one point of time no longer appear so marked or so salient at a later point. Divides that once seemed solid 'melt into air' (or statistical insignificance) over relatively short periods of time. This indicates that as ICTs spread they become perceived as necessities in people's everyday life and acquire a 'taken-for-granted' status that is central to the lifestyles of 'second' modernity (Ling, 2012). Of course, as long as the use of new technology continuously demands both economic and human capital resources, socio-economic divides are likely to remain influential, particularly in emerging economies and developing countries. Even so, the changes that can be anticipated and that indeed are already emerging within many developed economies – in education and life-long learning, in the 'immateriality' of labour, the 'democratisation' of the internet, the ageing of ageing societies, and the steady diffusion and diversification of families and households – make even the long-lasting divisions of capital and class seem more precarious points of reference.

Not only are such 'between groups' differences becoming more fluid over time, but the technologies' own generational identities seem to be increasingly short-lived. Nowhere is this more noticeable than in the rapid 'generational' trajectories of mobile telephony networks, so that the time from 1G to 5G occupies more or less the same chronological space of what was traditionally thought of as just one 'social' generation (Berger, 1960). Given such asynchronies, it seems improbable that whatever influences technology has upon the identity of social generations, they are unlikely to be strong stable or secure. Moreover, along with the rapid development of digital networks, most services in social and health care, culture, education and local governance will operate in digital marketplaces in the future, using different digital platforms.

In the digital societies of the future, the rapidly evolving tools and frameworks based upon the internet will frame and channel the economic and social lives of individuals over the whole life course. Naturally, people at different life stages will derive different meanings and experiences from their digital devices, and act differently in online environments. However, as people's everyday lives gradually shift from digital networks into the Internet of Things and further, into the Internet of Everything (including Virtual Reality), the positions, interactions and power relations of generations as well as the meanings associated with different life stages will be constantly redefined and reimagined. While we would not advocate abandoning the endeavour to understand the relationship between generations, life stages and the new digital technologies, we would argue that we need now to move beyond Mannheimian thinking, to embrace a more contingent and fluid understanding of these relationships. The work reported in this volume provides a rich resource from which to take that project forward.

References

Beck, U., Bonss, W. and Lau, C., 2003. The theory of reflexive modernization: problematic, hypotheses and research programme. *Theory, Culture and Society*, 20(2), pp. 1–33.

Berger, B. M., 1960. How long is a generation? *The British Journal of Sociology*, 11(1), pp. 10–23.

Bolin, G., 2016. *Media generations: experience, identity and mediatised social change*. London and New York: Routledge.

Bouchet, D., 1998. Information technology, the social bond and the city: Georg Simmel updated – about the changing relationship between identity and the city. *Built Environment*, 24(2/3), pp. 104–133.

Buckingham, D., 2013. Is there a digital generation? In: D. Buckingham and R. Willett, eds. *Digital generations: children, young people and new media*. London: Routledge, pp. 1–17.

Castells, M., 1996. *The rise of the network society: the information age: economy, society, and culture*. London: Wiley-Blackwell.

Frisby, D., 1997. Introduction to the texts. In: D. Frisby and D. Featherstone, eds. *Simmel on culture: selected writings*. London: SAGE, pp. 1–28.

Kertzer, D. L., 1983. Generation as a social problem. *Annual Review of Sociology*, 9, pp. 125–149.

Ling, R., 2012. *Taken for grantedness: the embedding of mobile communication into society*. Cambridge, MA: MIT Press.

Mannheim, K., 1997. The problem of generations. In: M. A. Hardy, ed. *Studying aging and social change: conceptual and methodological issues*. Thousand Oaks, CA: SAGE, pp. 22–65.

Oakes, G., 1984. The problem of women in Simmel's theory of culture. In: G. Oakes, ed. *G. Simmel: on women, sexuality and love*. New Haven, CT and London: Yale University Press, pp. 3–62.

Rainie, L. and Wellman, B., 2012. *Networked: the new social operating system*. Cambridge, MA: MIT Press.

Index

accountability 128, 130
actuality, generation as 25, 35
adaptive digital technologies 17, 210
addiction 176
advertising 206
affectivity 91
affectual solidarity 70, 76–77, 82, 83
affordances 91, 99, 143, 205–206, 213–214
ageing 13–14, 220; ageing populations 4–5, 102; care of old people 126, 129; generational analysis 39; 'successful' 17; *see also* older people
agency 71, 87, 89, 134, 135, 144
agreeableness 184–187, 190–195, 197
agriculture 136
ambivalence, intergenerational 71
Anttila, T. 5, 55–68
anxiety 125
apps 202
archetypes 168–169
Aroldi, P. 41
assistive technologies 4, 121
associational solidarity 70, 75–76, 82, 83
attitudes 167, 169, 219; digitalisation of domestic environments 170, 172, 176, 178; Finnish consumers 177; generational analysis 38, 40
autonomy 14, 99, 126; care professionals 128–129; older people 129; women's mobile phone use 92

Baby Boomers 150, 153, 155–156, 163n1, 169, 183–184; generational analysis 28, 32, 34–35, 38–39, 40; personality traits and computer use 189, 196, 197
Bakardjieva, M. 80, 106, 111, 140
Baron, R. M. 186
Bassett, C. 205, 213

Beck, U. 11–12, 15, 217
beliefs 38, 77
Bengtson, V. L. 70, 71, 74, 104
Beniger, J. 27
Berkowsky, R. W. 188
Berman, M. 25
Big Five personality traits 184–188, 190–195, 196, 197
'biological rhythm' 2
Bittman, M. 59
the body 14
Bolin, G. 2, 5, 23–36, 218
boundaries 126, 219
Bourdieu, P. 14, 40
Brannen, J. 60
BT Cellnet 201, 207
Byrne, D. 123

Calhoun, C. 11
Calnan, M. 129
cameras 94, 95, 97, 98, 152
card games 114
care of old people 6, 119–133
care professionals 120, 122, 123–124, 127–129
caste 6, 134–135, 137–138, 139, 142, 144
Castells, M. 56, 89
Castoriadis, C. 17, 19n2
Cathcart, R. 23
cellphones *see* mobile phones
change 25, 28, 34; *see also* social change
children: computer use 45; democratic families 78; emotions and mobile phone use 202, 203–204, 208, 209–211, 213; generational analysis 41; India 135–136, 140, 144; intergenerational solidarity 72; knowledge of technology 206; middle-aged and elderly people in Finland 155, 158–159, 160–161, 162;

mothers' mobile phone use 94–95; multiple influences 13; time coordination 65; *see also* youth
China 42, 103, 140
class 12, 134, 137, 142, 220; *see also* middle class
co-presence 205
coevals 25, 26
cohorts 12, 150, 153, 213; generational analysis 38, 40; media behaviour 28–29; middle-aged and elderly people in Finland 153–163; technology generations 15; *see also* generational analysis
collective memory 37–38
Colombo, F. 41
communication: care of old people 121–122, 130; digitalisation of domestic environments 170, 178; family 71, 72, 74, 75–82, 83; internet 183; personality traits 185; 'second' modernity 15–16; synchronised 58; technology-mediated 59, 69
community 12, 15
comparative approach 26–27
computers (PCs) 16, 149, 183–184; avoidance of time contamination 61; care of old people 120–121; children 72; consumption norms 152; generational analysis 44–45, 48; intergenerational solidarity 72–73; late middle-agers 168; leisure activities 187; middle-aged and elderly people in Finland 154–156, 158–159, 161–162; older people 106, 107, 108, 113; personality traits and computer use 185–186, 188–197; work-related use 187–188
Connidis, I. A. 71
conscientiousness 184–188, 190–193, 196, 197
consensual solidarity 70, 77–78, 82
consumerism 3, 12–13, 14, 18, 218; consumer society 152, 163; resistance to 59
consumption 3, 12, 43, 48, 169, 219; digitalisation of domestic environments 170; India 138; middle-aged and elderly people in Finland 154; moral framework of 177; norms 151–153, 162; studies of 167; third age 14
content analysis 74, 105–106, 203
control 91, 99
Correa, T. 185
Costa, P. T. J. 184

costs 142, 143
Coupland, D. 163n2
creativity 91
cultural capital 17, 131
cultural context 26, 28, 151
cultural fields 40
cultural identity 37
cultural practices 55, 138
cultural turn 13–14
Cuman, A. 211

daily schedules 56, 58–59, 63–65, 66, 71
data security 79–80
de-digitalisation 114–115
Deacon, D. 24
democratic family concept 78
demographic changes 134, 135–136
dependency 91
'destandardisation' 11, 12, 14
diffusion of innovations 104, 115–116, 153, 163
digital divide 17, 143, 150
Digital Generation 1
digital global generation 41
digital housekeeping 5, 103, 104, 111–113, 115, 116
digital immigrants 41, 149, 153
digital natives 41, 149, 150, 169, 174, 178
digital spectrum 1
digital technology 2, 149, 153, 167, 219, 220; accelerating pace of life 56; adaptive 17, 210; children's use of 140; cultural context 151; digitalisation of domestic environments 167, 170–179; networked society 11; older people 18–19, 102–118; public services 119; resistance to 106–107, 108, 111–112, 177; *see also* computers; information and communication technologies; internet; mobile phones
digital television 109–110, 111, 114, 152
disability studies 19
discrimination 137–138
dispositions 40
distinction 14
Dolničar, V. 5, 69–86
domestic appliances 108, 110
domestic environments 6, 167, 170–179
domestication 41–49, 104, 106–109, 114–115, 204–206, 213–214
Donner, J. 143
'dotnets' 28
'dutifuls' 28
dysfunctionality 174–175

e-book readers 3
e-Generation 150
e-health/e-welfare services 130
Edmunds, J. 41
education 122, 152, 183, 220; India 138,
    140, 142–143, 144n3; middle-aged
    and elderly people in Finland 153, 155,
    158–159, 160–161, 162
elderly people *see* older people
electronic emotions 6, 201–216
electronic patient records 127–128, 130
email 65, 183; communication norms
    81; emotions 202; intergenerational
    solidarity 74, 79, 81; mobile phone use
    in India 143; older people 106, 113;
    work-related 188
emotions: electronic 6, 201–216;
    hyper-coordination 64
empty nesters 90, 91, 98–99
entelechy 14, 206
entertainment: digitalisation of domestic
    environments 170; intergenerational
    solidarity 72; mobile phone use in India
    142; older people 151; women's mobile
    phone use 91
Estonia 4–5, 24, 26–27, 28, 30–33, 35n3
ethnicity 13, 83, 217
EU Kids Online 203, 204
Eurostat 183
events 25, 28–29, 31, 38
exclusion 75, 77
extended families 69, 73–74, 82
Extended Group Interview (EGI)
    73–74, 83
extraversion 184–188, 190–195, 196

face-to-face communication 59, 120,
    122, 128, 129
Facebook 18, 61–62, 63, 183, 209–210;
    generational analysis 32, 33; impact
    on other leisure activities 187;
    intergenerational solidarity 74, 75–76,
    77, 78; Messenger 62; mobile phone
    use in India 143; older people 108, 113,
    115; personality traits and computer use
    185, 187, 196
family 3, 5; care of old people 121, 123–127,
    130–131; digitalisation of domestic
    environments 171, 174; generational
    identities 219; household structure
    151; India 134, 141; intergenerational
    solidarity 69–86, 104; time issues for
    middle-aged employees 55, 58–61,
    64–65; *see also* grandparents; parents

feminism 87–88
fields 14, 40
filial piety 80, 103
financial circumstances 42–43, 48, 142
Finland 4–5, 151; care of old people
    119–133; consumption norms 152,
    153; digitalisation of domestic
    environments 167, 170–179;
    intergenerational solidarity 70, 72,
    73–83; middle-aged and elderly people
    149–150, 153–163; personality traits
    and computer use 189–197; social
    networking sites 183; time issues for
    middle-aged employees 57–66
Fonda, J. 14
Fortunati, L. 5, 102–118, 201
Foucault, M. 14
fourth age 17, 18, 124
functional solidarity 70, 78–79, 82, 83
functionality 173, 174

gaming 72, 108, 114, 207
Ganito, C. 5, 60, 87–101
gender 12, 13; digital housekeeping 103;
    India 135–136, 138–139; life course
    transitions 151; middle-aged and elderly
    people in Finland 154, 155, 158–159,
    162; mobile phone use 87–101; older
    people 103, 110–111, 115, 116;
    personality traits and computer use
    188–189, 194, 195; purpose of internet
    use 183; social generations 134;
    temporal experiences 65, 66; *see also*
    men; women
generation gap 26, 34, 38, 40, 109
Generation X 150, 155, 163n2, 169, 213;
    computer and internet use 183–184;
    first exposure to ICTs 153; generational
    analysis 28, 38–39; personality
    traits 197
Generation Y 150, 153, 169, 178;
    computer and internet use 183–184;
    generational analysis 38; India
    142; personality traits 197; *see also*
    Millennials
Generation Z 150, 153
generational analysis 24, 26–27, 28–35,
    37–51
generational archetypes 168–169
generational consciousness 2, 25–26, 32,
    37, 114, 178–179
generational dispositions 40
generational divide 11, 14, 149
generational entelechy 14, 206

generational technologies 17
generational theory 23, 25–26, 34
'generationing' 2, 3, 24, 25–26, 31, 34–35,
    218–219
Genie 201, 207
Germany 204
'gerontechnologies' 19
G.I. Generation 38
Gilleard, C. 1–8, 14, 40, 124, 217–221
globalisation 38, 41
Goffman, E. 204
grandparents 18, 103; health issues
    81–82; intergenerational solidarity 72,
    73, 75–77, 79–82, 83, 104; women's
    mobile phone use 98; young people's
    experience of older people's ICT use
    105–114; *see also* older people
Gumpert, G. 23

habits 49
habitus 14–15, 17, 18, 40
Haddon, L. 5, 37–51, 106, 204, 210, 211,
    213–214
Harper, R. 208
health 81–82, 168
hedonism 177
Helsper, E. J. 87
Higgs, P. 14, 40, 124
Hirsch, E. 204, 213
Hirvonen, H. 6, 119–133
hobbies 58, 65
Hochschild, A. R. 204
home care 121, 127, 130
household structure 151, 153–154, 162
housing *see* domestic environments
Howe, N. 39
hurriedness 56, 58–59, 62
Hyde, M. 153
hyper-coordination 63–64
Hyppönen, H. 130

ICT Development Index 82–83
ICTs *see* information and communication
    technologies
ideal types 91
identity 1, 3; caste 137; cultural 37;
    early experiences of technologies
    48; evolution of generational 4;
    'generationing' 25, 31–32, 34–35,
    218–219; identity politics 217–218;
    India 138; intragenerational 116; late
    middle-agers 175; new divisions of
    16–17; older people 114; role of the
    media 46; social change 2; third age 14;

women's mobile phone use 91; young
    adults 168, 178; youth 150
illiteracy 138, 139
immaterial labour 103, 104, 116, 220
incomes: computer and internet use 152,
    183; extraversion linked to 188; middle-
    aged and elderly people in Finland 153,
    155, 158–159, 160–161, 162
India 6, 134–146, 219
indirect generational relations 31
individualisation 3, 4, 12–13, 69; of the
    body 14; 'second' modernity 16; of
    society 218
individualism 13, 70
information and communication
    technologies (ICTs) 3, 5, 11,
    219–220; care of old people 119–133;
    consumption norms 151–153; cultural
    and social relations 17; electronic
    emotions 201–216; generational
    analysis 37, 40–48; generations and
    life course 150–151; intergenerational
    solidarity 69–86; middle-aged and
    elderly people in Finland 149–150,
    153–163; older people 18, 19, 102–118;
    public services 119; time issues for
    middle-aged employees 55–66; trust 6;
    see also computers; digital technology;
    internet; mobile phones
Instagram 74, 75, 76, 77
interfaces 108–109
intergenerational ambivalence 71
intergenerational relations 26, 34, 58,
    60, 72
intergenerational solidarity 69–86,
    103, 104
international generations 38, 41
internet: avoidance of time contamination
    61; care of old people 130–131;
    children 72, 206, 211; democratisation
    of the 220; digital global generation 41;
    Eurobarometer survey 109; Eurostat
    survey 183; intergenerational solidarity
    70, 72; late middle-agers 168; leisure
    activities 187; middle-aged and elderly
    people in Finland 150, 154–155,
    156–157, 158–159, 161–162; mobile
    phone use in India 139–140, 142–143;
    older people 4, 106, 107, 111, 122, 131;
    personality traits 185–186, 196; proxy
    internet use 140; 'second' modernity 16;
    women's mobile phone use 92, 95, 96,
    98; work-related use 187–188; *see also*
    mobile internet; social media

Internet of Things 220
iPad 114, 210
iPhone 95, 97
Italy 4–5, 41, 102, 103, 105–114

Jain, V. 142
Janković, B. 187
John, O. P. 184
Judge, T. A. 188
Jyväskylä Longitudinal Study of
    Personality and Social Development
    (JYLS) 189

Kekäläinen, T. 6, 183–200
Kemppainen, T. 6, 167–182
Kennedy, J. 103
Kennedy, T. L. M. 69
Kenny, D. A. 186
Kinnunen, M. 197
kinship system 134, 141–142, 144, 219
knowledge workers 55, 58, 66
Kokko, K. 6, 183–200
Kröger, T. 121
Kuhlmann, E. 129
Kundu, T. 138–139
Kunk, L. M. 126
Kuo, T. 187
Kuoppamäki, S-M. 6, 149–166,
    167–182
Kwan, C. and Y-H. 103

labour 3, 12, 220; *see also* work
Landers, R. N. 195
landscape metaphor 27, 34
language use 78
Laslett, P. 14
late middle age 167–168, 169, 170–172,
    174–177, 178–179; *see also* middle-
    aged people
Le Cornu, A. 1
learning: change in the direction of 34;
    older people 71, 115; pre-figurative 33
Lefebvre, H. 28
Leinonen, A. 121
leisure 3, 56, 66; late middle age 168;
    mobile phone use in India 143; older
    people 151; personality traits and
    computer use 6, 186–187, 188, 190,
    191–194, 196; tablet use 162
Licoppe, C. 59
life course perspective 1–3, 69, 99, 151,
    167–168; electronic emotions 202,
    212–213, 214; household structure 162;
    women 88–89

life situation questionnaire (LSQ) 189, 190
life stages 89–91, 99, 167–168, 202,
    214, 220
lifestyle 151–152, 168, 217, 219;
    individualisation of the body 14;
    marketing of 218; new divisions of
    16–17; 'second' modernity 12, 13;
    third age 14
Lim, S. S. 141
LinkedIn 33, 61
Livingstone, S. 206
location, generation as 25, 29, 35
Lost Generation 38
Lounsbury, J. W. 195
Luhmann, N. 120, 122, 124
Lüscher, K. 71

Mannheim, K. 1, 38, 204–205, 213,
    218–219; generational entelechy 14,
    206; generational theory 23, 25–26;
    social change 2, 217; social generations
    2, 37, 134
marketing 39, 169, 179, 201
marriage 138–139, 141–142
Marx, K. 25, 218
Mascheroni, G. 211
Maxwell, J. A. 91
McCrae, R. R. 184
McLuhan, M. 25, 31
McMullin, J. A. 71
Mead, M. 26, 33, 34, 204
media: generational analysis 26–27,
    28–34, 46–48; 'generationing' 25,
    34–35, 218; India 142; mass 2; media
    generations 23; media landscape 1, 27,
    34; older people 102–103; 'second'
    modernity 12
mediatisation 5, 23–24, 27, 34
memories 37–38, 46
men: digitalisation of domestic
    environments 171, 173; India 135, 136,
    138, 139, 141; life course transitions
    151; middle-aged and elderly people in
    Finland 158–159, 162; mobile phone
    use 88; older 103, 110–111, 115;
    personality traits and computer use 185,
    189, 191; purpose of internet use 183;
    see also gender
messaging 61, 207; intergenerational
    solidarity 75, 78, 82; older people 106,
    115; time coordination 64, 65; *see also*
    text messages; WhatsApp
micro-coordination 63–64, 91

middle-aged people 5, 149–150, 153–163; digitalisation of domestic environments 6, 167, 170–172, 174–177, 178–179; life stages 167–168; personality traits and computer use 6, 184, 189–197; shared experiences 219; social networking sites 183; time issues and ICT use 55–66; women's mobile phone use 90, 91, 96, 97–98; *see also* late middle age
middle class 42, 43, 110, 139, 171, 177
Millennials 38, 39, 150, 169, 178, 213; *see also* Generation Y
mobile internet: Eurobarometer survey 109; Genie service 201; India 142–143; middle-aged and elderly people in Finland 150, 153, 154–155, 159–161, 162; older people 106; women's mobile phone use 92, 95, 96, 98; *see also* internet
mobile phones 16, 149; care of old people 120–121, 124–127, 130; children 72; communication norms 81; connectivity 205, 207, 211; consumption norms 152; emotions 6, 201, 202, 207–212; Eurobarometer survey 109; gender and 5, 87–101; generational analysis 29, 32; generational identity 150; 'generational' trajectories 220; Genie service 201; India 134–135, 139–144; intergenerational solidarity 69, 74, 76, 82; late middle-agers 168; middle-aged and elderly people in Finland 150, 154–155, 157, 158, 161–162; older people 4, 18, 44, 106, 107–108, 111, 112, 115, 122, 131; online parenting 60; time coordination 64; *see also* smartphones
mobile technologies 2; impact on scheduling 63, 64–65, 66; multitasking 62–63; online parenting 60–61
modernity 11–13, 15–19, 25, 217, 218, 219–220
Mortimer, J. T. 88
mothers: India 141; intergenerational solidarity 75–76, 83; mobile phone use 90–91, 94–96, 99, 211; single 90, 91, 95–96, 99
movies 3, 143
MTV generation 1
multimedia messaging services (MMS) 98
multitasking 56, 58, 60, 62–63, 65
music 3, 113, 143

naivety 113–114
Näsi, M. 187
NEO-FFI questionnaire 190
nesting women 90, 93–94
Net Children Go Mobile project 203–204
Net Generation 1, 41, 150
'network society' 11, 13, 217
networked individualism 13
neuroticism 184–188, 190–193, 195, 196, 197
newspapers 108
Nintendo 108, 111, 114
Nintendo generation 1
normative solidarity 70, 79–81, 82, 83
norms: consumption 151–153, 162; intergenerational solidarity 80; women's mobile phone use 91
nostalgia 46

occupational status 122, 190, 191, 193, 194
older people 3–4, 18–19, 102–118; care of 6, 119–133; changes in attitudes 113–114; digital housekeeping 103, 104, 111–113, 115, 116; digital television 109–110; diversity 16–17; domestication 41–49, 106–109, 114–115; education and income 152; emotions 202; Finland 149–150, 153–163; fourth age 17, 18, 124; gender issues 110–111, 115; generational belonging 32; generational identity 25, 34–35; health issues 81–82; intergenerational solidarity 72, 76–77, 78; learning strategies 71; leisure activities 151, 187; life stages 167–168; mobile phone use 144, 209, 210, 211, 212; new ageing 13–14; shared experiences 219; social networking sites 183; third age 14, 16–17, 18, 124; 'we-sense' 2; women's mobile phone use 90, 91, 98–99; *see also* grandparents
online communities 17
online parenting 60–61
openness to new experiences 184–188, 190–195, 196, 197
Oreglia, E. 140
Ortega y Gasset, J. 23
Oyama, P. S. 104

Pant, S. 142
parents: intergenerational solidarity 72–73, 75–82, 103, 104; online parenting 60–61; parent-child contract 103–104; working 13; *see also* mothers

Path 75
PCs *see* computers
periodisation 15–16
personalisation 91, 94, 95, 96, 208
personality traits 6, 183–200
Petrovčič, A. 5, 69–86
photos 94, 95, 97, 98, 110, 113, 207
Pillemer, K. 71
policy 119, 121, 129
politics: cultural or identity politics
    217–218; generational analysis 39;
    India 139
popular culture 39
Portugal 4–5, 41, 87, 88, 89–99
post-modernisation 11, 13
poverty 136, 144n2
Prensky, M. 41
privacy 173, 178, 179
public services 119, 121
Pulkkinen, L. 189
Putnam, R. 40–41

quality of life 120, 127, 129, 131

race 134, 217
radio 2, 12, 16, 108, 218
recycling 18
'rhythm of ages' 23, 24
risk 175, 176, 178
risk management 128
Roberts, R. E. 70, 74
Robinson, J. P. 187
routines 93–94, 96
Rowe, R. 129
rural India 134–146

Sackmann, R. 15
safety: care of old people 127; emotions
    and mobile phone use 209; late middle-
    agers 168, 175, 178, 179; women's
    mobile phone use 91, 97, 99
Sayago, S. 71
Schrock, A. 205–206
'second' modernity 11–13, 15–16, 17, 217,
    218, 219–220
security 79–80, 178
self-awareness 35, 37–38
self-expression 14, 92, 93, 168
self-presentation 64, 202, 205
self-understanding 35
sexuality 13, 217
Shah, D. V. 184
Shanahan, M. J. 88
shared meanings 170, 171–177

Silent Generation 38, 39, 42
Silver Surfers 213
Silverman, D. 105
Silverstone, R. 106, 204, 213–214
Simmel, G. 19n1, 217, 218
simultaneity 60, 65
single mothers 90, 91, 95–96, 99
'situated knowledges' 99
skills: intergenerational solidarity 70, 74,
    77–78, 79; late middle-agers 174, 178;
    older people 113
Skype 17, 18, 71, 76, 77, 81, 108
Slovenia 4–5, 70, 72, 73–83
smart home solutions 167, 170, 178
smartphones: addiction to 176;
    children 206, 209; co-presence 205;
    consumption norms 152; digitalisation
    of domestic environments 167, 170;
    emotions 202, 208, 214; increase in
    use 149; India 135, 140, 142–143;
    intergenerational solidarity 69; middle-
    aged and elderly people in Finland
    160; older people 18, 107, 113, 210;
    third age 17; ubiquity of 207; *see also*
    mobile phones
Snapchat 211
social capital 131, 168
social change 2, 104, 217; generational
    analysis 23, 24, 34, 35, 38; India 134,
    135–139
social contract 103
social generations 1–3, 37, 134, 142,
    220; definition of 6n1; India 143–144;
    mobile phone use in India 139
social imaginaries 17, 18, 19n2
social media: emotions 202, 213; hyper-
    coordination 64; intergenerational
    solidarity 69, 75, 76, 82, 83; messaging
    207; mobile phone use in India 144;
    multitasking 62–63; older people 18,
    103; personality traits and computer
    use 185–186, 188, 191, 193, 194, 197;
    rise of 1; self-expression 168; staying
    outside 58, 61–62; *see also* Facebook;
    social networking sites
Social Media Generation 1
social networking 92, 94, 97, 169
social networking sites (SNS) 3, 33,
    35, 71, 106, 115, 183–184; *see also*
    Facebook; social media
social networks 72, 122, 151
social relationships 173, 175, 178, 179
social support 72, 82, 168
socialisation 87

socioeconomic status 131, 155, 158–159, 162
'soft experts' 144
softening schedules 64–65, 66
Soulet, M.-H. 91
Spain 210
Spotify 32–33
spouses 103
Srivastava, S. 184
Stanyer, S. 24
stereotypes 1, 78, 99, 111, 116, 178
Strauss, W. 39
stress 125
structural solidarity 70, 81–82, 83
support 4, 72, 77, 82, 168; *see also* technical assistance
surveillance 210
Sweden 4–5, 24, 26–27, 28–33, 35n2, 35n3
Swing Generation 39

tablets: consumerism 3; digitalisation of domestic environments 170; emotions 202, 208; increase in use 149; middle-aged and elderly people in Finland 150, 153, 159–161, 162; older people 106, 115; ubiquity of 207
Taipale, S. 1–8, 69–86, 217–221
Tammelin, M. 5, 55–68
Tang, H. 187
technical assistance 79, 80, 82–83, 108, 140; digital housekeeping 103, 104, 111–113, 115, 116; digital television 110
technofeminism 87
technology: assistive 4, 121; changes in 15–16, 23, 107; 'generationing' 218; impact on generational identities 220; living without 176–177; media 26, 27; modernity 12, 217; public services 119; technofeminism 87; technological determinism 41; technology generations 15; time-space compression 56; *see also* digital technology; information and communication technologies; mobile technologies
telephones 16, 44, 65, 109, 152; *see also* mobile phones
television 2, 12, 175, 218; Baby Boomers 184; digital 111, 114, 152; generational analysis 31, 33, 40–41, 43, 45–49; India 143; intergenerational solidarity 72; older people 102–103, 109–110, 114; women's mobile phone use 92

Tenhunen, S. 6, 134–146
text messages 78, 80, 98, 99, 207; *see also* messaging
third age 14, 16–17, 18, 124
time 28, 55–66, 178, 219; accelerating pace of life 55, 56–57, 58, 63; changing conceptions of 56, 63, 66; contamination of 56, 59–62, 63, 66; digitalisation of domestic environments 173; fragmentation of 56, 57, 59–60; generational theory 25–26; time coordination 58, 63–65, 66; time-space compression 56; women's mobile phone use 95
transfer of knowledge 115–116
trust 6, 119–120, 121–124, 126, 128, 129, 130–131
Turkle, S. 89, 91
Turner, B. S. 41
Twitter 74, 211

UMTS Forum 203–204, 208
United Kingdom 4–5, 42, 201, 204, 208
United States 28
upgrading 18
Urry, J. 205
Uusitalo, O. 6, 167–182

values 77, 81, 167, 169–170; digitalisation of domestic environments 170, 172, 174, 176, 179; Finland 177; generational analysis 40
vanity 177
VCRs 45–46, 153
Viber 81
Viinikainen, J. 188
Vincent, J. 6, 201–216
Virgin Media 206

Wajcman, J. 55, 59, 62, 87
War Generation 150, 155–156
'warm experts' 80, 111, 140
'we-sense' 2, 38
Weber, M. 91
Wellman, B. 69
WhatsApp 61, 65, 210; children 211; emotional sharing 64; groups 62, 63; intergenerational solidarity 74, 75–76, 82; older people 110, 113, 115
White, D. S. 1
Wilska, T-A. 1–8, 149–166, 217–221
Winkler, O. 15
women: care of old people 123–127; China 140; demands for equal recognition 217;

digitalisation of domestic environments 171, 173, 174, 176; hurriedness 58; India 134–135, 136, 138–139, 141–142, 144; life course transitions 88–89, 151; middle-aged and elderly people in Finland 154, 158–159, 162; mobile phone use 5, 87–88, 89–99, 134–135, 141–142, 144, 201; older 103, 110–111, 115, 116; personality traits and computer use 186, 189, 191; purpose of internet use 183; time coordination 66; time fragmentation 59–60; *see also* gender; mothers
work 3, 12, 13, 219; hurriedness 58; increases in intensity of 104; India 137, 139, 144n4; middle-aged employees 58; personality traits and computer use 187–188, 190, 191, 192–194, 195; tablet use at 162; time issues for middle-aged employees 55, 57, 60–61, 66; women's mobile phone use 92–93, 94
working class 42, 43

young adults: cohorts 38; digitalisation of domestic environments 6, 167, 170–173, 176–177, 178–179; intergenerational solidarity 70; life stages 167–168; social networking sites 183; women's mobile phone use 90, 92–93, 99
youth 1, 13; digital housekeeping 5, 103, 104, 111–113, 115, 116; electronic emotions 213; experience of older people's digital technology use 102, 104–116; generational belonging 32; generational identity 150; 'generationing' 25; household structure 151, 162; India 142; intergenerational solidarity 72–73, 77; Mannheim on 37; mobile phone use in India 134–135, 140, 144; personality traits 185; self-understanding 2; youth culture 40; *see also* children

zeitgeist 107, 115
Zhou, R. 187
Zukin, C. 28

For Product Safety Concerns and Information please contact our EU
representative GPSR@taylorandfrancis.com
Taylor & Francis Verlag GmbH, Kaufingerstraße 24, 80331 München, Germany

www.ingramcontent.com/pod-product-compliance
Lightning Source LLC
Chambersburg PA
CBHW071419050326
40689CB00010B/1903